Defending Putin's Empire

Defending Putin's Empire

Russia's Air Defence System

Mihajlo S Mihajlović

Frontline Books

First published in Great Britain in 2023 by
Frontline Books
An imprint of Pen & Sword Books Limited
Yorkshire – Philadelphia

ISBN 978 1 39904 307 6

A CIP catalogue record for this book is available from the British Library

Typeset by Mac Style
Printed in the UK by CPI Group (UK) Ltd, Croydon, CR0 4YY.

FSC
www.fsc.org
MIX
Paper | Supporting responsible forestry
FSC® C013604

Pen & Sword Books Limited incorporates the imprints of After the Battle, Atlas, Archaeology, Aviation, Discovery, Family History, Fiction, History, Maritime, Military, Military Classics, Politics, Select, Transport, True Crime, Air World, Frontline Publishing, Leo Cooper, Remember When, Seaforth Publishing, The Praetorian Press, Wharncliffe Local History, Wharncliffe Transport, Wharncliffe True Crime and White Owl.

For a complete list of Pen & Sword titles please contact

PEN & SWORD BOOKS LIMITED
47 Church Street, Barnsley, South Yorkshire, S70 2AS, England
E-mail: enquiries@pen-and-sword.co.uk
Website: www.pen-and-sword.co.uk
or
PEN AND SWORD BOOKS
1950 Lawrence Rd, Havertown, PA 19083, USA
E-mail: Uspen-and-sword@casematepublishers.com
Website: www.penandswordbooks.com

Contents

Note to the Reader and Acknowledgements		vii
Abbreviations		viii
Chapter 1	**Integrated Air Defence System (IADS)**	1
	Airspace Control and Surveillance System	4
	Fighter-Interceptor Force	6
	Missile Defence System	6
	Electronic Warfare and Countermeasures System	8
	Automated Control System	10
	Modern Russian Integrated Air Defence	12
Chapter 2	**Air Defence 'Electronic Eyes'**	17
	The Opponents	19
	Counter-Stealth Radar Systems	29
	Counter-Stealth Concepts	37
	Electronic Warfare	39
	EW Systems against Airborne Systems (REB-S)	41
Chapter 3	**Air Defence and Anti-Ballistic Missile Defence of the Aerospace Forces**	47
	Ancestors	47
	The Mighty S-300	51
	S-400 Triumf	83
	Defending the Fleet – Naval S-300F	94
	S-500 Triumfator	98
	S-350 Vityaz	101
	Pantsir	105
	Prospective Systems: 42S6 Morfey	113
	The Moscow Shield – Anti-Satellite Missiles	116
Chapter 4	**Ground Forces Air Defence**	118
	Tactical Air Defence	118
	Battlefield Threat – Countering Drones	125
	Legacy Systems	127

Chapter 5	**S-300V (9K81) Long-Range Missile System**	142
Chapter 6	**Medium-Range Army Air Defence Systems**	169
	Legacy: 2A11 Krug (SA-4 'Ganef') and 2K12 Kub (SA-6 'Gainful') Missile Systems	169
	Successor: 9K37 Buk (SA-11, SA-17) and 9K317M – Buk M3 Viking	174
Chapter 7	**Short-Range Air Defence**	192
	Tor Missile System	195
Chapter 8	**Gun and Missile Systems, and Point Defence**	212
	2K22 Tunguska (SA-19 'Grison')	212
	Point Defence and MANPADS	216
	Self-Propelled Anti-Aircraft Guns (SPAAGs)	220
	MANPADS	225
Appendix		233
	NATO Codenames for Missile Systems	233
	NATO Codenames for S-300 and S-400 Missiles	234
	NATO Codenames for S-300, S-400, S-500 Systems Radars	234
	NATO Codenames for S-300V Radars	235
	NATO Codenames for Radars that are in Use (Including Older Types used by Other Countries)	235
	Most Common Russian Abbreviations	235
Notes		237
Bibliography		240
Index		242

Note to the Reader

Due to the book's size constraints, this work is a very broad overview of the history and modern applications of Russian air defence systems. It is the sole source for every modern Russian air defence system currently in use and still to be fielded by the Russian military. The Russian military project names for the individual systems are different than those used in the West. The author has chosen to use the original designations, pairing them with the Western designations when they appear for the first time. Detailed Western designations can be found in the appendix. Due to space constraints, the author has not included detailed technical characteristics (which can be found through the links in the Bibliography).

Acknowledgements

The images in this work come from the files listed in the Bibliography, the Ministry of Defence (MoD), public domain sites and author's archives. Some of the contemporary photographs come from Russian military websites and publications. Other pictures came from sources that are named. As with all published works, authors depend on friends for assistance in reviewing their work.

Abbreviations

AAA	Anti-Aircraft Artillery
AAMS	Anti-Aircraft Missile System
ACS	Automated Control System
AD	Air Defence
ADMS	Air Defence Missile System
AESA	Active Electronically-Scanned Array
AHH	Active Homing Head
APAA	Active Phase Antenna Array
ARM	Anti-Radar Missile
ASAW	Aerospace Attack Weapon
AWACS	Airborne Warning And Control System
C2	Command and Control
CCP	Combat Control Post
CEC	Cooperative Engagement Capability
CP	Command Post
c-UAS	Counter-Unmanned Aerial System
CV	Combat Vehicle
CVLO	Counter Very Low Observable
CW	Continuous Wave
DEAD	Destruction of Air Defence
DEW	Directed-Energy Weapon
EA	Electronic Attack
ECM	Electronic Countermeasures
ELINT	Electronic Intelligence
EW	Electronic Warfare
IADS	Integrated Air Defence System
IRM	Intermediate-Range Missile
LM	Lockheed Martin
LO	Low Observability
LRM	Long-Range Missile
MANPADS	Man-Portable Air Defence System
MEZ	Missile Engagement Zone
MoD	Ministry of Defence
OED	Optoelectronic Device

PGM	Precision-Guided Munition
RCS	Radar Cross Section
SA	Surface-to-Air
SAM	Surface-to-Air Missile
SAMC	Surface-to-Air Missile Complex
SARH	Semi-Active Radar Homing
SEAD	Suppression of Air Defence
SPAAG	Self-Propelled Anti-Aircraft Gun
SRM	Short-Range Missile
TELAR	Transporter Erector Launcher and Radar
TLC	Transport and Launch Container
UAES	Universal Automation Equipment System
UAV	Unmanned Aerial Vehicle
UBCP	Universal Battery Command Post
UCAV	Unmanned Combat Aerial vehicle
UHF	Ultra High Frequency
VHF	Very High Frequency

Chapter 1

Integrated Air Defence System (IADS)

The national air defence system of Russia is assigned a wide spectrum of missions. In peacetime, an effective air defence system is a major deterrent factor. Its role is significant in defending national borders and airspace and keeping them under close surveillance. In times of tension or conflict, its role may be decisive (Fig.1-1).[1]

An effective air defence system permits:

- early warning of the country's military and political leaders about enemy preparations for an aerospace attack or about its initiation;
- coordinated transfer of the country and its armed forces to full combat status;
- effective repulsion of initial and subsequent high-density airspace attacks;
- continuous functioning of the military command system, government and national economy;
- direct protection of the main group of troops on the battlefield, naval forces and vital military installations, as well as elements of the country's economy and infrastructure over the entire national territory.

The creation and improvement of the air defence system is one of the major objectives of military construction in Russia. A key goal centres on creating an operationally effective and economical air defence system employing the characteristics of all modem weapons to their maximum effect, capable of reliably defending all vital military installations and civilian facilities.

Russian experience in building modern air defence systems shows that the best variant to defend the state and its armed forces is an integrated air (aerospace) defence system (IADS) made up of subsystems, elements and aerospace defence assets designed to counter hostile aerospace attacks, operating under the overall direction of a common command and control authority. Such a system offers the advantage of utilising the full capabilities of its information-gathering and combat subsystems. It synchronises and controls the activities of air defence forces via automated channels and is able to deal with all types of existing and future aerospace attack weapons under heavy hostile attacks and electronic countermeasures. It also features the capability to quickly adapt to a new environment.

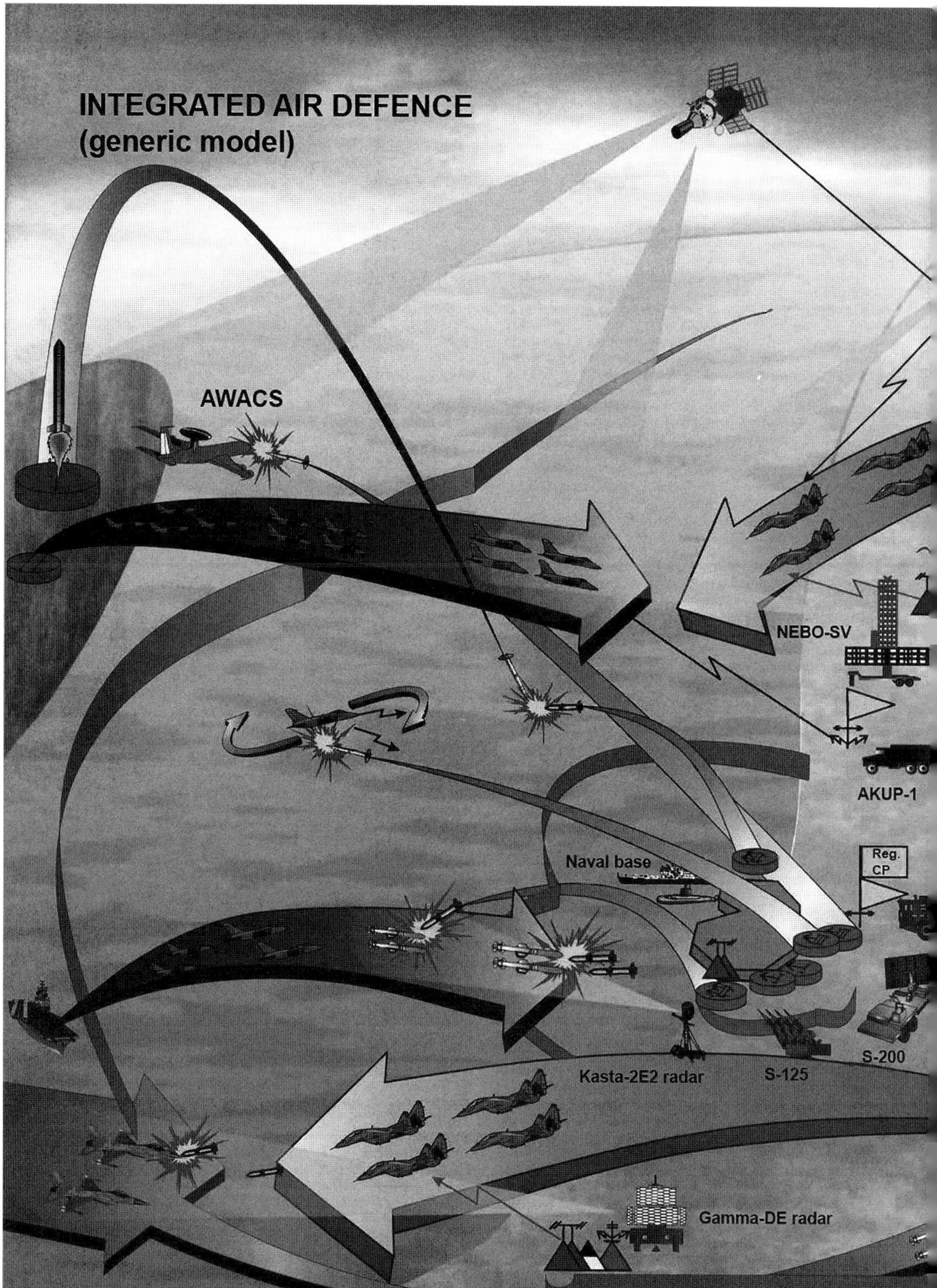

Figure 1-1: Integrated air defence – generic model. (*Source: PVO I PRO XXI veka*)

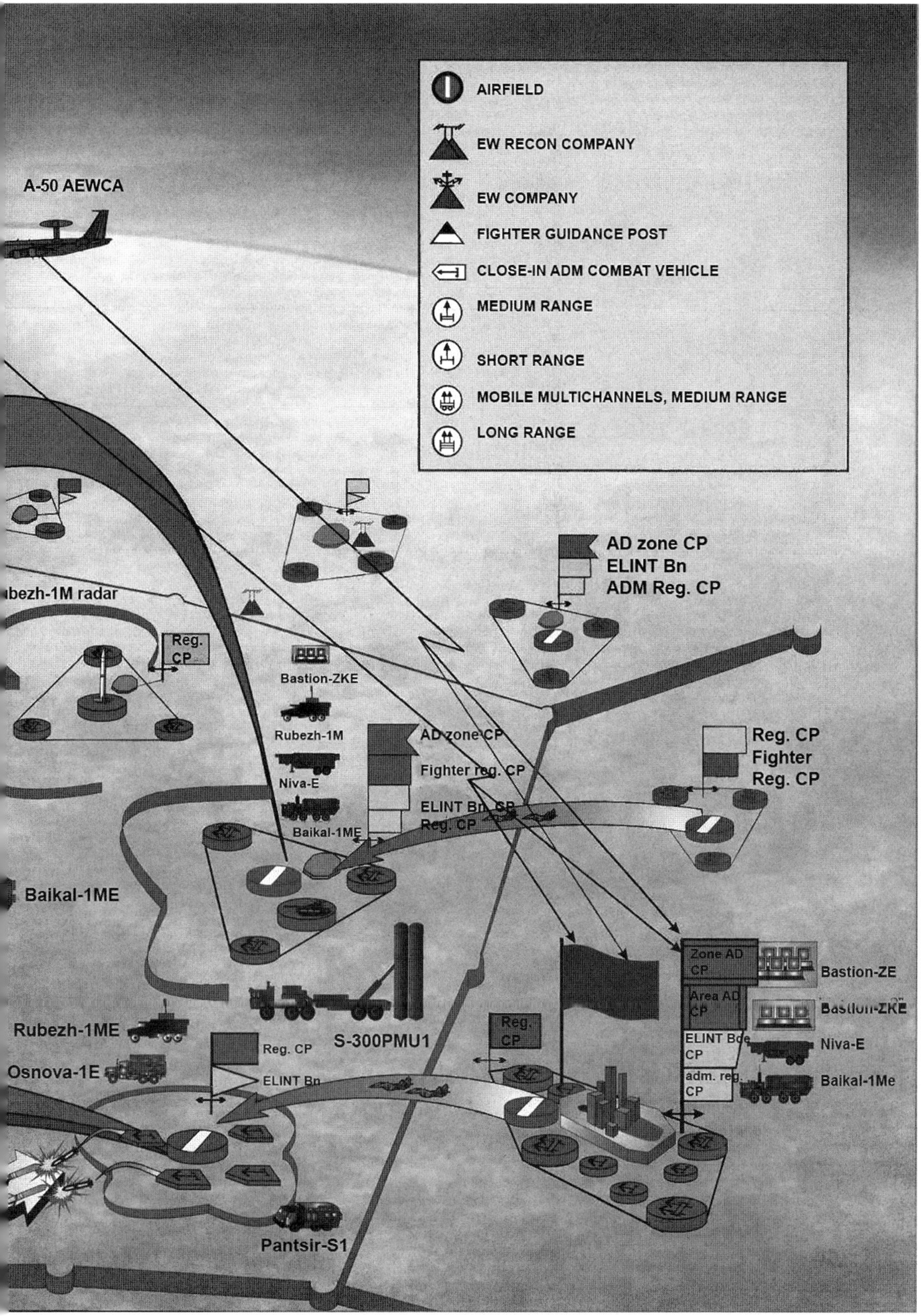
AIRFIELD
EW RECON COMPANY
EW COMPANY
FIGHTER GUIDANCE POST
CLOSE-IN ADM COMBAT VEHICLE
MEDIUM RANGE
SHORT RANGE
MOBILE MULTICHANNELS, MEDIUM RANGE
LONG RANGE
A-50 AEWCA
AD zone CP
ELINT Bn
ADM Reg. CP
bezh-1M radar
Reg. CP
Bastion-ZKE
Rubezh-1M
Niva-E
Baikal-1ME
AD zone CP
Fighter reg. CP
ELINT Bn CP
Reg. CP
Reg. CP
Fighter
Reg. CP
Baikal-1ME
Zone AD CP
Area AD CP
ELINT Bde CP
adm. reg. CP
Bastion-ZE
Niva-E
Baikal-1Me
Rubezh-1ME
Osnova-1E
S-300PMU1
Reg. CP
ELINT Bn
Reg. CP
Pantsir-S1

The organisation, structure and development of air defence are subordinated to the following basic principles:

- distribution of aerospace threat situation data to users in a centralised manner;
- the responsibility of a single authority for the organisation of air defence over the entire national territory and for the engagement of intruders;
- flexibility of the air defence system and its capacity to build up resources in any region of the country, should military tension begin to mount;
- pursuit of a well-coordinated military and technical policy aimed at a further improvement of the air defence system as a whole and its subsystems in particular;
- effective utilisation of integrated air defence; and
- assets and their centralised command and control subsystem.

Structurally, an integrated air defence system comprises air defence regions ('okrug') and areas. It is essentially a combined war system made up of several integrated and interrelated subsystems.

An integrated air defence system includes:

- airspace control and surveillance system;
- fighter-interceptor force tasked to provide air cover;
- missile defence system;[2]
- electronic warfare and countermeasures system; and
- automated command and control system.

Airspace Control and Surveillance System

The aerospace surveillance system comprises intelligence-gathering assets of all the armed services, including ground-based, sea-based, air-based and space-based radar, and radio, electronic and optoelectronic equipment. The appropriate high-credibility intelligence unveiling current enemy intentions and preparations for war and disclosing the composition, location and actions of his aerospace forces can be obtained through the use of all of them in their entirety to permit air defence personnel to use the potential of the air defence system to the maximum possible extent (Fig.1-2).

The airspace surveillance system is multi-layered. The first layer is subordinated to the highest authorities and uses such intelligence-gathering assets as space-based radio, electronic, radar and optoelectronic intelligence-gathering facilities and land- and sea-based electronic intelligence assets. The second layer comprises air-based radar and electronic intelligence assets, ground-based electronic intelligence assets of the air defence troops and civil aviation traffic control assets. The third layer operates ground-based radars, whose primary role is to supply information to fighter aviation and to air defence missile forces.

One of the principal elements of airspace surveillance and integrated national air defence systems is a radar-based data-gathering system. It envisions the creation of a single, continuous, automatically-controlled radar field, with continuous low-altitude radar fields over certain areas to protect vital installations or the creation of near-border (maritime) low-altitude automatically-controlled early warning zones. The low-altitude radar cover can be extended if the general airspace surveillance system includes airborne and shipborne surveillance, and weapons-guidance radar.

In peacetime, the integrated automatically-controlled radar surveillance system carries out its dedicated missions in the interests of air defence, including continuous

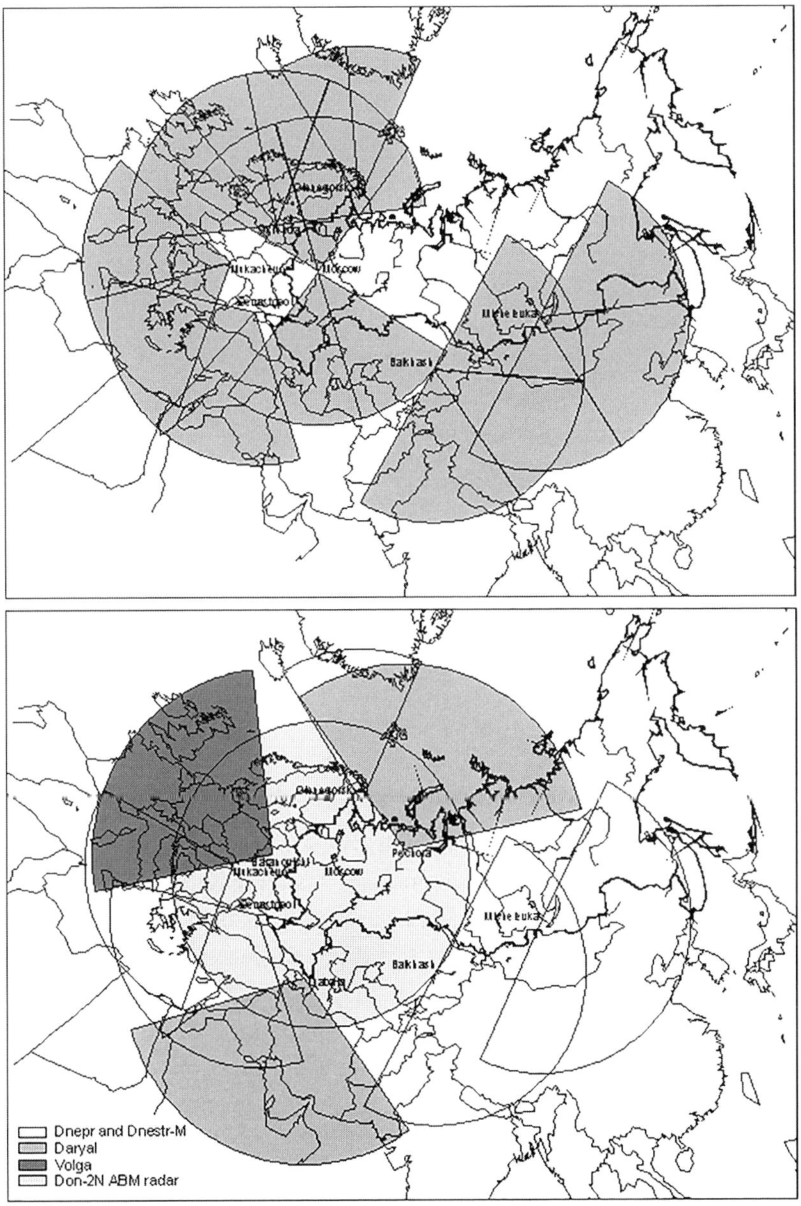

Figure 1-2: Russian aerospace cover – sample. (*Source: Pavel Podvig,* Science and Global Security *10(1), January 2002, 21–60*)

surveillance of airspace, transmission of air-threat situation data to superiors to warn them of mounting tension and of the beginning of air attack, and monitoring of air traffic across/along national borders and over the entire territory of the country. In wartime, the system furnishes operational information and intelligence to the command centres and air defence weapons sites, and to electronic countermeasures assets. The availability of electronic reconnaissance units, intelligence-gathering and information stations of the country's air defence command centres and air defence regions and areas of up-to-date automation complexes of the Fundament type and the Nebo-M, Barier-E, Gamma-SE, Gamma-DE, Kasta-2E2, Desna-ME and Protivnik-GE radar systems capable of operating in active and standby modes at high, medium and low altitudes makes it possible to create a multiple-band electromagnetic field.

Fighter-Interceptor Force

Fighter-interceptors make the entire air defence system extremely potent and dynamic. Their primary mission is to defeat enemy aircraft armed with precision-guided weapons, electronic countermeasures aircraft, airborne early warning and control aircraft and other air threats. They also engage in a manoeuvrable aerial combat with all types of manned aircraft and engage cruise missiles at a wide range of altitudes and speeds, in any weather, by day and night, at far and near approaches to installations being protected. Structurally, the fighter-interceptor subsystem of the air defence system is multi-layered and features an integrated automated battle-management capability aimed to control fighter-interceptors in service with the Air Force and Navy. The interceptor force operates modern and upgraded aircraft like the Su-27, Su-30MK, Su-35, MiG-29 and MiG-31 fighters (Fig 1-3) and the A-50 and A-100 airborne early warning and control aircraft. The operations centres of air defence regions and areas, the command posts of fighter aviation divisions and regiments and the vectoring posts of fighter aircraft are fitted out with automation equipment, such as the Rubezh-1ME and Rubezh-2ME, for example.

Missile Defence System

The missile defence systems provide the main source of firepower to air defence. Built from a point or point-region defences it is well planned, organised and timed for specific lines, directions, heights and sectors (or zones). Moreover, it combines zones defended by surface-to-air missile (SAM) and anti-aircraft artillery units deployed with combat formations. Russia has three main components – Air and Missile Defence Forces as a part of VKS, ground forces air and missile defence (V-PVO – PVO Sukhoputnykh Voysk)[3] which is independent from the Air Defence Forces, although coordination of their respective operations remains necessary, and naval air defence as a part of the Russian Navy.

The main principles underlying the organisation of the missile defence system are the development of integrated missile defence systems based on up-to-date long-, medium-

Figure 1-3: Su-35 and Mig-31. (*Source: Russian MoD*)

and short-range multi-channel guided SAMs for various purposes (for example S-300 (Fig. 1-4), S-400, S-500 of various modifications, S-350, Pantsir-S1, Buk-M2 and M3 (Fig. 1-5) and Tor-M2); information-gathering and automated control systems (Baikal-1ME, Senezh-M1E), which combines them and ensures their effective operation; multi-layered organisation of air defence of vital areas and facilities of the country; ability to counter any type of modern air threat from potential enemies, including precision-guided munition (PGM) carriers and weapons in flight, in any operating environment; high immunity of SAM systems to enemy weapons and electronic countermeasures (this is done by enhancing the mobility of air defence missile units, concealment of combat

Figure 1-4: S-300PM.

formations, engineer organisation of firing positions, employment of different types of air defence missiles in a single grouping and quick replacement of disabled elements); and close cooperation between air defence groupings, as well as with units of other arms such as Army Air Defence.

The main task of the air defence missile forces is to defend vital military installations, important civilian facilities and the state infrastructure against high-density air attacks by manned and unmanned weapons systems. Moreover, they can defeat an enemy's strike aircraft, airborne early warning and control aircraft and electronic countermeasures aircraft, as well as reconnaissance/strike aircraft at long range.

Electronic Warfare and Countermeasures System

The purpose of the electronic warfare and countermeasures (ECM) system is to disorganise control of hostile air attack weapons while they are in the air and to jam airborne radars. ECM units protect key military installations and vital facilities of the national economy to prevent their location by an adversary's reconnaissance assets and their attack from the air. The ECM units can operate both autonomously and in cooperation with the combat units in order to enhance the efficiency of air defence. The ECM system can perform successfully if its electronic reconnaissance, electronic countermeasures (Krasukha [Fig. 1-6], SPN-2, SPN-3, SPN-4 and R-9SA4U) and automation facilities, used to

Figure 1-5: Buk-M2 and Pantsir-S1. (*Source: Russian MoD*)

allocate targets and control air defence operations, are combined. It can use passive countermeasures, including chaff, smoke and aerosols, which change the electromagnetic properties of the medium; and absorbent coatings, etc., which considerably reduce the reflecting properties of objects being protected.

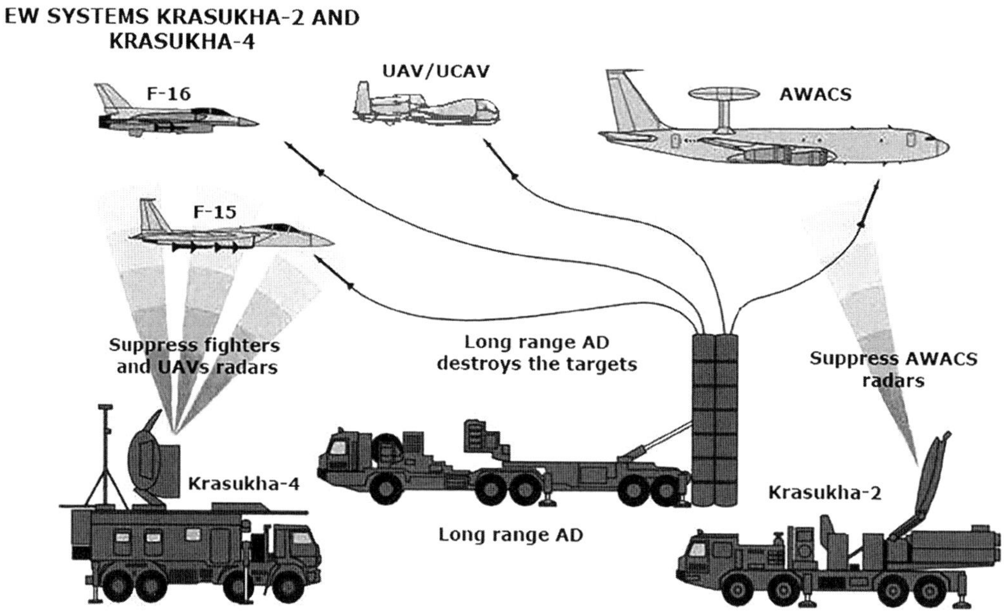

Figure 1-6: Krasukha EW systems.

The ECM system is capable of suppressing multifunctional and special-purpose radars carried on board combat aircraft, radio altimeters installed in cruise missiles, short-wave and ultra-short-wave communication lines used by manned aircraft, and the receivers of navigation systems.

Automated Control System

The automated control system concentrates real-time control of different air defence assets operating at different organisational levels in the hands of a single authority and ensures that the characteristics of all combat systems are employed to their maximum effectiveness (Fig. 1-7).

The air defence forces control system features a multilevel structure and comprises the strategic component, including the main command post of the Commander-in-Chief of the Air Force; the operational component, including command posts of air defence regions equipped with the Bastion-ZE system; the operational-tactical component, including area air defence command posts equipped with the Universal-1E system; and the tactical component, including the command posts of air defence missile, fighter aviation and electronic countermeasures units fitted out with appropriate automation facilities.

Progressive refinement of the integrated air defence system, modernisation of air defence weapons and equipment, and the creation of a single automated control system uniting the air force and the air defence troops makes it possible to enhance the combat capabilities of Russian air defence forces, combine all air defence resources of the Armed Forces into a single entity with a view to the specific features of each region, and ensure

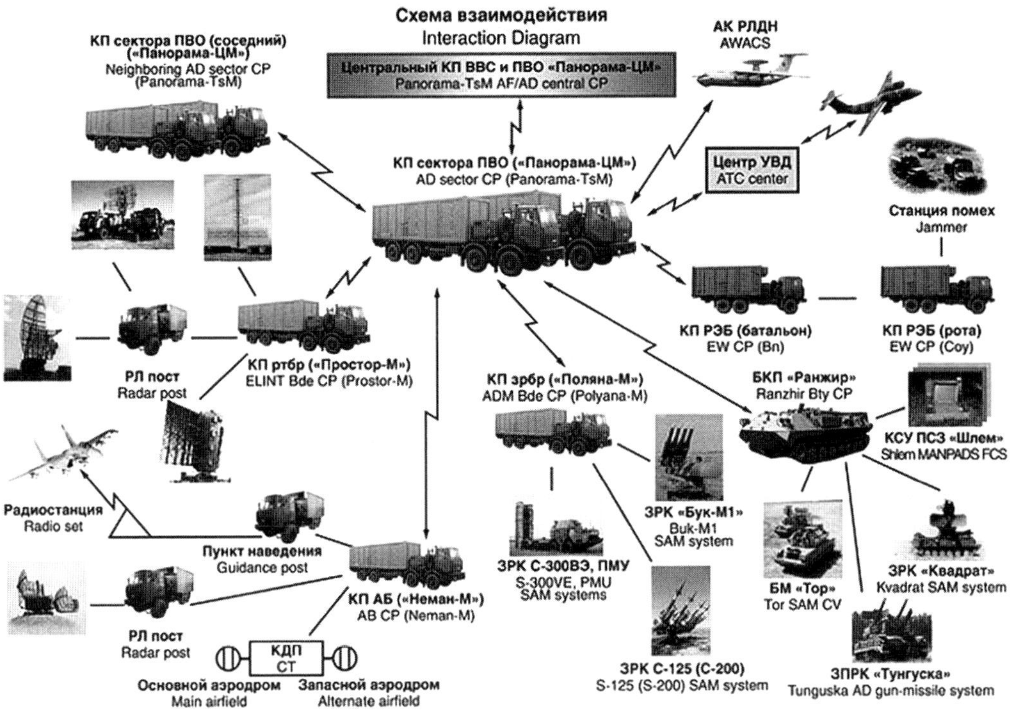

The Agat Panorama TsM Air Defence Area/Sector Mobile Command Post is a good example of the highly integrated systems approach taken in the design of contemporary IADS. It also illustrates the level of penetration achieved by COTS computing technology in modern Russian designs. Note that both legacy and contemporary missile batteries are supported, as well as VHF band and microwave radars (Agat).

Figure 1-7: The Air Defence Area/Sector Mobile Command Post.

balanced development of air surveillance, the fighter force, missile defence, electronic countermeasures and automated control systems.

The integrated air defence system is one of the major components making up the country's overall defence system. It serves as a deterrent to potential threats in peacetime and is a decisive factor in seizing and holding the strategic initiative in the event of a military conflict.

To reach a new qualitative level of efficiency of the air defence armament system of the Air Force, the thrust of development is toward comprehensive harmonisation of intelligence-gathering activities and strike and defensive assets. The primary focus of this effort involves the development of modular combat and intelligence-gathering systems integrated into a single automated information and battle-management system enabling air defence personnel to carry out both their dedicated air defence missions and non-strategic missile defence missions.

Modern Russian Integrated Air Defence[4]

A modern IADS is one of the most formidable threats that an air force can be tasked to confront. Given the level of overmatch possessed by NATO against any potential state adversaries in terms of combat aircraft and associated aerial enabling capabilities, it is unsurprising that both Russia and China have invested significant resources into developing ground-based methods to deny Western air forces access to their airspace. Russia, in particular, develops and manufactures the most potent SAM systems in the world and has done so since the mid-Cold War.

When discussing the issue of ground-based air defences and the threat they pose to NATO forces, policy and media discussions typically focus on long-range, so-called 'strategic' SAM systems such as the S-400 (SA-21 'Growler') due to their ability to project a missile engagement zone (MEZ) over large areas of territory. However, it is crucial to understand that these systems are intended to be deployed as part of a multi-layered IADS rather than as standalone batteries. The S-300VM/4 (SA-23 'Gladiator'/'Giant') and S-400 series are designed as modular systems, able to interface with, control and enhance the capabilities of older, short-range systems in addition to their own organic radar and launcher vehicles.

An S-300VM/4 or S-400 battalion will include at least one command vehicle, such as the D4M1 Polyana or 55K6E, which functions not only as a command-and-coordination centre for the battalion itself, but also as a data fusion and relay node. These command vehicles are linked to other IADS elements by multiple radio datalinks and are also able to leverage local infrastructure such as WiFi, mobile networks and landlines laid at pre-prepared firing positions to improve command and control (C2) resilience. The sophisticated fire-control and acquisition radars[5] which form part of the battalion can be used to provide longer-range and more accurate target data to older SAM systems such as the S-300, Buk-M1-2 and S-200 that are linked up and controlled via the command vehicle. This technique can greatly enhance the effectiveness of older systems which are limited in terms of performance more by their radar capabilities than by their missiles.

This modular architecture also allows S-300V or S-400 units to bypass the radar horizon limitations of their own organic radar assets by using radar tracks generated by third-party sensors. These might be ground-based in the form of medium- or even short-range mobile SAM units such as Buk-M2 or Buk-M3 batteries, which are generally sited much closer to potential enemy threats than the strategic SAMs. They might also be from airborne assets in the shape of the A-50M and the new A-100 AWACS, or MiG-31BM interceptor flights surveying the battlespace from high altitude and at standoff ranges.

Russia has relied much more heavily than the West on ground-based air defences as a core pillar of its great-power competition strategy. With long land borders to the east, south and west, the Soviet Union and later the Russian Federation saw a multi-layered IADS as essential to its national defence capabilities. As Western dominance in the air environment increased following the end of the Cold War and especially in local conflicts, Russian reliance on its IADS and the priority afforded to continued development and modernisation of the key systems has also increased. The admission of Poland and the Baltic States to NATO following the end of the Cold War, however, has significantly changed the potential importance of these traditionally defensive systems within the context of any standoff with Russia over these countries. The long engagement range offered by modern strategic SAMs allows Russia to threaten NATO's freedom of access to much of the airspace of these Eastern member states without the systems themselves ever leaving Russian territory, especially from the area of Kaliningrad (Fig. 1-8).

This capability is provided in large part by two 400km-class missiles; the 40N6 and 9M82MD, which have been developed for firing by the S-400 and S-300V respectively. Both the S-400 and S-300V are designed to fire a range of missiles out of common launch tubes to cover multiple engagement range brackets and target types. For example, the S-400 uses the 400km-range 40N6 missile and the 250km-range 48N6E3, as well as the much smaller and more agile 120km-range 9M96E2 and 40km-range 9M96E. This design philosophy allows these strategic SAM systems to save the largest, most expensive missiles for those engagements where extra reach is really needed, using medium- and short-range missiles wherever possible. The smaller size of the medium- and short-range missile types also allows more ammunition to be carried in launch tubes, ready to fire, per battery than if all missiles carried were the very-long-range types.

The Russian Ministry of Defence officially accepted the 40N6 for active service in October 2018, and it has also been sold to China to equip the latter's S-400 systems which were previously supplied by Russia. There is much less clarity around the status of

Figure 1-8: Kaliningrad S-400 engagement zone.

the 9M82MD. However, since the 40N6 has now entered service it seems fair to assume that Almaz-Antey – the parent company for the design bureaus which manufacture both the 40N6 and 9M82MD – has managed to solve the active seeker guidance, cueing and aerodynamic control issues surrounding this class of hypersonic long-range SAM. Since a long-range equivalent to the S-400's 40N6 for the S-300V remains a priority for Russian IADS planners, the 9M82MD will likely enter service soon, if it has not done so already. Not content with having developed the S-300V and S-400 as the backbone of its long-range 'strategic' SAM systems, Russia is actively testing an even longer-ranged derivative with greater anti-ballistic missile capabilities, named the S-500. As if to illustrate Russian long-range SAM design capabilities, a prototype S-500 system successfully destroyed an aerial target from a distance of almost 500km during testing in 2018. Due to the radar-horizon issues discussed previously – as well as different target speeds, altitudes and headings – the range of these systems in practical terms is often significantly less than advertised. This is especially true against low radar cross-section (RCS[6]), highly agile and aware targets such as fighter aircraft, but this should not distract from the fact that Russian strategic SAMs can project a high-threat MEZ over hundreds of kilometres, especially against enabler aircraft like tankers and AWACS. Radars positioned further forward or on raised terrain can cue in long-range active missile shots, and A-50M and MiG-31BM interceptors could potentially supply targeting data unaffected by the radar horizon if successfully connected by datalink to the ground-based IADS.

Russia has also been investing heavily in developing and upgrading a wide variety of different radar types, both for use as part of SAM systems and as standalone systems to feed into the IADS as a whole. In the past 15 years, most have been specifically designed to improve detection ranges against low-observable (stealth) and low-flying targets including fifth-generation fighters and modern cruise missiles. Any stealth aircraft design is a compromise between aerodynamic properties and visibility from different angles in various parts of the electromagnetic spectrum. For example, the US F-22 Raptor is extremely difficult to detect from almost any angle in the X-band of the electromagnetic spectrum which is typically used in fire-control radars. However, its airframe shaping is less effective at reducing returns when illuminated by radars in the metre and decimetre wavelengths. On the other hand, radars operating at significantly shorter or longer wavelengths face varying trade-offs in terms of effective range for a given power level, resolution and radar horizon.

The Russian approach has been to develop multiple classes of digital radar operating across a broad range of the radar spectrum, scanning for targets from multiple different angles and ranges to allow the returns to be cross-referenced. The idea is that this multi-static, multi-frequency approach will overcome many of the advantages of stealth aircraft by ensuring a sufficiently high effective resolution to allow detection and tracking at much greater ranges. A good example of this approach is the 3D multiband RLM-M Nebo-M radar which incorporates different-frequency transmitter and receiver elements, as well as passive receivers to generate a multi-static, multi-frequency picture in one system. Naturally, the Nebo-M is designed to feed directly into either S-400 or S-300V battalions' command vehicles, and increase the long-range and anti-stealth capabilities of the whole IADS through them. Through this sort of innovative radar technology, it is likely that Russia's IADS in Eastern Europe has a limited capability to detect and track stealth aircraft like the F-22, B-2 and F-35 under certain conditions, albeit at shorter ranges than traditional combat aircraft. This does not, however, translate directly into an ability to complete the kill chain by successfully guiding SAMs to intercept those stealth aircraft, which are themselves highly lethal, mobile and designed specifically to destroy, evade or suppress strategic SAM systems. However, Russian radar technology will only continue to improve in this regard and the true combat performance for both sides' systems under actual warfighting conditions is almost impossible to predict with certainty.

Russia's IADS is much more than simply strategic SAMs fed by a broad range of early-warning, anti-stealth and fire-control radars. The mobile medium-range and short-range SAM systems which form part of every Russian army manoeuvre element are also a vital component. Systems like the medium-range Buk-M2 (SA-17) and the short-range Tor-M2 (SA-15) and Pantsir-S1 (SA-22) ensure that any Russian brigade positioned ahead of a strategic SAM unit presents a formidable initial obstacle to any would-be suppression of air defence (SEAD) mission. In an Eastern European context, this means that in any scenario where NATO forces were faced with massing or aggressive Russian ground forces, those Russian forces would not only be a challenge on the ground but act as an extension of the IADS. Significant numbers of medium-range BUK-M2 SAMs near the line of contact and the strategic long-range S-400 and S-300V batteries further back would mutually support and enhance each other's capabilities. Meanwhile, the presence of large numbers of short-range SAMs, man-portable air defence systems (MANPADS) like the Igla-S (SA-24) and Verba (SA-25) series, as well as short-defence systems like the Pantsir-S1 would make low-altitude flight extremely hazardous for both aircraft and cruise missiles over a considerable area. The Verba MANPADS can be linked to the broader IADS through the system's automated control system, giving the operator helmet-fed indications of approaching enemy aircraft or helicopters before they are visible to the naked eye. The presence of MANPADS and radar-guided anti-aircraft artillery (AAA)/point-defence SAMs such as the Pantsir-S1 and Tunguska (SA-19 'Grison') make the low-level environment near Russian forces very dangerous for aircraft, whilst the larger SAMs are at their most effective against targets flying at medium altitudes and above. The Pantsir-S1 also provides integrated point defence to S-400 and S-300V batteries, deploying with them to shoot down incoming cruise missiles and anti-radiation missiles. This means that in addition to the challenges of finding and getting into weapons range of an active strategic SAM battery within the IADS, SEAD/DEAD forces would need multiple near-simultaneous weapon deliveries to have a high probability of a kill against each SAM asset. In other words, Russia could use the fact that its ground-force formations are extremely well provided with their own SAMs and other air defences such as MANPADS and radar-guided AAA, all of which can interface with the longer-range strategic S-400 and S-300V systems, to present a multi-layered challenge to NATO air forces in any Eastern European flashpoint scenario.

This multi-layered physical defence network made up of SAMs and AAA is further strengthened by sophisticated electronic warfare capabilities. The US Department of Defense notes that Russian IADS also contain systems designed to 'jam aircraft navigation, communications, target acquisition systems, and guided weapons'. Systems such as the Krasukha-4 1RL257 broadband jammer, the R-330Zh Zhytel GPS and satcom jammer and the SPR-2M RTUT-BM munitions-fuze jammer ensure that Western aircraft, sensor and weapons systems would be less reliable and suffer degraded performance in any operation against Russian forces compared to normal conditions.

In broad strategic terms, this means that Russia can present a sufficiently dense and sophisticated IADS to make sustained NATO air operations over the Baltic States and significant parts of Poland prohibitively costly during the first phases of any military clash in the region. NATO relies very heavily on traditional fast jets such as the F-16, the Typhoon and the Rafale for much of its rapidly-deployable firepower. This is a major regional advantage for Russian forces which rely on ground-based artillery and heavily armoured formations for the bulk of their firepower. The IADS coverage would also provide a buffer area of relatively safe airspace for Russian Aerospace Forces' fighters to operate against enemy ground forces during the first phases of any clash, despite said fighters being technically and operationally outmatched by the leading NATO air forces in a head-to-head clash. NATO air forces would be able to mount a viable SEAD/DEAD effort with the help of a combination of stealth fighters like the F-35 and standoff munitions from air, naval and ground-based launchers. However, such an effort would need careful coordination as a joint force to achieve 'pulses' of temporary access into the IADS and slow degradation of key radars and C2 nodes. Getting all the required forces (most of them American) into theatre and ready to fight, with the required weapons stocks and enablers in place, would take weeks. The SEAD/DEAD campaign itself would also take weeks to degrade the IADS to the extent whereby something like semi-permissive airspace could be established over the area of operations for non-stealth NATO aircraft. Such an effort would also require kinetic strikes on targets on Russian soil to destroy key radars and C2 facilities, with significant political risk and escalation implications.

With the first-mover advantage in terms of mobilisation and a greatly reduced distance for heavy forces to cover compared to US, UK, French or German forces, Russia can outmatch NATO on the ground in the Baltic States in the initial phase of any conflict. The strength of IADS for Russia, then, is that they offer a way to keep NATO's airpower occupied and at arm's length for the first weeks of any conflict. With most of NATO airpower committed to SEAD/DEAD efforts and only able to achieve temporary inroads into the defences in large, pre-planned strike packages rather than ranging freely over the battlespace, IADS offer Russia enough potential breathing space to establish a fait accompli on the ground. As a result, it helps an otherwise strategically-outmatched military power to project a credible military threat to NATO's eastern flank.

Chapter 2

Air Defence 'Electronic Eyes'

Stealth technology is the most potent tool and symbol of US military power. For Russia, that is a challenge that they had to face straight on. Russian officials admitted in 2001 that they used remains from the USAF F-117 stealth fighter shot down over Yugoslavia to improve their air defence systems. A senior Russian aerospace official said that they were able to test their system against the broken pieces. Of course, Russia will never say what information they were able to get and are likely to try to mislead and downplay what they recovered. The fact is, anti-stealth radars were rapidly developed afterwards. The early Nebo VHF radar at the MAKS air show in 2001 was the ancestor of the huge active electronically-scanned array shown in 2013. Stealth modifications to tactical aircraft were confirmed a couple of years later when engineers from Moscow's Institute for Theoretical and Applied Electromagnetics spoke at a London conference about RCS reduction work on the Sukhoi Su-27 family.

The Russian Defence Ministry's 2nd Central Scientific & Research Institute (2nd TzNII[1]) and its facilities, in Tver, tested RCS models of the F-117, B-2 and many other aircraft (Fig 2-1 and 2-2).

Figure 2-1: CNII VKKO radar research institute. (*Source: Voenaya Priemka*)

A typical conventional aircraft signature strategy is shown in a) and a stealth aircraft signature strategy might be as shown in b). ,here several main spikes contain most of the RCS signature. A modern stealth aircraft signature strategy is where there are a couple of main spikes that contain most of the RCS signature. The total RCS integrated over all directions will not be much better than that of a non-stealthy platform. By pushing most of the RCS into a few large spikes then everywhere else can be much lower. If those directions are in areas that the threat cannot exploit, then the platform can be stealthy (like B-2). The idea is to design a platform in such a way that there are only a few RCS spikes in carefully controlled directions. The goal of the radar is to be able to detect, track and lock onto the target by exploiting those spikes.

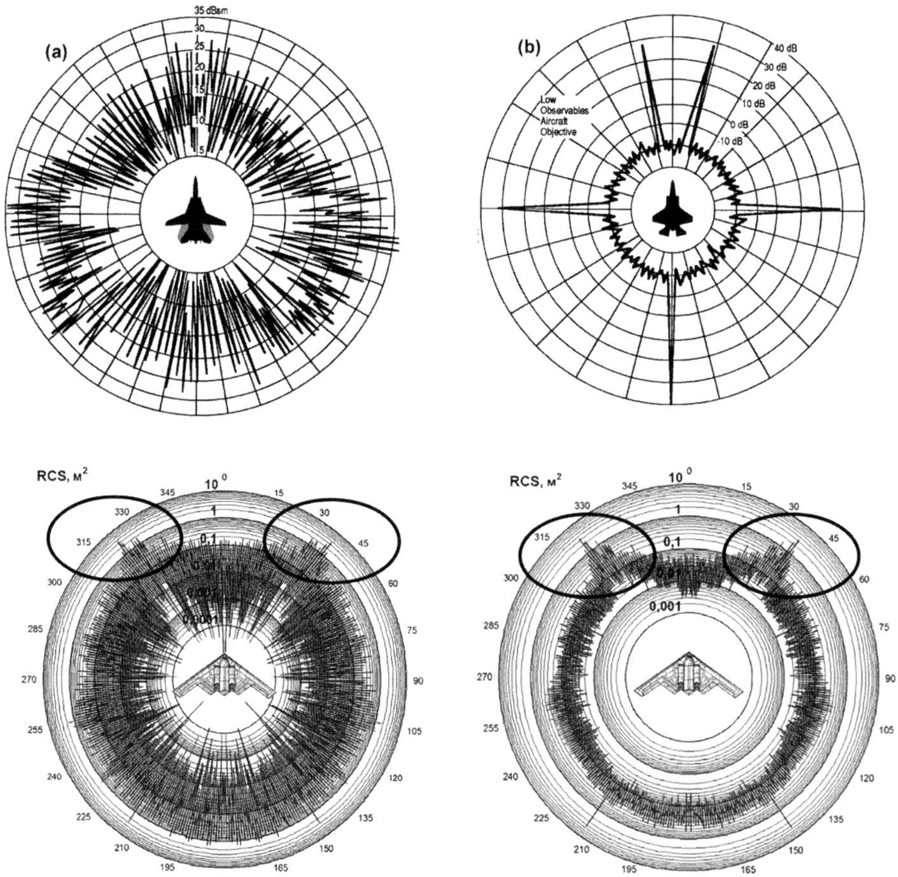

Circular diagram of instantaneous RSS at electromagnetic illumination at frequencies of 10 GHz (3 cm wave length)

Circular diagrams of non-coherent RCS at electromagnetic illumination at frequencies of 10 GHz (3 cm wave length)

B-2 circular RCS for 10 GHz/3cm radar which is a common frequency in fire control radars. (Source: Raseyanie Elektromagnetnih Voln, modified by author)

Figure 2-2: Typical non-stealth and stealth RCS (top) and B-2 simulated RCS (bottom).

Tactics and procedures for the attackers were improved, as were counter-stealth measures for the defenders. Some of the manuals have been rewritten and corrected. The F-117A, now officially retired (since 2008), was a revolutionary aircraft which pushed the boundaries of aerodynamics and stealth into new areas. New stealth aircraft have been developed, and they are and will be involved in conflicts and wars to come. Air defence has also evolved; there are constant improvements with new systems introduced. It is a never-ending process. There are three major fields where these technologies clash:

- Stealth aircraft.
- Counter-stealth detection and tracking.
- Air defence missiles.

The Opponents

The F-117A, B-2 (Fig 2-2, Fig 2-3) and B1-B can be regarded as the three emblematic low-observability aircraft of the late 1980s. Having realised the capabilities offered by low-observability technology, the US went on developing a number of stealth jet fighters, such as the F-22A. Lockheed Martin was the prime contractor and Boeing the main partner (Fig. 2-4).

The Lockheed Martin (LM) F-35 Lightning II (Fig. 2-5 and 2-6) is a general fighter with stealth capabilities currently in production. There are three variants, the F-35A CTOL (Conventional Take-Off and Landing), the F-35B STOVL (Short-Take Off and Vertical-Landing) and the F-35C CV (Carrier Variant). The F-35 is based on the Joint Strike Fighter (JSF) programme, which started in the mid-1990s. In 2001 the LM X-35 won the JSF competition over the Boeing X-32. Consequently LM was awarded the System Development and Demonstration contract to develop the F-35, based on X-35. The development of the F-35 is funded primarily by the US but also by several other partner nations. The F-35's first foreign buyer was Israel.

It is claimed that the F-35 fuselage design was a compromise between cost and requirements and some capabilities were 'sacrificed': RCS is low in the X-band (8–12 GHz) and in the Ku-band (12–18 GHz), while it is not so low at lower frequency bands. The aim is the breaking of the kill chain:[2] even if the F-35 is detected by surveillance radar, it may not be easy to engage it with a fire-control radar, which usually operates in the X or Ku bands. The F-22, on the other hand, presents a lower RCS from all aspects and at more frequency bands, of course at a considerably higher cost (Fig. 2-4, 2-7).

The production F-35 presents a slightly higher RCS than the prototype X-35 since more volume was required for internal equipment and armament bays. The curves of the redesigned fuselage will incur an RCS increase from some certain directions. It was calculated that the RCS would remain very low from the frontal sector – to be precise, from a sector of 29° in front of the aircraft. However, the RCS will not be so low from the lateral aspect or the rear. The researchers at Air Power Australia created a 3-D model of the underside of the fuselage and tried to calculate the RCS using the POFACETS algorithm developed at the Naval Postgraduate School of the USN.

In any case, there is no doubt that the F-35 exhibits stealth capabilities, maybe not as good as the F-22 but probably better than any other aircraft. To estimate the maximum detection range for the F-35, first there should be an estimation of its RCS, and then a calculation, using the radar equation and the logic mentioned before, with respect to the detection range for a standard target used for comparison purposes. As a 'standard target' for the comparison, a $1m^2$ RCS target is used. A target of $1m^2$ RCS corresponds

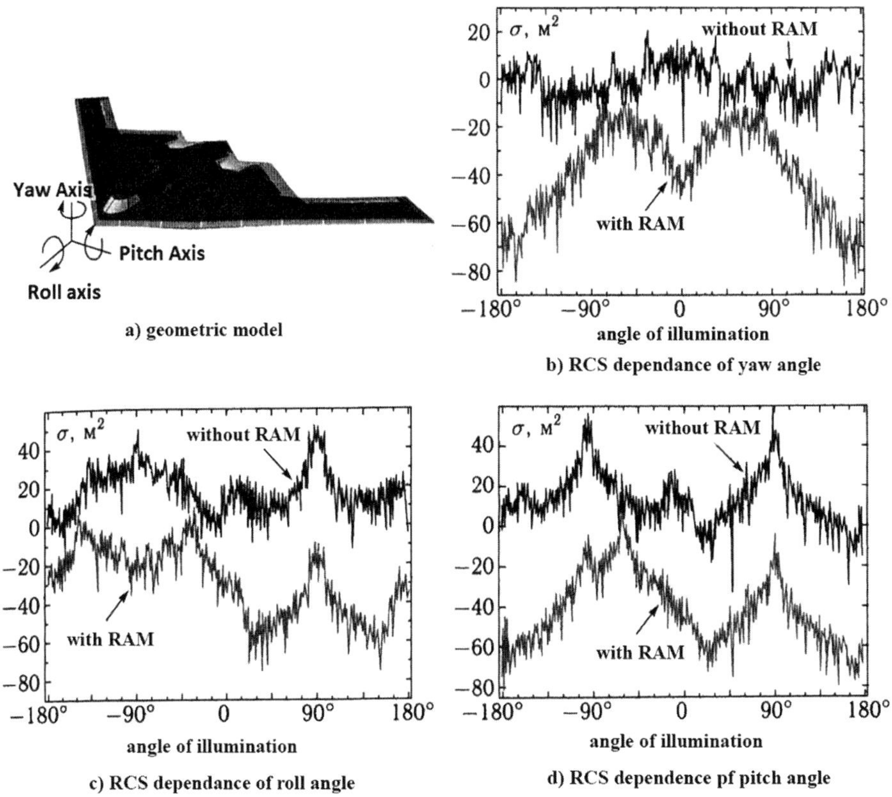

Calculated RCS values for B-2

With and without RAM (Radar Absorping Material)

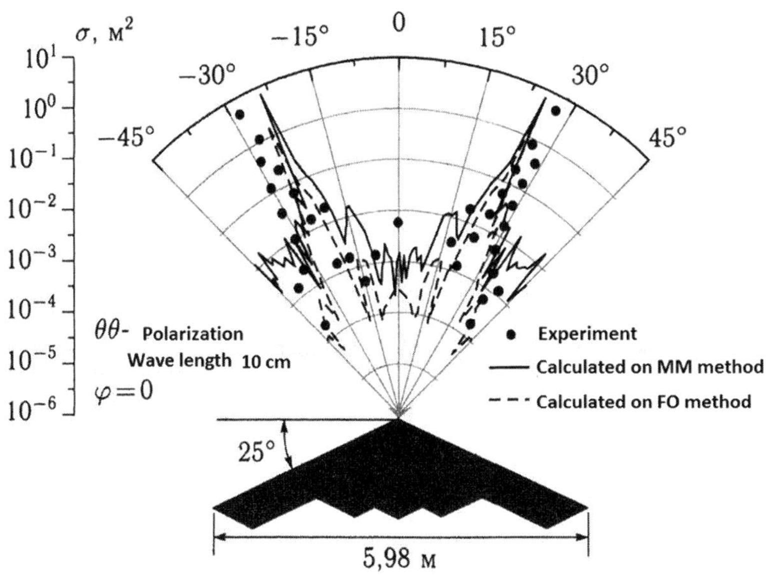

B-2 model monostatic RCS diagram

Figure 2-3: CNII VKKO B-2 calculated RCS.

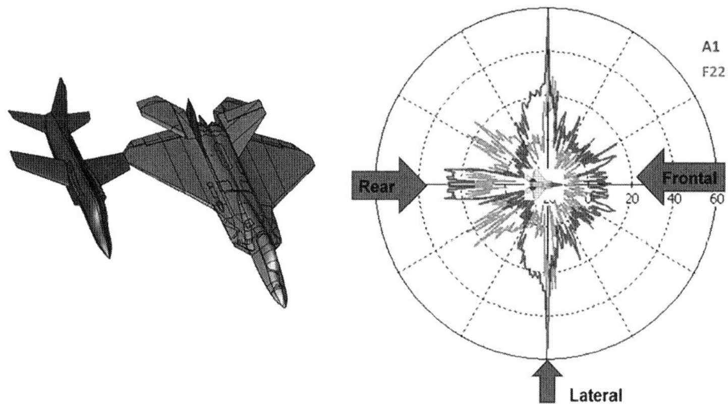

Comparison of the sizes of the AMX-A1 and the F-22 (left). Monostatic RCS plot of both planes, at the frequency of 10.5GHz (right). (Source: Radar Cross Section of a stealthy aircraft using electromagnetic simulation in the X and in VHF/UHF Bands, IJRAME)

Figure 2-4: F-22 Raptor monostatic RCS.

Figure 2-5: F-35 Lighting II. (*Source: USAF*)

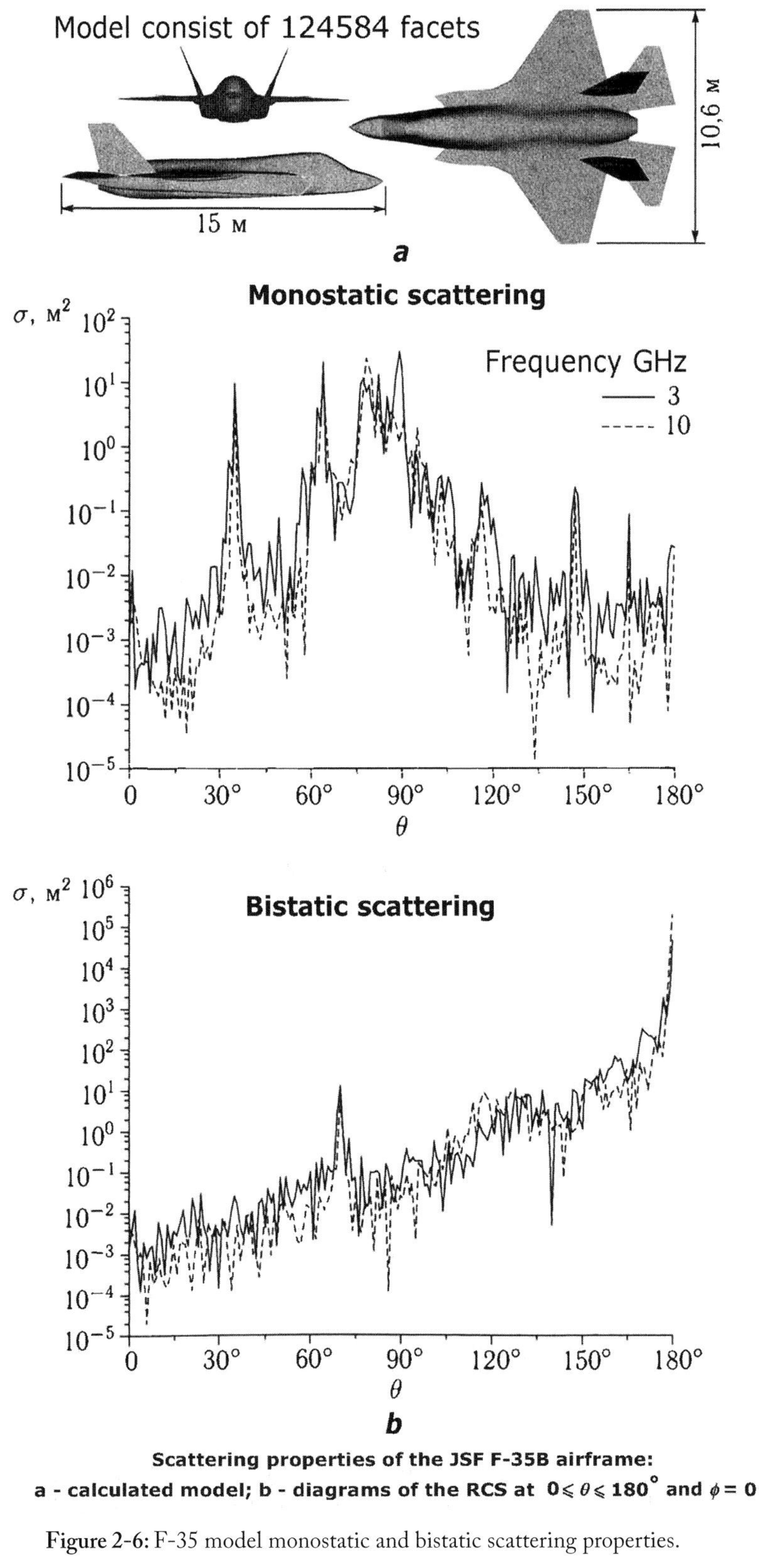

Figure 2-6: F-35 model monostatic and bistatic scattering properties.

to a small fighter, such as the Northrop T-38 Talon. Simulated RCS is shown in Fig. 2-7 and Fig. 2-8.

The detection range for a 64N6E search radar of the S-300 PMU-1 system (operating in the S-band with a maximum range of 300km), for a 1m^2 RCS target is calculated to be 200km. For the 30N6E1 engagement radar of the same system operating in the X-band, with a maximum range of 150km, while the detection range for a 'standard target' is 100km.

Boeing proposed a low-observability (LO) variant of its proven F-15E fighter, designated F-15SE Silent Eagle. Initially Boeing declared that the F-15SE would

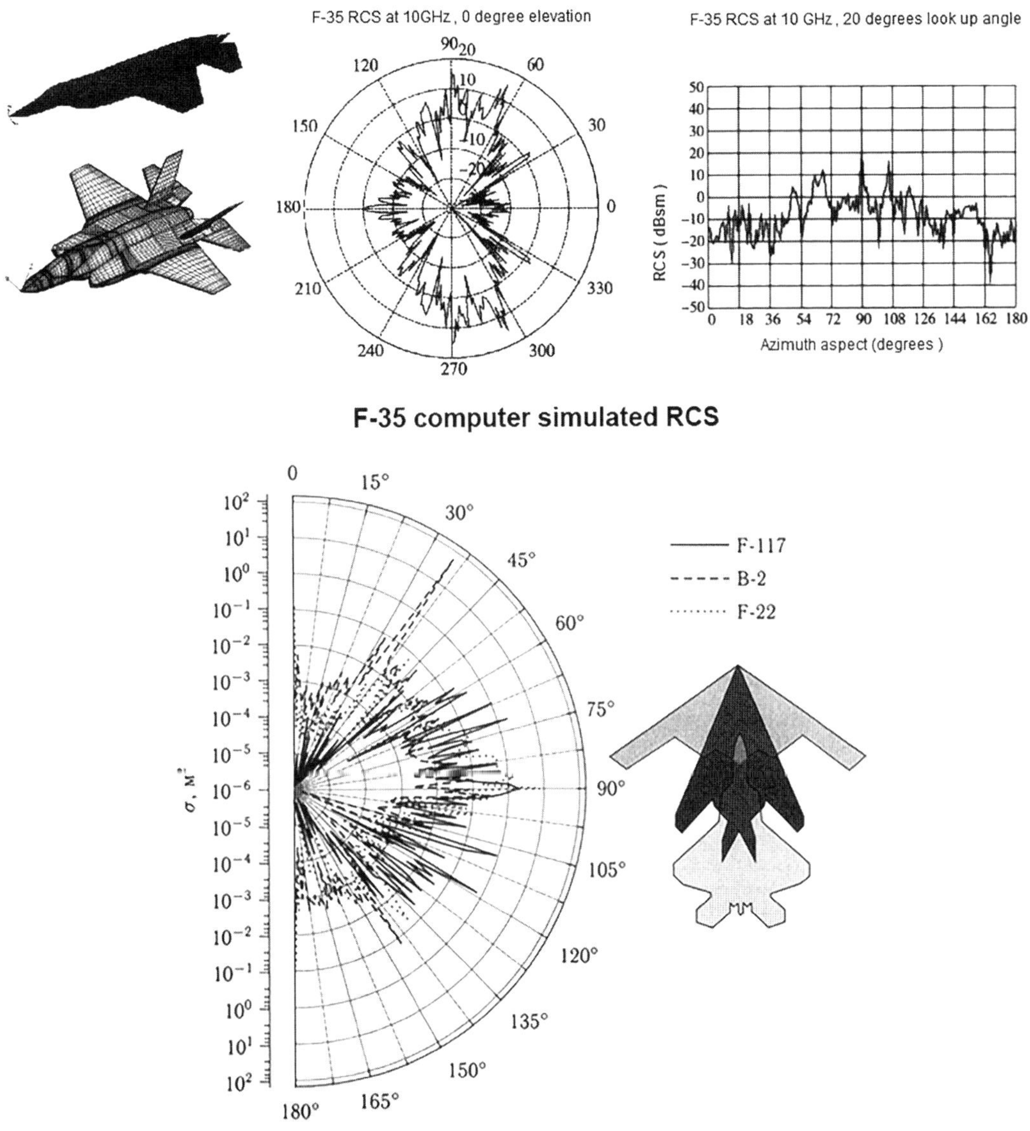

Figure 2-7: F-35, B-2, F-117 and F-22 simulated RCS comparison.

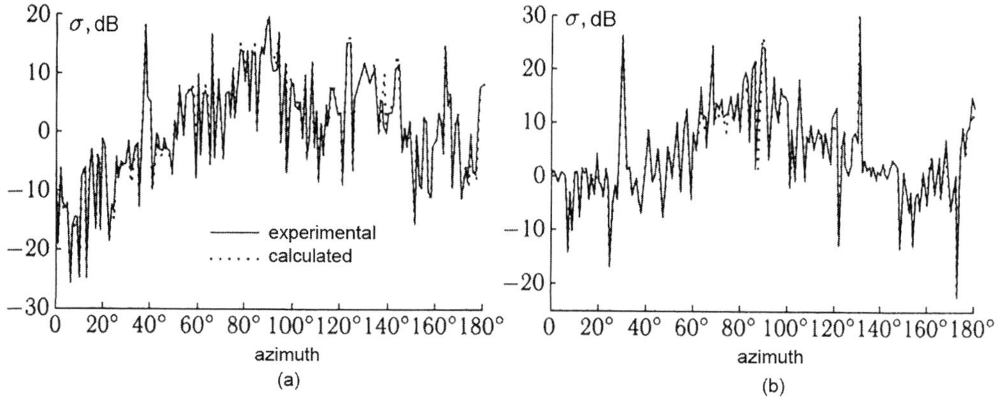

F-22 (a) and F-35 (b) 1:36 scale models RCS

The F-35A model with the radar nose cone, created with the help of Blender 3D suite

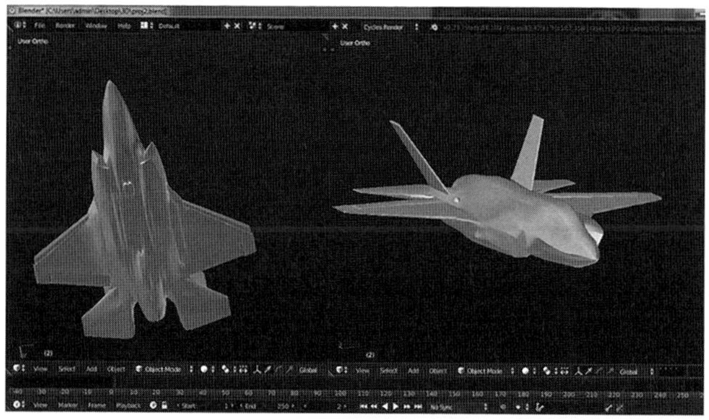

RCS polar plot for the F-35A model, at 10 GHz, seen from below (depression angle 10°). RCS is relatively small in a wide sector in the front, apart from the peaks produced by the leading edges of the wings (approximately at 35° off-axis), attaining higher values at the sides (due to the wings and the fuselage)

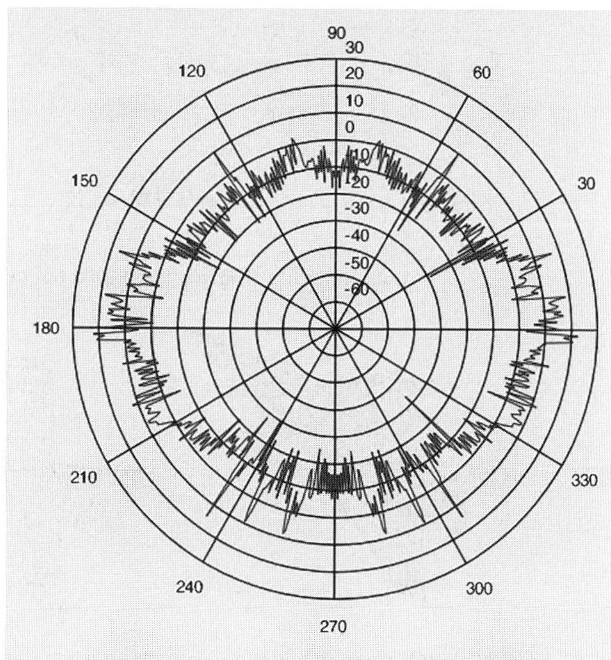

Figure 2-8: F-22 and F-35A comparison (top) and simulated RCS (bottom).

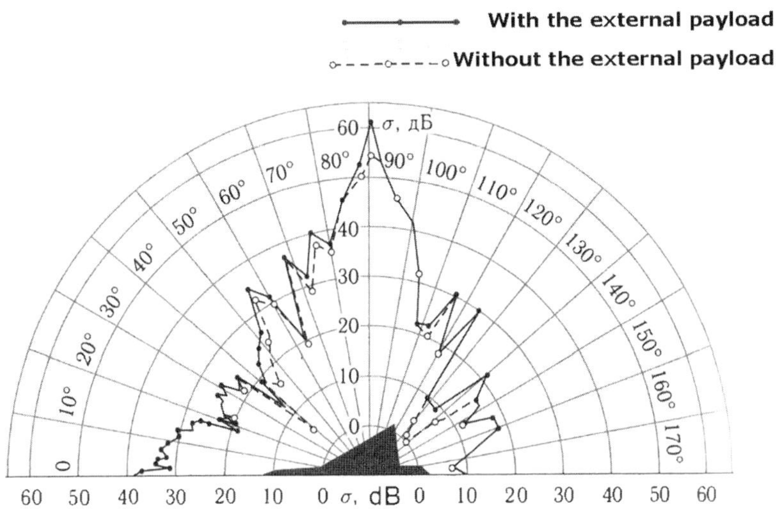

Calculated RCS diagram for EFZ000 for 3 cm wavelength

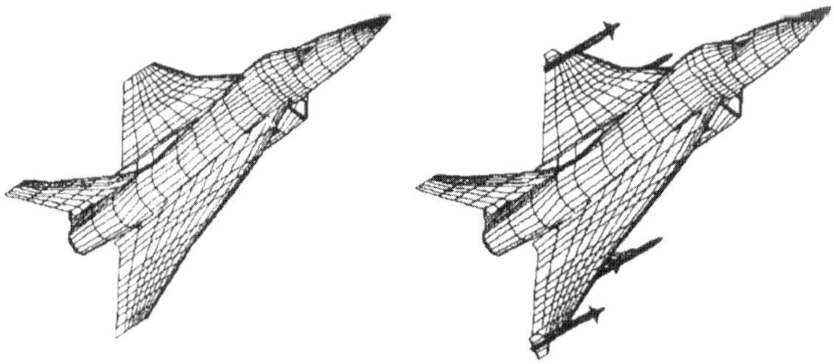

EF2000 Typhoon geometric model without and with external payload

Figure 2-9: Eurofighter RCS.

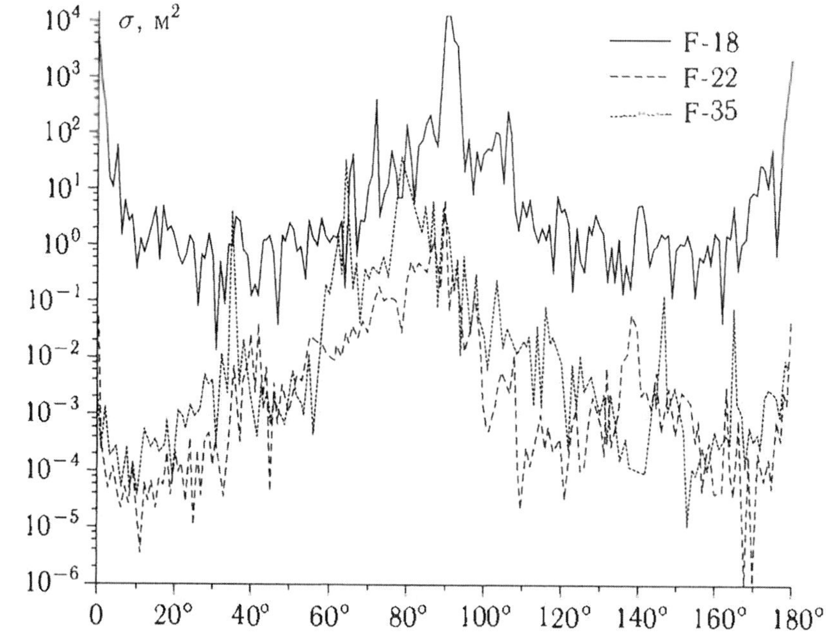

RCS for F-18, F-2 and F-35 fueselages at the wavelength of 3.2 cm

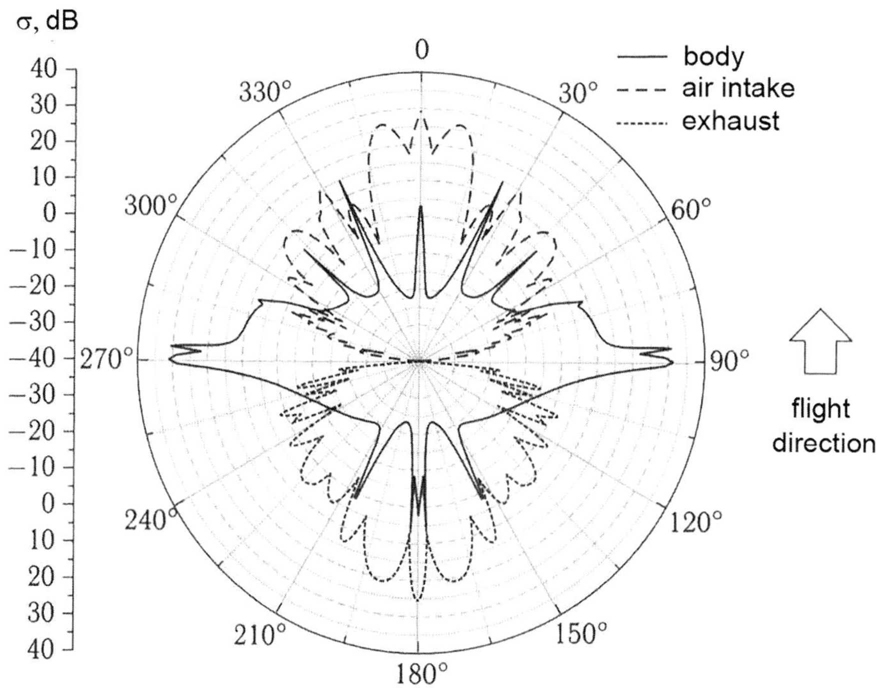

F-18 RCS for 10 cm wavelength

Figure 2-10: F-18, F-22 and F-35 RCS comparison (top) and F-18 RCS for the 10cm wavelength (bottom). (*Source: Harakteristiki Radiolokacionih Zametnosti Letalnih Aparatov*)

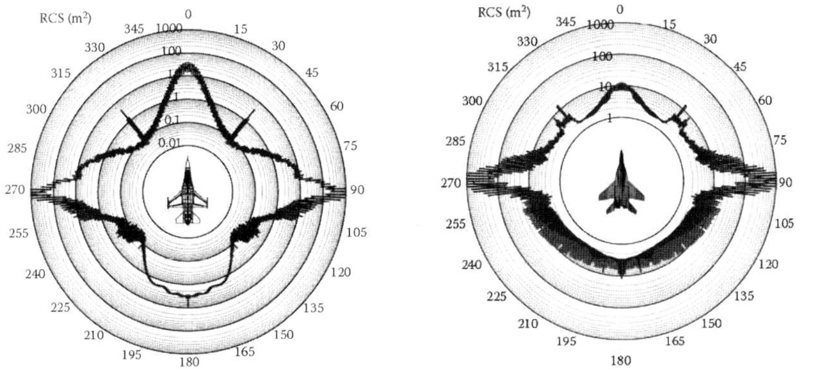

Circular diagrams of noncoherent RCS of F-16 (left) and MiG-29 (right) aircraft model given its radar observation at carrier frequency of 3 GHz (10 cm wavelength).

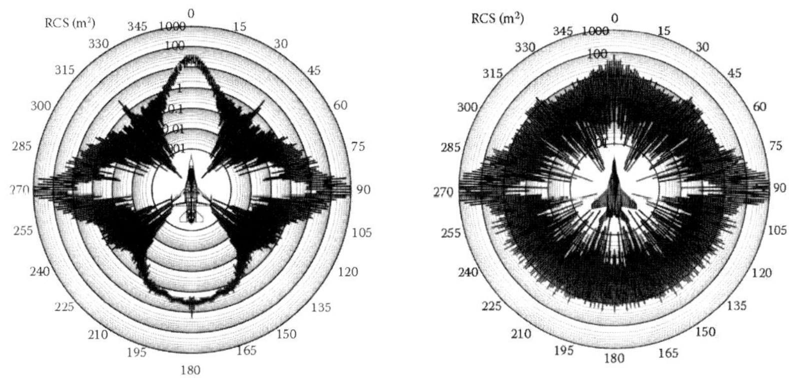

Circular diagrams of instantaneous RCS given radar observation of F-16 (left) and MiG-29 (right) aircraft model at carrier frequency of 3 GHz (10 cm wavelength).

F-16 and MiG-29 RCS

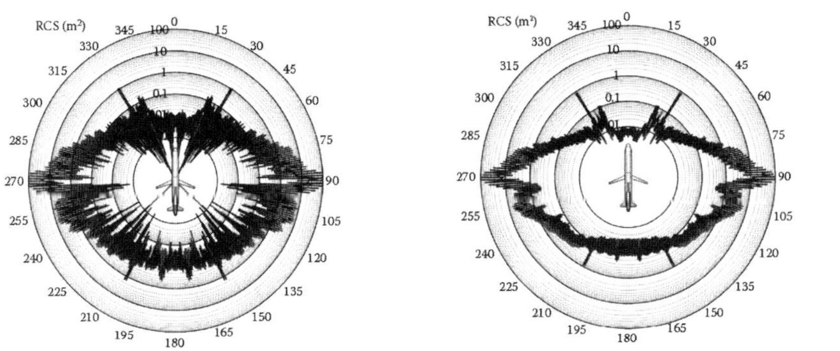

LEFT: Circular diagrams of instantaneous RCS given radar observation of AGM-86 ALCM model at carrier frequency of 3 GHz (10 cm wavelength).

RIGHT: Circular diagrams of noncoherent RCS of AGM-86 ALCM model given its radar observa-tion at carrier frequency of 3 GHz (10 cm wavelength).

AGM-86 Tomahawk RCS

Figure 2-11: F-16, MiG-29 and AFM-86 RCS. (*Source: Raseyanie Elektromagnetnih Voln*)

The F-16C model, with the radar nose cone, created with the help of AUTODESK 3ds MAX software

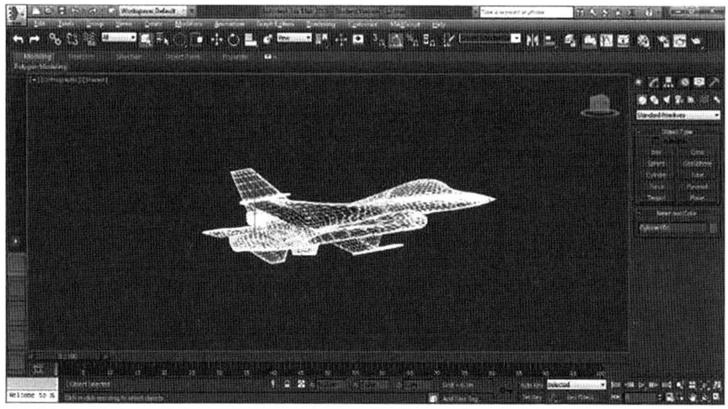

RCS polar plot for the F-16C model, at the same level, at 10 GHz (the plane nose is pointing at 90°)

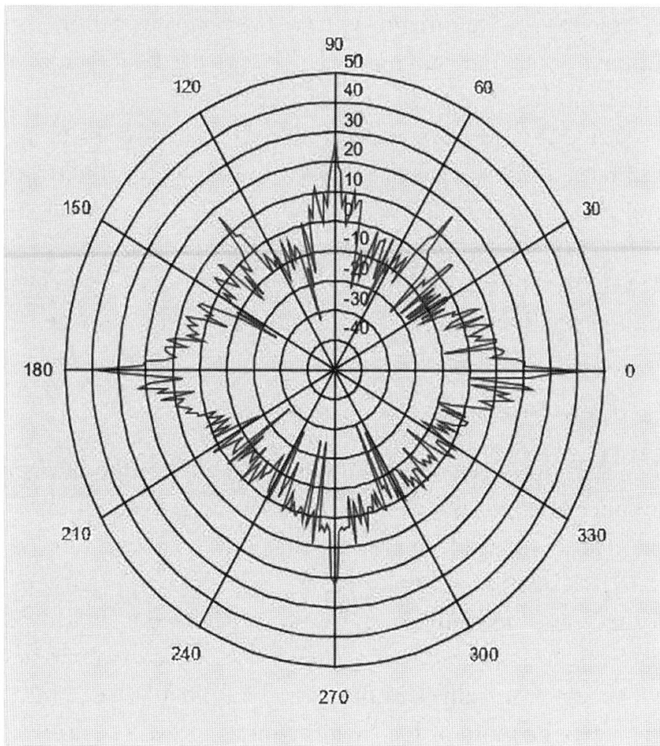

Figure 2-12: F-16C model and RCS plot.

exhibit an LO level comparable to that of a fifth-generation aircraft, implying the F-35. A Boeing spokesman clarified that they meant that 'the Silent Eagle could meet the level of stealth approved by the US government for release to international customers', a point still reflected in their most recent description of the aircraft. Also, Boeing had extensively applied LO techniques to the F/A-18E/F Super Hornet. Furthermore, in August 2013, Boeing started flight-testing the 'Advanced Super Hornet', a new variant of the F/A-18E/F Super Hornet, with conformal fuel tanks, an enclosed weapons pod and 'signature enhancements' designed to substantially increase range and reduce radar signature.

China is developing the Chengdu J-20 and more recently the smaller Shenyang J-31, both twin-engined. It is speculated that the Chinese used parts of the downed F-117A to reverse-engineer the structure and stealth coating of their planes.

In Europe, LO techniques have been applied to Rafale (Dassault Aviation) and Eurofighter Typhoon (EADS), drastically reducing their radar signatures, even though technically they are not stealth aircraft. The Rafale is supposed to employ active techniques to hide from enemy radars, using its advanced countermeasures suite (Fig. 2-9).

On the subject of LO aircraft, one should also mention the TF-X, a fifth-generation fighter being developed by Turkish Aerospace Industries in partnership with SAAB AB, according to the Turkish press. The first flight is scheduled for 2023. In the next decade, more than 250 TFX are expected to serve alongside the 100 F-35s which Turkey intends to procure. At the time of writing, there is an ongoing dispute between Washington and Ankara about the purchase of the Russian S-400 missile system, which may delay or cancel the Turkish F-35 programme.

Beside the new planes, the older US F-15, F-16 (Fig. 2-11 and 2-12) and F-18 are still the most numerous in the NATO air forces. There are also MiG-29s and AGM-86 cruise missiles (Fig. 2-11).

In conclusion: every modern opponent aircraft in service and the ones still in development has a unique RCS that represents a fingerprint that can be detected, tracked and engaged by the air defence (AD) system in service.

Counter-Stealth Radar Systems[3]

The US approach to stealth has seen a combination of technologies employed, to produce the overall effect of 'stealth'. Active emissions by aircraft radar and data links have been reduced by the adoption of what are termed 'low probability of intercept' (LPI) techniques. These typically rely on the use of very wideband frequency-hopping techniques, noise-like waveform modulations, and sometimes pseudorandom scan patterns, to made radar and data-link/network emissions very hard to detect. A modern active electronically-scanned array (AESA) radar with the ability to hop across a gigahertz or more of bandwidth, using spread spectrum modulated pulse trains, will be all but invisible to the crystal video receiver technology radar threat-warning systems of the late Cold War era. The radar signatures of aircraft and missiles present a much more challenging problem, for a variety of good reasons. The most prominent of these is that threat radars may be operating across a range of wavelengths, from around 10m down to less than a centimetre. This has important implications for the two primary technologies employed in producing very low observable (VLO) capability, shaping and materials.

Materials are often touted as the solution by parties who do not understand the physics well. For example, 'apply this magical coating and your aircraft will vanish off their screens'. The reality is that coatings and materials are usually only effective over a fairly narrow band of frequencies, and often to get good effect a considerable depth or thickness is required, resulting in weight and volume penalties. Central to the difficulties with radar-absorbent and lossy materials[4] is the 'skin effect', where radio-frequency electrical currents induced by an impinging wave tend to concentrate in the surface of an object. With highly conductive materials like aluminium skins, this layer is extremely thin for most frequencies of interest, making such skins excellent reflectors. Absorbent or lossy coatings, however, must be much less conductive to produce effect, and this results in much greater skin depth. As a result, a very thin coating or laminate which might be highly effective against a 10 GHz radar is apt to be ineffective against a 10 MHz or 100 MHz radar as the skin depth becomes many millimetres or centimetres deep.

The most common approach to this problem is the use of radar-absorbent structures, an example being the leading edge on the B-2A 'batwing' bomber, which has the depth to accommodate complex absorbent structures which are highly effective over a very large bandwidth. This is a more difficult problem for fighters, as volume and weight are critical problems. However, airframe shaping is where the biggest gains are to be had in making aircraft stealthy; in fact the rule of thumb is that the first one-hundredfold reduction in radar signature is produced by smart airframe shaping, and the remaining 'fuzzball' of minor reflections is then soaked up by absorbent or lossy materials.

For example, a conventional fighter design might have a radar cross section of $1m^2$ in the centimetre wavelength band, but an equivalent design with proper stealth shaping might be only $0.01m^2$. Further application of absorbent materials in the right places then drives that down to 0.001 to $0.0001m^2$.

The effectiveness of shaping is, like the effectiveness of materials, dependent upon the wavelength of the threat radar. Where the flat area, facet or leading edge is much larger in dimensions than the wavelength of the radar, the rules of geometrical optics apply, and reflections can be very precisely bounced away from the threat radar. The aligned leading edges, aligned planforms and facets or flat areas seen in the F-117A, B-2A and F-22A are all extremely effective down to wavelengths of the order of tens of centimetres, or in the instance of the B-2A down to metres. In frequency terms, fighters are stealthiest in the X-band and S-band, while the B-2A is stealthy down to the VHF band.

Where the shaping features are comparable in dimensions to the wavelength of the radar, an effect called 'resonance' occurs, resulting in the induced electrical charges in the skin of the target running back and forth and waves then re-radiating from edges, tips, or other prominent shapes. For fighter-sized aircraft the resonance region is primarily in the UHF frequency band. In this so-called 'resonance scattering region' it becomes very difficult to control the direction and shape of reflections. Some techniques, employing for instance resistive and magnetic materials along edges, are often used but in general fighter-sized targets are no longer marble- or golf-ball-sized reflectors.

This effect becomes exacerbated as the wavelength reaches a metre or more, where the radar signature becomes effectively proportional to the physical size of the reflecting feature. This is termed the 'Raleigh Scattering Region'. VHF band radars which operate typically between 3m and 1m in wavelength occupy this region for typical fighter-sized targets.

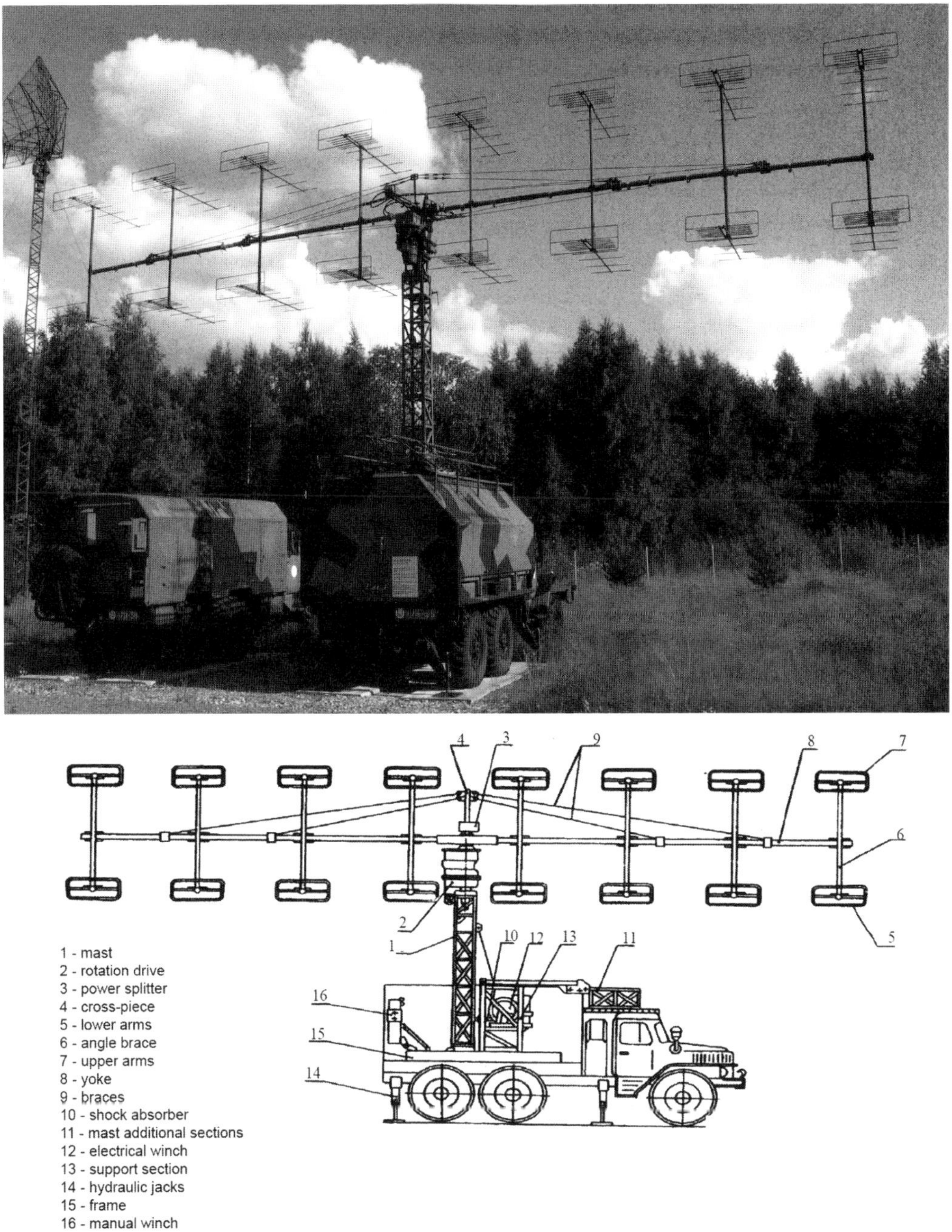

Figure 2-13: Modernised P-18 radar.

Historically, stealth designers have focused their efforts in the centimetre and decimetre bands, since these are where most fire-control, engagement, air-intercept and missile-battery acquisition radars operate. The aim of the stealth effort was thus to disrupt the 'kill chain' by denying opportunities to launch and guide missiles, or frustrating the missile seekers and thus disrupting terminal missile guidance. If we look at operating bands

Figure 2-14: Vostok E-6S 2D VHF radar design, using a unique wideband 'Kharchenko' square ring radiating element design, in a diamond lattice pattern. (*Source: KB Radar*)

Figure 2-15: 39N6E Kasta 2E1. (*Source: Vitaly Kuzmin*)

Modern air defence radars: 1 – X-band 9S19 Imbir radar; 2 – S-band 9S15 Obzor-3 radar; 3 – S-band 9S18M1 Kupol radar; 4 – VHF-band 1L13 Nebo-SV radar (four transport units – hardware cabin, rotary antenna device, diesel power station, trailer with interrogator antenna device); 5 – radar of type Yenisei; 6 – RM of SHF band (RLM-S module) being part of radar complex 55ZH6M Nebo-M; 7 – RM of UHF band (RLM-D module) being part of radar complex Nebo-M; 8 – radar of VHF band 1L119 Nebo-SVU; 9 – RM of VHF band (RLM-M module) being part of radar complex Nebo-MM; 10 – RM of VHF band (RLM-M module) being part of radar complex Nebo-M

Figure 2-16: Modern Russian air defence radars.

Rendering of Almaz-Antey 55Zh6ME Nebo ME deployed. The VHF-band component is at the right of the image, the S/C-band component is at the left of the image, the L-band component in the foreground, and the data fusion system, in the background. All components are carried on high mobility BZKT BAZ-6909 series vehicles. At least one hundred of these advanced systems will be acquired for the Russian air defence.

Figure 2-17: New Russian NEBO-M counter-stealth radar. (*NNIIRT image*)

for typical Soviet-era missile battery engagement guidance and illumination radars, we find the following: SA-2's SNR-75 ('Fan Song') in the upper S-band or lower X-band; the SA-3's SNR-125 ('Low Blow') in the X-band; the SA-4's 1S32 ('Pat Hand') in the X-band; the SA-5's 5N62 ('Square Pair') in the S-band; the SA-6's 1S91 ('Straight Flush') and the SA-8's ('Land Roll') radars in both the X- and S-bands; and finally the SA-10's 30N6 ('Flap Lid') and SA-12's 9S32 ('Grill Pan') in the X-band.

Where a defender is reliant on search and acquisition radars operating in the S-band – examples include the widely-used Soviet/Russian P-30 ('Big Mesh'), P35/37 Bar Lock, P-40 ('Long Track'), 19Zh6/36D6 ('Tin Shield'), 64N6 ('Big Bird'), or US AN/TPS-43 and AN/SPY-1 Aegis – then a by-product of good stealth is surprise as beyond a certain detection range the stealth aircraft is invisible. Operators of Russian air defence equipment will be willing customers for upgrades to legacy systems that were considered ineffective against stealth aircraft. Upgrade packages are on offer for the VHF band P-14 ('Tall King') and P-18 ('Spoon Rest D') (Fig. 2-13) and the UHF band P-15/15M/19 ('Flat Face' and 'Squat Eye)', and customers can also purchase a range of new-build VHF radars, including the 55Zh6-1 Nebo UE ('Tall Rack'), the 5N84AE Oborona-14 ('Tall King'), the 1L13-3 Nebo SV, the 1L119 Nebo SVU, and the Vostok E (Fig. 2-14). The latter two are entirely new post-Cold War designs. The trusty 'Flat Face' and 'Squat Eye' UHF radars remain in production in digital solid-state form as the 39N6E Kasta 2E1 and 2E2 (Fig. 2-15).

Many of the new Russian designs are phased arrays, and at least two of the VHF designs are AESAs, dispensing completely with all vacuum-tube technology, and

Figure 2-18: NEBO-M counter-stealth radar on display (top) and on duty (bottom).

embedding transmit-receive modules in the antenna subsystem (Fig. 2-16). Typically, the computers and software used for digital signal and data processing in these radars are commercial off-the-shelf types, no different from their Western counterparts, even using large LCD display panels. Russian literature claims the use of the latest Space Time Adaptive Processing algorithms for clutter rejection which, given the known skills base in mathematics and physics in Russian research institutes, is a credible claim. If a Western manufacturer were asked to design a VHF radar, the technology and components it would be built from would be much the same.

Russia is leading the counter-stealth development programmes. Russian marketing literature and numerous interviews with chief designers or senior design engineers invariably focus on the issue of counter-stealth capabilities in these radars. Key points raised repeatedly in interviews are Raleigh and resonance mode scattering versus geometrical optics scattering, and skin depth impairing the performance of radar-absorbent coatings. These are precisely what radio frequency physics and the extensive unclassified US engineering literature on stealth identify as key limitations. More than one Russian designer has publicly commented on the F-117A, famously known in the West as a 'ball bearing-sized target' in the S-band and X-band, as a '0.5m²' sized or beach-ball-sized radar target in the VHF band. It is likely that this claim is the result of detailed scientific analysis of radar tapes from the Balkan campaign. Russian and Belarusian designers have claimed detection ranges of up to 330km against fighter-sized stealth aircraft, claims consistent with cited range specifications for these radars.

Figure 2-19: One of the NEBO-M interior and screens presenting detection of the small quadcopter. (*Source: Still from documentary* Voennay Priemka)

The flagship of the Russian counter-stealth radar effort is the digital 55Zh6M Nebo-M radar (Fig. 2-17 and 2-18). This design is a genuine three-dimensional AESA radar system, with three individual networked radars on three separate high-mobility BAZ-6909 8x8 vehicles, and a fourth vehicle which performs data fusion from the three radars and target tracking. One radar operates in the VHF-band, one in the L-band, and one in the S or C-band. The VHF-band RLM-M radar is the largest mobile 3D VHF-band radar ever built anywhere. The design could accommodate configurations with different mixes of radars, such as replacing the C or S-band RLM-S component with an L-band RLM-D or VHF-band RLM-M. The use of networked data fusion permits this system to cue the RLM-S and RLM-D components to stealth targets detected initially by the RLM-M component (Fig. 2-20).

The Nebo-M evolved in part from the earlier 1L117 Nebo SVU mobile VHF-band radar, at least one example of which was sold to Iran some years ago. The Nebo SVU included some sophisticated anti-jamming features. Curiously the Nebo-M's numerical designation is based on the very different 55Zh6UE Nebo U/UE 'Tall Rack', a gargantuan fixed 3D VHF-band radar with a characteristic and unique T-shaped antenna. These systems are supplemented by the Rezonans N/NE marketed by Rosoboronexport as a 'Stealth Air Target Early Warning Radar'. It is a large multi-static relocatable VHF-band radar system, carried on several vehicles. Technical disclosures have been scarce (Fig. 2-19).

Counter-Stealth Concepts[5]

Counter-stealth or counter-very low observable (CVLO) techniques encompass possible techniques that overcome the effects of stealth design methods. While many technologies and techniques have been proclaimed to be CVLO panaceas, closer examination suggests otherwise. Broadly, there are two approaches in overcoming a stealth design. One is the brute-force approach of finding ways of making a sensor that is much more sensitive, able to find a much fainter target; the other is to build a sensor that can see the stealth design in some area in which it was not designed to be stealthy.

The brute-force approach in radar design usually involves increasing the peak and average microwave power the radar produces. This is usually not cheap, and often introduces other problems such as providing enough power to drive the radar, getting rid of waste heat, and making sure key components in the radar are not overstressed electrically or thermally. This is a commonly-favoured approach in land-based or naval radars, as the requirements can be challenging for compact airborne radars. Due to the inverse square law behaviour of radars, maintaining detection range against a target which reflects 1/100th of a conventional target requires a 100-fold increase in the emitted power of the radar. While doubling or quadrupling power output in a radar may be feasible, increasing it tenfold or a hundredfold usually is not.

Two techniques which can alter the radar's 'duty cycle' are to increase the density of pulses the radar emits, and to increase its 'dwell time' or how long it spends looking in a given direction. The former inevitably increases the power requirement, while the latter increases search times. Since the aim of radars is to find and track targets, increasing dwell times can seriously degrade effectiveness. Mostly, the brute-force approach is a loser's game, especially against highly stealthy targets like the B-2A and F-22A. Much less stealthy targets yield some payoff.

The alternative of building sensors that can see the aircraft from directions or at wavelengths where it was not designed to be very stealthy is a much better game plan, and this is also where most current investment by the Russians and Chinese can be seen.

There are numerous ways in which this game can be played, and combinations of multiple techniques can be quite effective, especially against designs with poor or otherwise limited stealth performance. A technique that is often overstated in effectiveness is the use of networked radars and data fusion techniques, similar to the US Navy Cooperative Engagement Capability (CEC) system. CEC collects and simultaneously fuses tracking data from multiple shipboard search radars, the intent being to share tracking data across the fleet even if some targets are too distant to cleanly track for some radars, or below the radar horizon for others. In the CEC system a target blip might be a fusion of intermittent or partial tracks from half a dozen different radars.

Defeating stealth targets using networking and data fusion presupposes that some radars can see the target some of the time, and also that the target's stealth is poorer from some directions and aspects than others. Suffice to say, an aircraft with excellent 'all-aspect' stealth such as a B-2A will not be susceptible to this technique, since all of the radars in the network are equally blind. Even the F-22A is not particularly exposed, as its weakest areas in the beam aspect are not exposed long enough to seriously matter. Much more exposed are the compromised J-20, Su-57 and F-35, as their side and rear aspects present many more tracking opportunities. In some designs, the frontal hemisphere of an aircraft is stealthy but the rear hemisphere is not.

A networked data-fusion system is thus not a panacea, but is potentially quite effective against stealth designs that do not have genuine 'all-aspect' stealth capability. There are technical challenges in designing such systems, as the constituent radars must be built to not discard poor-quality radar returns from point targets, which typical radars automatically reject as 'false alarms'. Also, a lot of computing power is needed to sift and sort the collected data to determine which returns amount to a real target track. To date only the US and Russia have demonstrated the ability to build such a system.

The alternative game plan of exploiting aspect limitations in target stealth shaping is to exploit wavelength limitations. This area has been the focus of most Russian and Chinese activity in CVLO system design. It relies on the basic physics of stealth shaping, where a straight edge or flat facet can only reflect sharply in one direction, and if its geometrical size is larger than two or more wavelengths. A straight edge or flat facet which reflects the radar illumination away in a tight beam (technically a 'lobe') must be many wavelengths in size. If not, its reflection smears out over a wide range of angles, making it easier to detect.

In stealth fighters this effect is most prominent, as their size puts hard limits on the wavelengths where their forward and aft fuselages can still cleanly bounce illumination away. Typically, performance that is reasonable in the 3 GHz decimetre wavelength S-band degrades with varying rapidity as the wavelength increases through the L-band, UHF-band down to the metre-wavelength VHF-band.

Electronic Warfare

In recent years, Russian electronic warfare has attracted an unusual amount of attention. New Russian electronic warfare equipment in eastern Ukraine – and also in Syria – has caught the world's attention.

Electronic warfare (EW) is defined as military action involving the use of electromagnetic and directed energy to control the electromagnetic spectrum or to attack the enemy. Nearly every military action, from command and control of an entire integrated air defence system to precision guidance of an individual weapon, depends on effective use of the electromagnetic spectrum. Radar systems have become a vital element of nearly every military operation. Since these systems operate across the entire electromagnetic spectrum, much of the EW effort is concerned with countering radar systems. All of the equipment discussed under this heading is specifically designed to counter radar systems. These actions are classified as electronic attack (EA), which is a part of EW (Fig. 2-20, Fig. 2-21).[6]

Electronic warfare is somewhat like a chess game – a series of moves and counter-moves within the electromagnetic spectrum. As one side develops jamming techniques to counter radar systems, the other develop counter-countermeasures to negate them. In response, the former develops newer techniques and their adversaries respond with

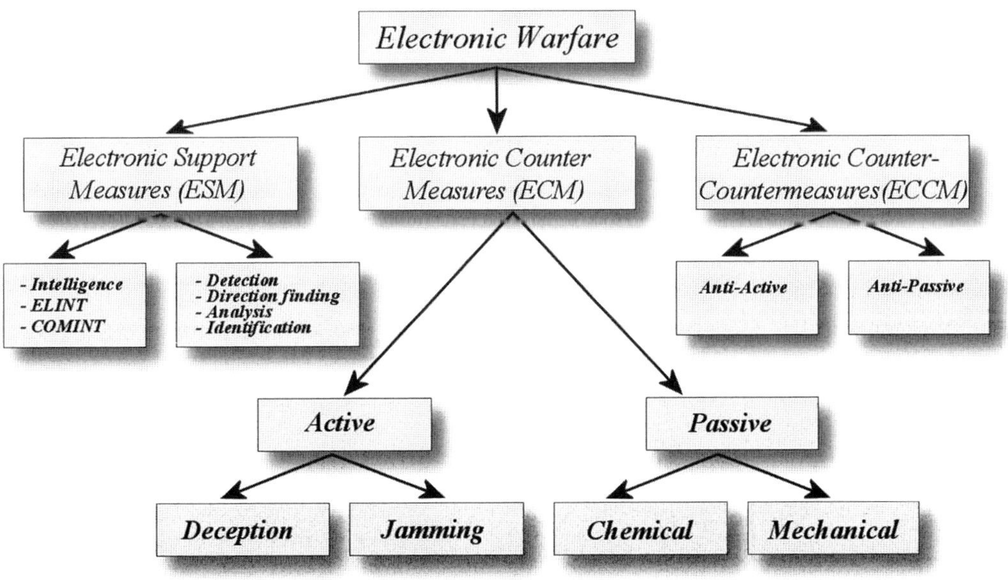

Figure 2-20: Electronic warfare – typical Western classification. (*Source:* Electronic Warfare Handbook)

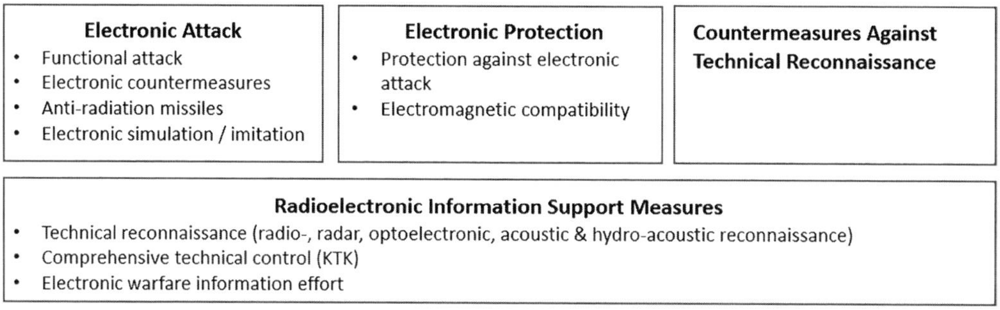

Figure 2-21: Electronic warfare. (*Source:* Russian Electronic Warfare – The Role of Electronic Warfare in the Russian Armed Forces)

newer modifications to their radar systems. This sequence can continue for decades. The development and application of radar counter-countermeasures are classified as electronic protection, also a part of EW.

In the Russian military, electronic warfare has the following definition: 'Electronic warfare is a set of coordinated activities and actions encompassing radioelectronic attack on adversarial radioelectronic and information-technical objects, radioelectronic protection of radioelectronic and information-technical objects, countermeasures against technical reconnaissance and radioelectronic information support measures.' This definition differs from the earlier Soviet and Russian definitions in a number of respects. The first and most apparent difference is that it is divided into four areas, rather than the usual two, the additional two being countermeasures against technical reconnaissance and information, and radioelectronic information support measures. Second, the offensive side of traditional Soviet and Russian EW, 'electronic suppression', is replaced by electronic attack. In this way, the diversity of offensive EW weaponry has been broadened to include means capable of destroying electronic equipment. Correspondingly, the range of protective measures included in radioelectronic protection has also broadened. Third, by replacing the previous 'radioelectronic equipment and systems' with 'radioelectronic and information-technical objects', the types of enemy targets that can be subject to EW measures, as well as friendly systems in need of EW protection, have also been increased. The targets of EW are thus not limited to equipment and systems directly active in the electromagnetic spectrum (EMS), such as radiocommunications equipment, radar, electro-optical sensors, and so on. Underlying systems such as computers, data storage and energy-supply systems now also constitute viable targets for EW measures.[7]

One of the most discussed topics in the Russian EW literature is the role of EW in modern air defence. The increased use of UAVs, PGMs and stealth technology has changed the preconditions for an air defence based around missile systems. Aircraft and missiles flying at either very low or high altitude, at hypersonic speed, or which come in very large numbers (swarming) are particularly difficult targets. The discussion has mainly been about how EW can provide complementary means to offset the shortcomings of traditional air defence, and there are discussions about strengthening the Armed Forces Air Defence divisions with complementary EW means. There are discussion in

Russia that the status of EW units in ground forces operations should not be one of combat support. Instead, their role should be made equal to the four main combat arms: motorised rifle, tank, artillery and air defence. Thus, in ground forces operations EW should not been seen as complementary to air defence capabilities, but as a capability in its own right. EW has increasingly prominent role in air defence, the ambition being to achieve greater coordination in EW operations and the efforts to address the challenge of sustaining high levels of innovation and production in the EW industry.

The most conspicuous example is the more significant role anticipated for EW means in future air defence. Combating UAVs and cruise missiles with air missile defence systems, for example, is perceived as too slow, too costly and above all too inefficient. This growing emphasis on EW in air defence is apparent in Russian-Belarusian air defence cooperation and the development of directed energy weapons (DEW) capabilities, and is the main argument among the Russian EW community for a further increase in the role of EW in the Russian Armed Forces. The enhanced role of EW in air defence is not just limited to combating these types of new threats head on. The role of EW means is also highlighted in reducing an adversary's surveillance and targeting capabilities as well reducing the signature of troops and objects.

EW Systems against Airborne Systems (REB-S)[8]

The capability to detect and suppress aerial onboard electronic systems such as radar, airborne communications systems or cruise-missile homing is an important task for Russian EW. These capabilities are found in particular in the REB-S battalions subordinated to the Ground Forces EW brigades or the independent REB-S battalions subordinated to the Air and Air Defence Armies of the Aerospace Forces. Systems for jamming airborne communications and satellite navigation are primarily found in the Borisoglebsk-2 (Fig. 2-22) and the Diabazol complexes, whereas the Moskva-1 EW command and control complex and the radar-jamming complexes of the Krasukha family, Krasukha-2 (Fig. 2-23) and Krasukha-4 (Fig. 2-24), are intended to suppress airborne and space-based radar systems. These systems target on-board radar systems of all kinds, but the role of reducing the effectiveness of aerial warning and control (AEW&C) takes special precedence. All three of these complexes are more or less further developments of earlier ones that have been in the Soviet and Russian EW inventory since the 1970s and 1980s. Systems specially intended to combat UAVs have also recently been introduced.

The Moskva-1 complex (Fig. 2-25), produced by Kvant, is sometimes described as a passive radar. However, this should probably not be confused with passive radar in the sense of systems that use reflections from existing sources of illumination in the environment. Instead, its description as 'passive' concerns its alleged capability to provide the location of emitting flying objects through electronic intelligence (ELINT) without revealing its own position, as a radar system would. The Moskva-1 is mainly a command complex with some ELINT capabilities that is able to link together up to nine Krasukha-type jamming systems located at different sites, and transfer target data to Air Defence

Figure 2-22: Borisoglebsk-2.

Figure 2-23: Krasukha-2O.

Figure 2-24: Krasukha-4S.

command and control systems. The Moskva-1 is able to triangulate the position of the emitting aircraft or cruise missile at a distance of up to 400km. The complex consists of three systems based on as many Kamaz trucks. One truck holds an ELINT system and the other two trucks are command vehicles. The Moskva-1 complex has been developed as a replacement for the AKUP-1, which was developed in Soviet times.

The Krasukha family of jamming complexes consists today of the Krasukha-2O and the Krasukha-4S. Development of both systems began early in the 1990s, with the larger Krasukha-2O system mounted on a BAZ-6910 vehicle and the Krasukha-4S on a Kamaz-6350 truck. The Krasukha-2O is primarily designed to suppress airborne early-warning aircraft, such as the Boeing E-3 Sentry or the Northrop Grumman E-8 JSTAR. It is largely a more mobile and modern version of the Soviet Pelena-1 jamming system. It is probably usually procured together with the Moskva-1 complex, and possibly also together with Krasukha-4S.

The Krasukha-4S is mainly designated to suppress the airborne interception radar of fighter and interceptor types of aircraft, but also drones, reconnaissance aircraft and satellites in low earth orbit. Development of the complex began as early as 1994, but state trials did not end until 2009. Serial production began in 2011 and the first deliveries took

Figure 2-25: Moskva-1.

Figure 2-26: Avtobaza-M ELINT.

place in 2013. The system was first ordered by the Strategic Rocket Forces (RVSN) to provide a means of jamming US Lacrosse-type radar-imaging reconnaissance satellites. There is not much information on the rate at which the complex has been procured. Eighteen systems were delivered in the period 2014–15 (nine complexes, as each complex consists of two vehicles per system). The Krasukha-4S is largely a successor to the SPN-4 jamming system, with reduced deployment time and a range that is three times greater. The KRET company started testing a newly developed successor to both the Krasukha-2O and the Krasukha-4S. The new system is supposedly able to block threats regardless of whether they are from an aerial or a space-based system.

The Krasukha and Moskva-1 complexes are the most recently developed Russian EW complexes against aerial targets, but older systems are still being modernised in large numbers. In 2014, one-third of the total production capacity of EW systems against aerial targets was used for modernisation. The Avtobaza-M ELINT system (Fig. 2-26) and the SPN-4M (Fig. 2-27) jamming system are both modernised versions of older systems. Both are intended for the Russian Armed Forces as well as the export market. The letter 'E' in the system designation often represents an export version.

Parodist is another newly-developed radar and communications jamming system against aerial targets (REB-S). Compared to the Krasukha complexes, it has been less talked about. It is supposedly a multifunctional jamming system designed to counter the

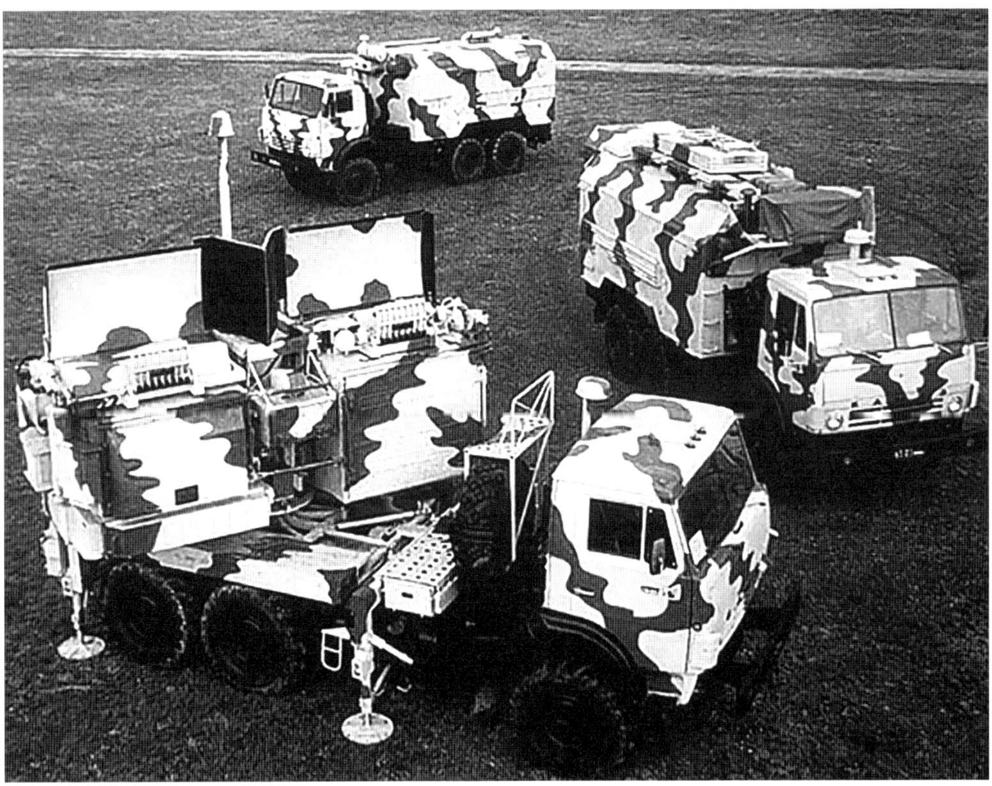

Figure 2-27: SPN-4M high-power X-band jammer.

Northrop Grumman E2 Hawkeye airborne early-warning system. The extent to which this complex has been procured is unknown (as of June 2022).

State trials of the new EW system, the Shipovnik-AERO developed by OPK, ended in 2017. The system is intended to combat an enemy's UAVs by attacking their control transmissions, but is also able to locate where the UAVs' control signal is transmitted from. The system provides different solutions for attacking UAVs. One is to first analyse the control signal, then suppress and replace it, thereby taking control of the UAV. Another is to force it down by creating an area with fake navigation signals (GPS). The system can also attack cell phone communications, as well as Wi-Fi and Wimax networks.

The Russian military possesses numerous EW systems and the majority of them are engaged in the war in Ukraine (Fig. 2-28).

Figure 2-28: Russian EW in Ukraine. (*Source: pro-Ukrainian infonapalm.org*)

Chapter 3

Air Defence and Anti-Ballistic Missile Defence of the Aerospace Forces[1]

Ancestors[2]

The first Soviet surface-to-air missile was the S-25/S-25M Berkut/Sosna (SA-1 'Guild'). It was created against long-range intercontinental bombers (B-36, B-47 and B-52) with lots of target channels. It had twenty target channels per regiment (system) but this capability demanded such a huge infrastructure that it made the system static both in location and in the direction of the engagement zone. It was also far too expensive to build them elsewhere than around Moscow. Another factor was that less-important targets simply did not need so many target channels and missiles (Fig. 3-1).

A more scalable, cheaper and easily-deployable system was needed with 360-degree launch capability. This became the SA-75/S-75M Dvina, Desna/Volkhov (SA-2 'Guideline') family with a single target channel that could be set in any direction. It was far cheaper and more flexible with a similar engagement range to the S-25/S-25M (Fig. 3-2).

In the Vietnam conflict it became evident the USA could jam them in many ways to reduce their effectiveness, especially against agile fighters and strike aircraft. In 1966 71 per cent of the guidance with Dvina SAMs were performed with auto target tracking while in late 1967 this dropped to 4 per cent. Only manual target tracking could be applied with three-point guidance.

Figure 3-1: S-25 (SA-1 'Guild').

Figure 3-2: S-75 (SA-2 'Guideline').

Regardless of continuous development, both the SA-75 and S-75M were inadequate against low-level targets. A shorter-range, low-level capable system was needed. The S-125 Neva (SA-3 'Goa') had the low-level capability which the S-25 and SA-75/S-75 families lacked (Fig. 3-3). Against low-level targets detection range generally is less because of the terrain and curvature of the Earth. Therefore, it was pointless to create (at that time) a longer-range system with low-level capability as the main goal, especially when another goal was to make the new system cheaper. The Neva was basically a scaled-down and simplified S-75M Volkhov for short-range and low-level purposes. The antenna configuration was different, and the LORO guidance type was the only one available for the Neva. It had more missiles ready to launch, even in its initial configuration – four launchers with two missiles on each which later increased to four missiles on each. The missile still had a solid booster stage, but the main motor was

Figure 3-3: S-125 (SA-3 'Goa').

Figure 3-4: S-200 (SA-5 'Gammon').

changed to solid propellant which made handling the missiles easier. The smaller missile also had better turning capability.

But the Neva could be jammed with (almost) the same methods as the previous SAM system. Used in combination with the SA-2, area defence and denial was still not possible. A very long-range SAM was needed but with a different guidance principle and antenna because of known jamming methods. The new S-200 Angara/Vega/Dubna (SA-5 'Gammon') family appeared. Angara had a range of 'only' 150km, but the later upgraded Vega-M had 250km, and the final iteration, the Dubna, had 300km. Finally, the Soviet Union had area-denial capability (Fig. 3-4).

The S-200 was immune to every type of jamming which was usable against the S-25/75/125 because of its monopulse continuous wave (CW) radar and semi-active radar homing (SARH) guidance. Its high target speed made it usable against the AGM-28 Hound Dog missile (both at high level/high speed and low level/low speed) and the Mach 3.0-capable AGM-69 SRAM. Because of the huge range required, liquid propellant had to be used for the main motor which was a step backward compared to the S-125M Neva. The huge missile needed a booster stage, and the system had an exceptionally large minimum engagement range of 17km.

In the early 1970s the PVO, using SAMs and fighter-interceptors, was prepared against every threat. The AGM-28 could be downed both at low level (slower) and at high level at higher speed (17km and about Mach 2.0), as well as the B-58 Hustler. Even the Mach 3.0-capable B-70 and AGM-69 SRAM missile could be downed at least by S-200 SAMs. The PVO introduced the MiG-25 high-speed interceptor but the B-70 never entered US service.

In the 1970s the only effective SAM in theory was the S-125M Neva considering its minimum engagement altitude limitation and neglecting all other operational factors. These were the reaction time and other target parameters which seriously reduced the effectiveness of the Neva. The only problem was that no Neva batteries were ever deployed around Moscow. Even if Soviets had assumed reliable low-level engagement capability against cruise missiles, just to fill the gaps in the S-25 Berkut SAM ring would have required an insane amount of S-125M batteries. The inner air defence ring around Moscow included twenty-two regiments (sites). Without any reserve and with minimal or no overlapping engagement zones, 132 Neva batteries would have been needed just for the inner ring, but they could provide an engagement range of only 20km. A different solution was urgently needed to solve the problem.

The new task was creating a SAM system that was capable of engaging and destroying targets at very low altitudes (30m or lower) including large-scale attacks. This basic demand meant that the new SAM had to have multiple target channels. Designing a new SAM system only for a single goal would not be economical. Therefore, it had to have at least the same engagement range as the S-75M against targets at medium and high altitudes. With these specifications, as a first step it would be possible to replace the S-25B Berkut around Moscow, and the S-75M Volkhov and S-125M Neva around other larger cities and key military installations such as the Vladivostok or Murmansk naval bases.

The long-term goal was much more ambitious. Not only the S-25M, S-75M and S-125M but even the long-range S-200 family had to be replaced with a new S-300 variant. This was not a simple task. The leadership wisely selected an incremental development method. It was not intended to replace every previous SAM system in a single large step. At that time nobody had any idea how long it would take to reach that original goal. Even just between the first deployment of the S-300PT and the S-400 (S-300PMU3) 30 years passed . . .

The Mighty S-300

Hard beginning

Having received a huge number of reports on the combat operations of the S-75 in Vietnam, General Designer Aleksandar Raspletin carefully analysed them and formulated three basic principles for building a future system:

1. All facilities should be placed on mobile vehicles so that the system has a minimum deployment time.
2. All radio equipment must be built on the latest element base: the radar must have a phased antenna array.
3. To achieve the maximum rate of fire, the launch of missiles should be carried out vertically, followed by the guidance of the missile towards the target. The missile must be solid propellant, safe to operate and always ready to fire.

In December 1966, the Military-Industrial Commission issued a task to the Design Bureau (Konstruktorski Biro) KB-1 to develop a unified new-generation S-300 system for the Air Defence Forces, the Navy and the Ground Forces, designed to combat both current and future air targets. In March 1967, A. Raspletin died. The acting head of the design bureau Boris Bunkin was not approved for a whole year.

The Minister of the Radio Industry Valery Kalmykov, his deputy Pyotr Pleshakov and Veniamin Efremov, who had just assumed the position of scientific director of the Research Institute (NIEMI), supported the Prism project, proposing to use it as a basis to create a unified S-500U system capable of engaging not only aircraft but also ballistic missiles.

The chief designer of the strategic missile defence system, Grigory Kisunko, said that the Minister of Radio Industry, V. Kalmykov, did not represent the whole complexity of creating a mobile missile defence system, and that even if successful, the complex might overcome obsolete ballistic missiles, but it couldn't cope with the new missiles being developed.

Finally, Bunkin was approved as the head and general designer of the enterprise. Having met with the command of the Air Defence Forces, he proposed to continue work on the creation of a unified S-300 system.

The GRAU[3] categorically objected. The main supplier of weapons for the Ground Forces, it was interested in developing a system capable of combatting enemy tactical ballistic missiles, but the Air Defence Forces and the Navy were not interested in tactical ballistic missile engagements. The problem reached the General Staff.

The Chief of the Scientific and Technical Committee of the General Staff, Pavel Kuleshov, organised a discussion of the issue with representatives of the customers of the Air Defence Forces, the Ground Forces (SV[4]) and the Navy.[5] Efremov made every effort to convince the participants that the Ground Forces urgently needed a system capable of fighting enemy tactical ballistic missiles. However, the parties continued to stand their ground and fierce disputes continued. Behind Bunkin was the experience of participating in the creation of all the air defence systems in the country. Behind Efremov was the only 2K11 Krug complex adopted for service. At first, disagreements arose between the two chief designers but soon they turned into an irreconcilable confrontation. After long, almost anecdotal, meetings and arguing between the chief designers facilitated by the head of the GRAU, a final agreement was reached to create one system with three modifications.

The Decree of the Central Committee and the Council of Ministers 'On the creation of a unified S-300 system' was issued on 27 May 1969. Per the decree, the designers had to create the most unified versions of the system capable of effectively dealing with air targets flying at an altitude of up to 25km, at a range of up to 75km. By a decision of the Military-Industrial Commission, the anti-aircraft version for the Air Defence Forces received the S-300P designation (P from PVO),[6] for the Navy S-300F (F from Flot) (Fig. 3-5), and the anti-missile and anti-aircraft version for the Ground Forces' S-300V (V from Voiska). All variants were to be equipped with the same Pyotr Grushin V-500 missile.

It soon became clear that complete unification was not possible. Bunkin decided to place all the elements of his system on wheeled all-terrain vehicles. Grushin made a preliminary design of a missile, the maximum speed of which did not exceed 1,200m/s. Such a missile could not engage ballistic targets.

The Ground Forces insisted on the development of tracked all-terrain vehicles for continuous escort of tanks on the march and during operations. To combat ballistic targets, Efremov needed a missile with a speed of 2.4km/s and an interception altitude of 35km for the Ground Forces S-300V. According to one recollection, Grushin himself refused this work. According to others, the secretary of the Central Committee of the CPSU, Dmitriy Ustinov, and the head of the GRAU, Kuleshov, insisted on handing over the missile to the Lyulyev design bureau.

The radar facilities of the air defence and naval systems had many differences. Only the Grushin missile for Air Defence and the Navy turned out to be the most unified.

On a par with the performance specifications, among the main criteria the S-300P developers were guided by were also the minimum number of required personnel and items of equipment to reduce the life-cycle cost of the system, as well as achieving the characteristics necessary to repel air threats whose emergence was expected in the coming decades.

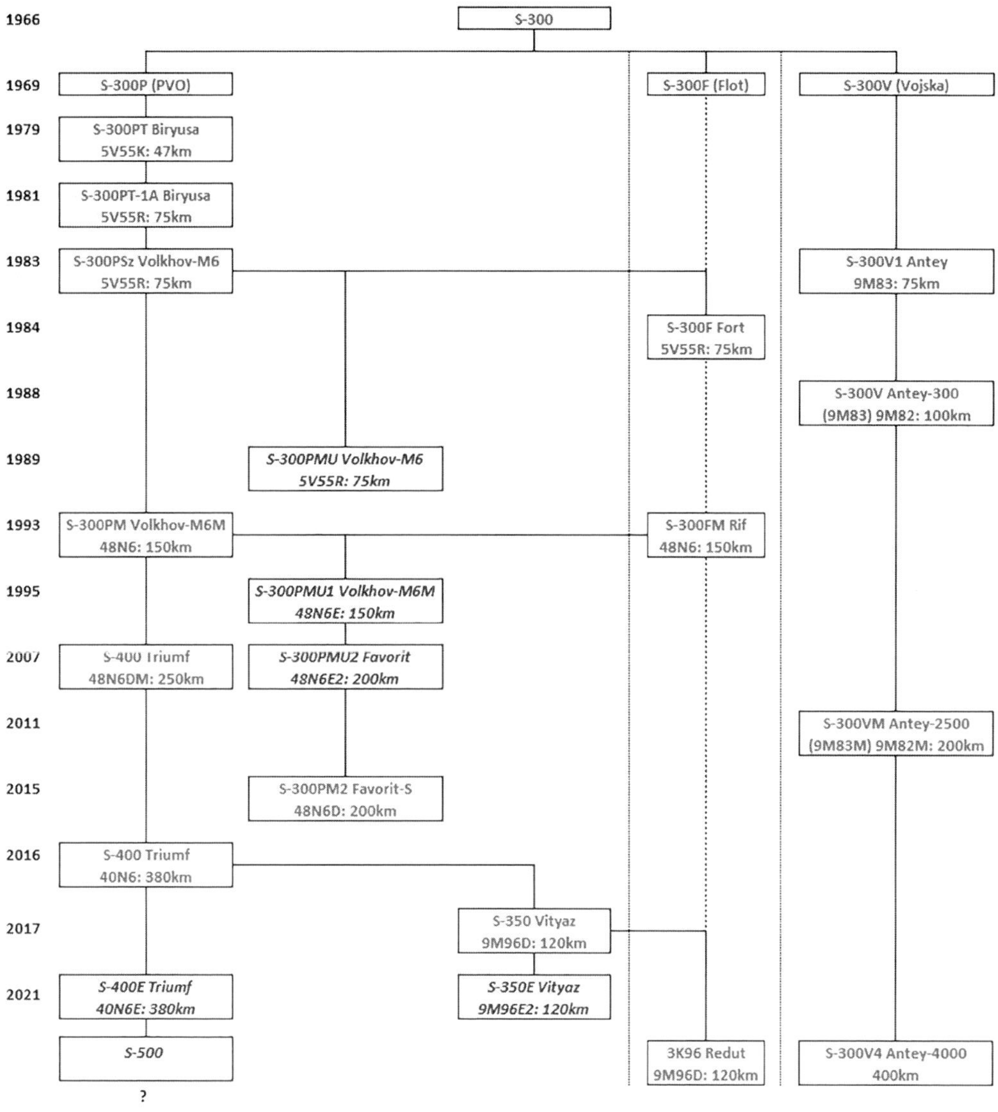

Figure 3-5: S-300 family tree.

The 5V55 missile developed for the S-300P also fully met these criteria. Its development relied upon analysis of all previous experience with similar efforts accommodating many of the trends in missile technology available at that time, embodying the most advanced design, manufacturing and testing technologies. For example, a number of innovative technical solutions were used during the development of the 5V55. The use of a transport and launch container (TLC), in which the whole life-cycle of the missile was to take place – from assembly at the factory to launch – occupied one of the central places among them.

In turn, the requirement for a high rate of fire led to a number of decisions aimed at minimising the duration of pre-launch operations and flight-time to target. For the

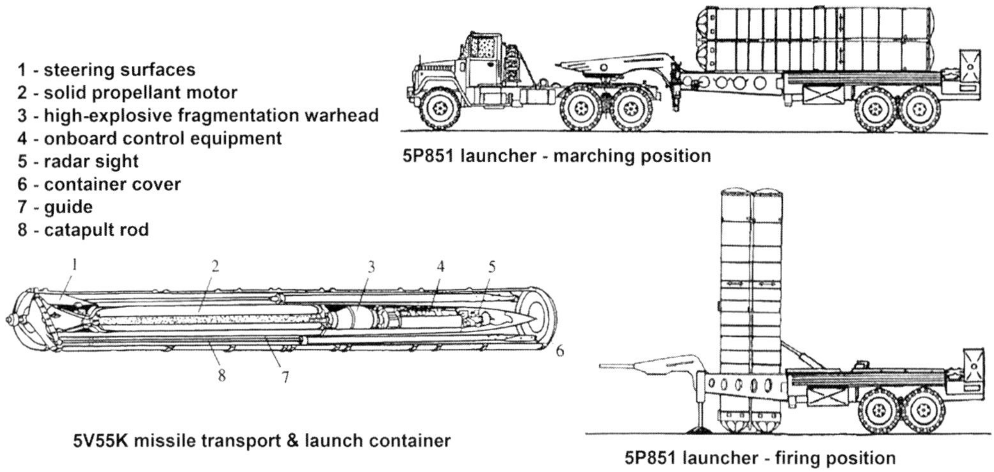

Figure 3-6: 5P851 launcher and 5V55K missile.

first time for this type of missile, a forced vertical launch from the TLC was proposed (Fig. 3-6). This helped greatly increase the system's rate of fire since all the missiles were directly on the launcher and ready for immediate launch; this allowed the effective all-around engagement of enemy aircraft and missiles flying in from different directions.

With such a launch, the sustainer motor of the 5V55 starts at an altitude of 20 to 25m. This minimises the effects of the gas jet on the nearby components of the system. For a quick turn toward a target after the engine start, the missile is equipped with a special gas-dynamic system.

S-300PS (90Ж6)

The first variant, the S-300P/PT, entered service with the Air Defence Forces in 1979. It was followed by the S-300PS (S for self-propelled) where all elements were mounted on self-propelled wheeled chassis. A improved version designated S-300PS (export version S-300 PMU) was adopted in the mid-1980s. Increased cross-country capability was one of its features: in this version all the components of the system were carried by MAZ-543M tractor trucks and their deployment from the ready-to-launch position took a mere five minutes.

The main element of the S-300PS missile battalion is the 5N63S (Fig. 3-7) command post (CP), consisting of a target illumination and guidance radar (Radiolokator Podsveta i Navedeniya – RPN) in an F1S container – a transceiver cabin with an interrogator, and a combat control cabin (Kabina Boevoga Upravleniya – KBU) in a F2K hardware container). The gearbox is mounted on the F20 chassis based on the MAZ-543M vehicle. The chassis includes a 5S17 power supply system with two gas-turbine power units and a power take-off generator (from the vehicle's MAZ engine) and a telescopic antenna-mast for communication with a higher command post, and an automatic control system. The design of the F20 chassis allows combat to be carried out directly 'from the wheels' after the machine is installed on hydraulic supports (levelling errors are calculated by a

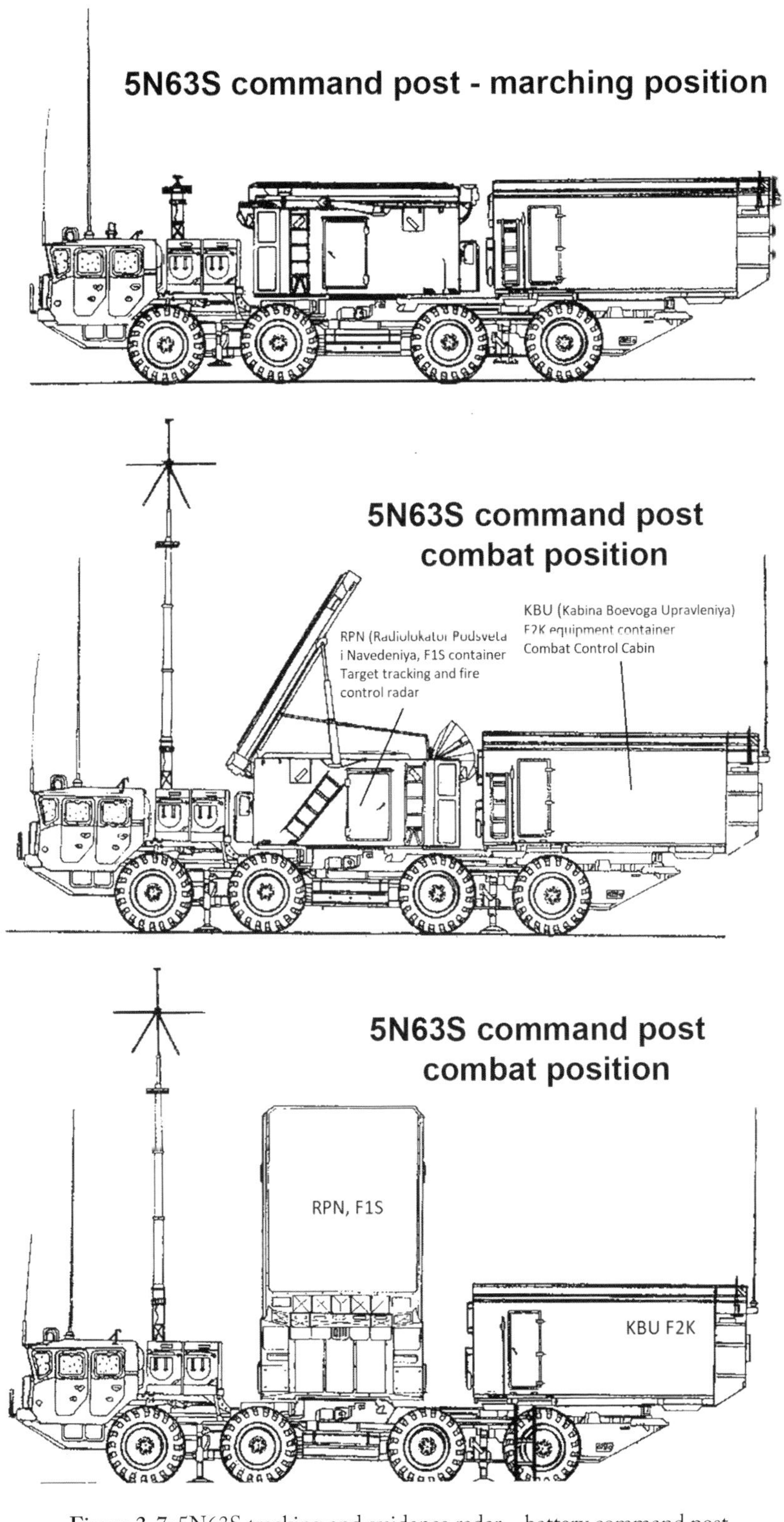

Figure 3-7: 5N63S tracking and guidance radar – battery command post.

Figure 3-9: 5P85S launcher.

launchers and the F2K container. If there is time, external power supply systems (SVEP) are connected to the corresponding users. The rate of fire is 3–5 seconds, and up to six targets can be engaged at the same time with twelve missiles (two missiles per target). There is a mode of shooting at ground targets as well.

The exchange of information with the system command post (CPS) is carried out through the antenna-mast device (AMU) installed on the F20 chassis. When the battalion is more than 20km from the system CP, the AMU FL-95 (FL-95M, FL-95MA) is included – a telescopic truss mast up to 25m high based on the chassis of a ZIL-131N vehicle – for the implementation of a stable exchange of telemetric information on the air situation and the conduct of operations. After redefining the coordinates of the target with the help of the target illumination and guidance radar, it is acquired for tracking and, if necessary, fired upon. The horizon is automatically scanned, where low-altitude targets may appear. The TsVK of the complex evaluates the interference situation, both passive and active, and suppresses it.

To expand the capabilities for detecting and tracking low-altitude targets during the deployment of the anti-aircraft battalion and units of the radio engineering troops (RTV) in wooded or rugged terrain, since the 1960s air defence forces have used stationary towers to raise the antenna posts of the missile guidance stations, and surveillance and target-tracking radars. To expand the capabilities for detecting low-altitude targets, the battalion is given a 5N66M low-altitude detector (NVO) mounted on a universal mobile tower adopted in the late 1970s (Fig. 3-10).

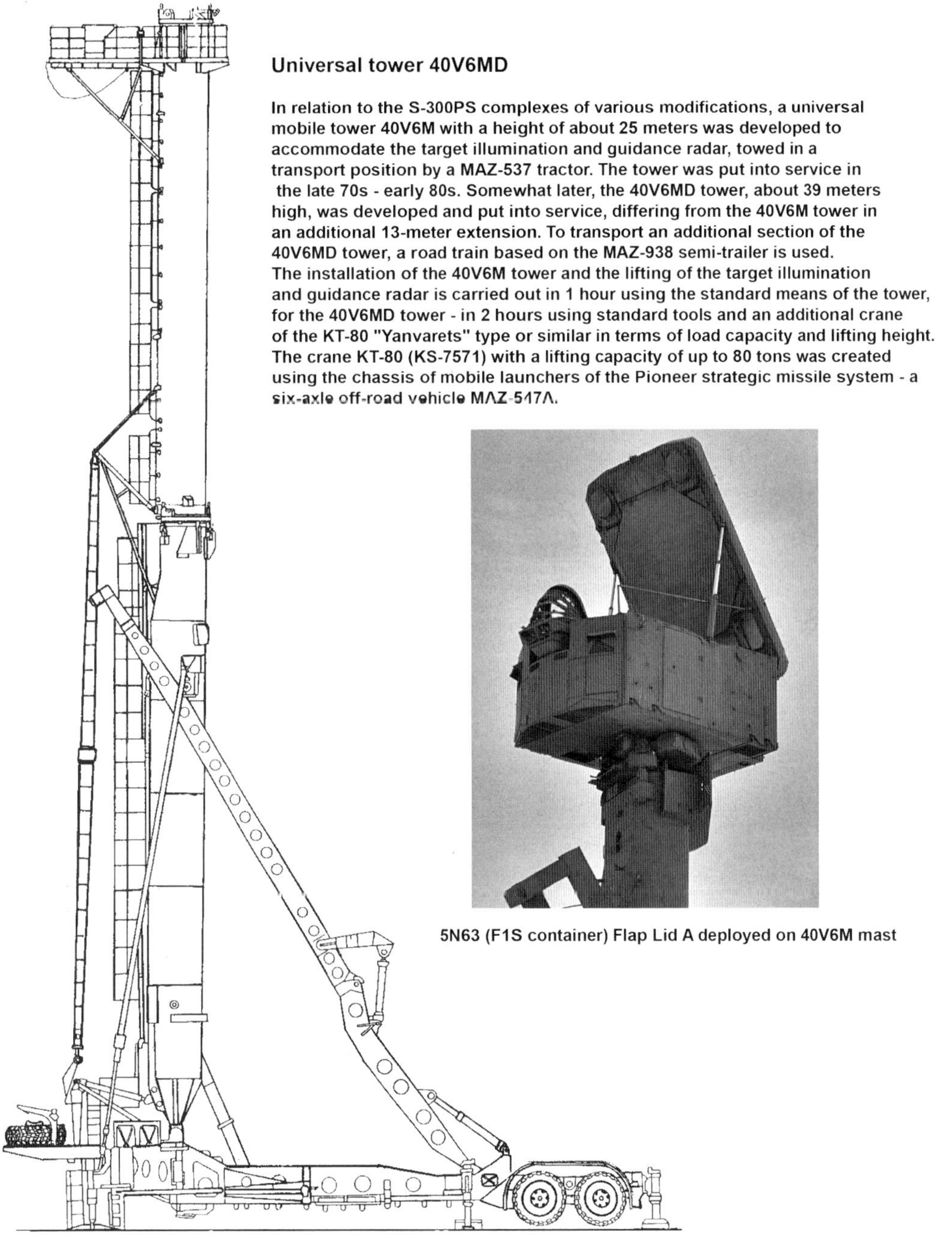

Figure 3-10: 40V6MD tower with 5N63 radar container.

Figure 3-22: 54K6E command post.

attached autonomous reconnaissance and target designation assets. It entered service in 1993.

The new system, due to the improvement of the hardware and the use of the new 48N6 missile (export version 48N6E) with a combined guidance system, expanded the range of speeds of engaging targets up to 6,450km/h, the field of view of the illumination and guidance radar (RPN) was increased, and the maximum range of guaranteed destruction of an aerodynamic target increased to 150km, of a strategic cruise missile flying at an altitude of 6–100m to 28–38km, and of a theatre ballistic missile to 40km. The system's capabilities for conducting autonomous operations were improved, and training

Figure 3-23: 5N64S (top) and 64N6E (bottom) long-range target-acquisition radar.

Figure 3-26: 30N6 tracking and guidance radar and CP.

The system can engage strategic and tactical aviation, cruise missiles, air-launched missiles, tactical and theatre ballistic missiles and other aircraft in the entire range of combat conditions including in a difficult jamming environment, with both active and passive interference. The sequence of firing at targets is determined automatically and recommendations are made at the moment of launching missiles – the number of missiles. Permission to launch a missile is given by the commander. Targets are tracked automatically by tracking radar; manual mode can be used in extensive jamming conditions. The system can simultaneously fire at up to six targets. The target can be engaged with one or two missiles with a rate of fire of 3 seconds (the first launch is made by the operator; the second launch is automatic: S-300 variants have the firing parameters recorder for evaluation of the engagement).

The illumination (engagement) and fire-control (guidance) radar provide the following sectors of view (elevation x azimuth):

- 1^0 x 90^0 – low-altitude target detection mode.
- 13^0 x 64^0 and 5x64^0 – mode for detecting aerodynamic targets at medium and high altitudes.
- 10^0 x 32^0 – detection of ballistic targets.

According to the target designation, the RPN detects a target in the additional search sector (40x40 or 20x20), captures it and switches to automatic tracking. In a difficult jamming environment, manual tracking mode can be used. When the target is hit, the target and missile channels are released to enable the next target to be engaged.

All launchers of the towed version of the system are the 5P85TM (export version). The RPN guidance radar consisting of the F1E (F1M) antenna post and the F2E (F2M) hardware container mounted on an F20M chassis based on the MAZ-54ZM vehicle. The composition of the F20M chassis is similar to that of the F20 chassis of the S-300PS system. The weight of the chassis is 45,500kg, including 11,500kg and 9,100kg hardware containers which house operator workstations, a multiprocessor computer, a signal processing system and built-in functional control equipment.

All 5P85TM launchers are of the same type and are mounted on semi-trailers towed by KrAZ-260 trucks. Each launcher provides transportation for four missiles, automatic pre-launch preparation and launch of missiles on command from the RPN. To communicate with the engagement radar, each launcher is equipped with a disk-shaped antenna which is retractable while on the march.

The system uses the 48N6 missile, which has more advanced onboard equipment and guidance methods than the various versions of the 5V55. The launch of the single-stage 48N6 missile (export version 48N6E) is carried out with an ejection to a height of 25m. The operating time of the solid-propellant single-mode propulsion engine is up to 12 seconds. After acceleration to a speed of 1,900–2,100m/s and after the motor runs out of fuel, the missile flies by inertia. The launch weight of the missile is 1,900kg; the weight with the container is 2,580kg. The length of the missile is about 7.5m, and the mass of the

Figure 3-27: 48N6 launch.

the SAM. The coordinates of the target and the missile are determined by the RPN, which are used to determine the mismatch between the missile's position relative to the calculated trajectory and the missile control commands are formed, which are transmitted to the SAM via the RPN. A few seconds before the interception point of the missile with the target, commands are issued to the radio fuze to initiate the warhead. At the moment of warhead detonation, the parameters of the missile relative to the target are recorded in the RPN. According to these, the results of shooting are automatically evaluated. Despite the great variety of modern AD missile systems, the general approach of their operating principle is approximately the same.

The system is in constant evolution since as it has considerable growth potential, including significant expansion of the engagement zones for aerodynamic and ballistic air attack weapons and missile kill effectiveness. These qualities have been realised to a large extent in the S-300PMU2 Favorit missile system.

S-300PMU2 Favorit

The S-300PMU2 Favorit ('Favourite') universal mobile multi-channel missile system is designed for the defence of the most important assets of the state and its armed forces from massive strikes by advanced modern aircraft, strategic cruise missiles, tactical and theatre ballistic missiles and other means of air attack, in the entire range of altitudes and speeds in intense active and passive interference.

The Favorit system is a further development of the S-300PMU1 system and the 83M6E system controls (Fig. 3-29). It has the following new qualities and capabilities:

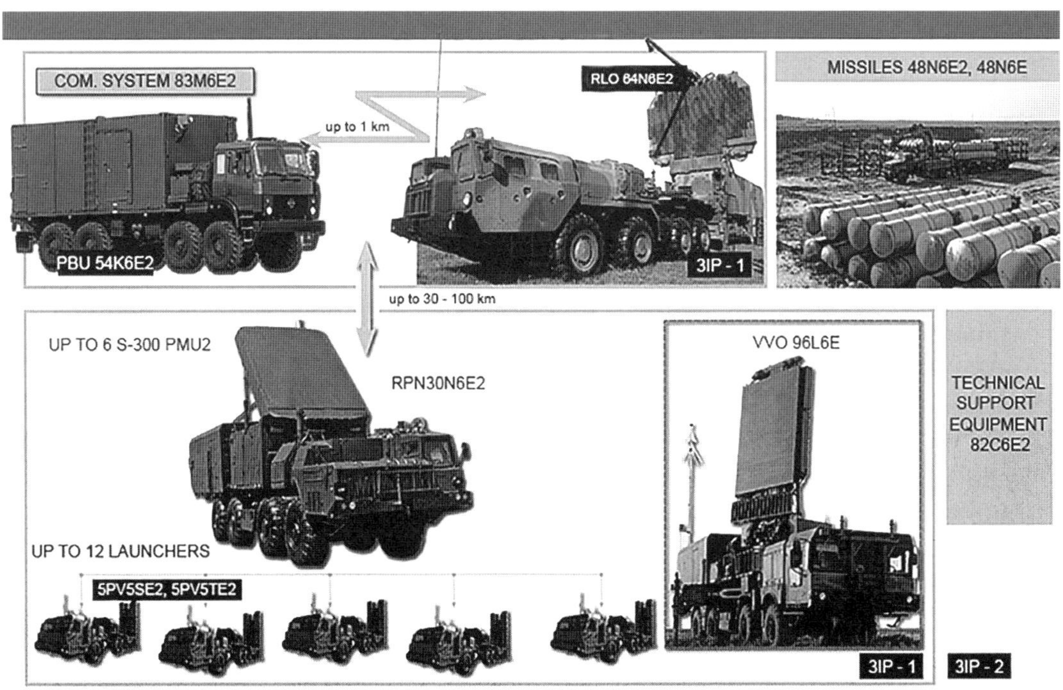

Figure 3-29: S-300PMU2.

- The search characteristics of the 83M6E2 controls for detecting and tracking ballistic targets have been expanded while maintaining the sector for detecting aerodynamic targets.
- The far boundary of the zone of destruction of aerodynamic targets has been increased to 200km, including when firing in pursuit.
- The efficiency of the system has been increased when working on aerodynamic targets, including low-flying ones, in an environment of extensive jamming.

The effectiveness of hitting ballistic targets with the 48N6E2 missile has been increased, ensuring the detonation of the target's payload, which was not provided for when firing the 48N6E missile. The warhead of the new missile passed a long stage of ground testing, and its combat effectiveness has been confirmed by successful flight tests.

When designing the system, the idea was to integrate it into various air defence systems. The battalion's command post vehicle has a different configuration of antenna system to provide communication with a higher command post. The composition of the main combat and additional means does not differ practically from those of the S-300PMU1 system. To improve the characteristics of the system in autonomous combat operations, a new-generation autonomous target-designation system is used – the 96L6E radar (Fig. 3-30).

The 96L6E three-coordinate mobile radar station is designed to search, determine nationality, classify and track air targets. Information from the 96L6E radar for support of the S-300PMU2 system (it can also be used for the S-300PMU and S-300PMU1 systems) can be transmitted via a cable or an information-exchange radio link. The radar station, consisting of an antenna post and a control cabin, is mounted on the chassis of a MAZ-7930 off-road vehicle. If necessary, the antenna system can be mounted on a 40V6M (40V6MD) universal tower. The 96L6E radar was developed by the Lira design bureau and is produced by the Lianozovo Electromechanical Plant.

The S-300PMU2, like the S-300PMU1, can be supplied in two versions: a mobile launcher based on a MAZ vehicle or a 5P85TE2 towed launcher based on a semi-trailer towed by a KrAZ truck tractor. The new 48N6E2 missile used in the complex is an improved version of the 48N6E with a maximum target engagement range of 200km. A new autopilot, warhead and radio fuze have been developed, and the solid rocket motor has been modernised.

The typical structure of a S-300PMU2 unit includes combat and maintenance assets and assigned facilities (Fig. 3-31). The 83M6E2 control system includes:

- 54K6E2 combat control centre,
- 64N6E2 acquisition radar (Fig. 3-32),
- maintenance facilities including the SPTA sets, external power supply sources and vehicles, and
- supplementary equipment including the antenna-mast assemblies and repeaters to extend radio-communication range.

Figure 3-30: 96L6E.

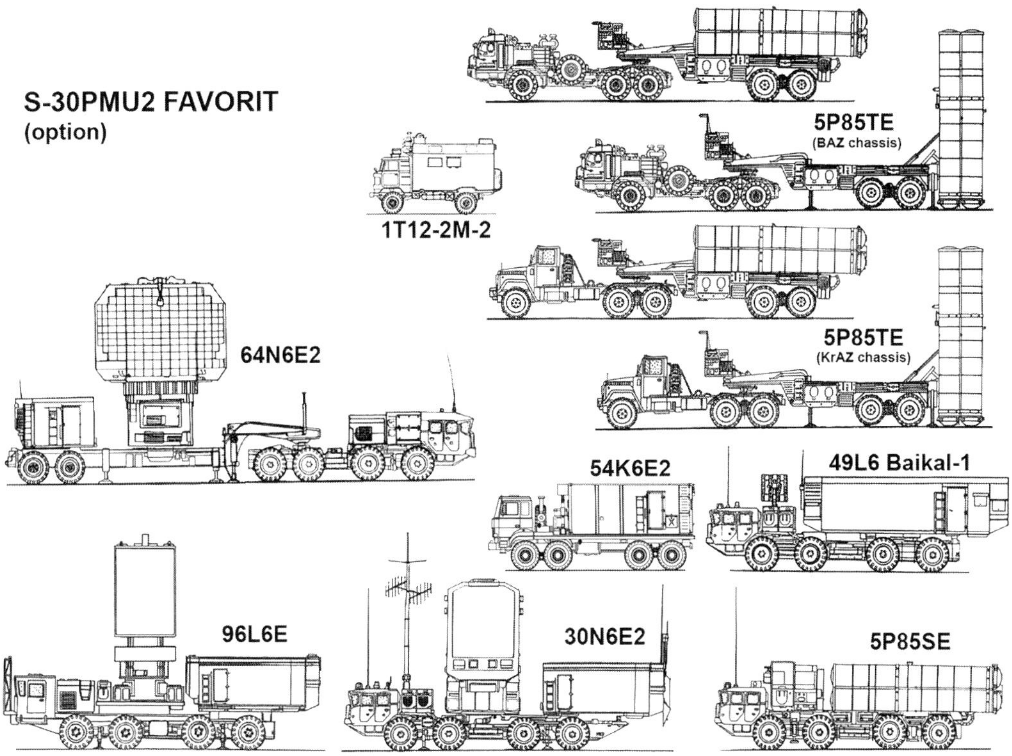

Figure 3-31: S-300PMU2 configuration (one of the options).

Figure 3-32: 64N6E2.

The combat assets include:

- 30N6E2 multi-role illumination and guidance radar,
- up to twelve self-propelled 5P85SE missile launchers (or 5P85TE missile launchers on semi-trailers) – four SAMs on each,
- 48N6E2, 48N6E (5V55R, 5V55K) missiles (Fig. 3-33), and
- 1T12-2M-2 survey vehicle.

Figure 3-33: 48N6E2 launch from 5P85SE.

Figure 3-34: 22T6E2.

The maintenance assets include:

- 82Ts6E2 missile maintenance and storage assets (5T58E2 transporter vehicles, 22T6E2 (Fig. 3-34) loader vehicles and other assets),
- 48N6E2 weight-size mock-up and 48N6E2UD combat training missile,
- a set of auxiliary means for S-300PMU2 ADM system, and operating manuals, and
- external power sources for radars and missile launchers.

The assigned facilities include:

- 96L6E all-altitude or 76N6 low-altitude target acquisition radars,
- 40V6M mobile antenna tower, and
- maintenance and repair assets.

The ALTEK-300 simulator system for crew training with the 83M6E2 and S-300PMU2 has also been developed. The Favorit system was not delivered to the Russian army but rather it was used as a base for the new S-400.

S-400 Triumf

In the late twentieth and early twenty-first century the following trends became apparent in the development of air and space attack weapons:

- Development of low and extremely low flight altitudes and sharp reduction in their visibility in the basic physical fields through the integrated use of stealth technology.
- Increase in the number of air threats in air defence weapons operation areas through the use of unmanned vehicles.
- Equipping all air attack weapons with highly-effective EW equipment and use of precision-guided weapons
- Growth in production and adoption of non-strategic ballistic missiles, primarily tactical and theatre missiles, as well as the production of medium-range ballistic missiles by some countries.

An opportunity to analyse the potential of the most effective air attack weapons became available also as a result of their use during operations in Iraq and Yugoslavia. The need

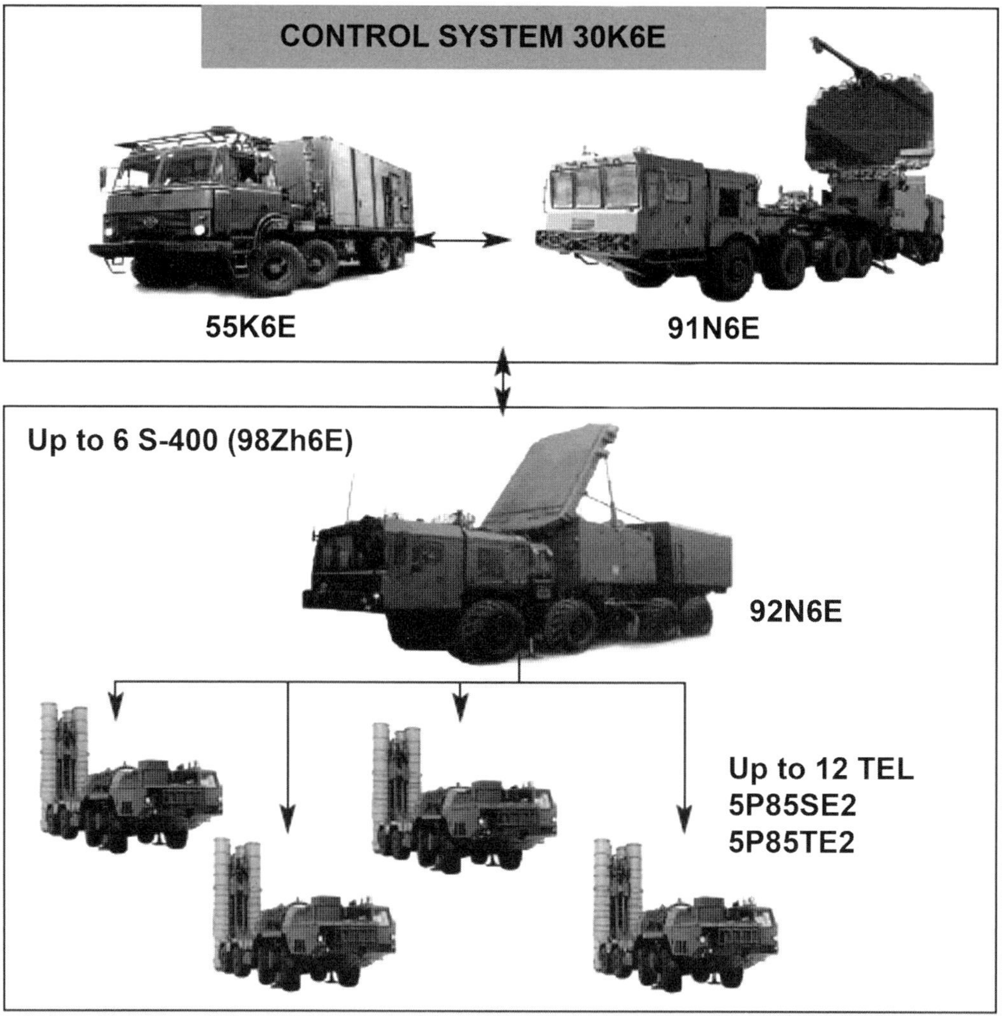

Figure 3-35: 30K6E control system.

to effectively accomplish aerospace defence missions in these circumstances became the focal point in developing the new generation of systems.

All assets of the Triumf (Triumph) system (Project 98Ж6) are mounted on self-propelled wheeled all-terrain chassis, have built-in self-contained power supplies, orientation and survey control, communications and life-support systems. In addition, provision is made for using ADMS assets in specialised shelters, with removal of the equipment containers of the multi-functional radar, command and control post, and radar system from their self-propelled chassis.

Time to deploy from marching position to operational readiness is 5–10 minutes. The prime developer of the Triumf ADMS is Almaz-Antey. Among its other developers are the Fakel Design Bureau (missile development), Research Institute of Instrumentation (acquisition radar system for the command post), and Special Engineering Design Bureau (launcher development).

The S-400 Triumf/SA-21 (Fig. 3-35 and 3-36) mobile multi-channel air defence missile system is a new-generation system to effectively engage practically all modern and future air attack weapons, including medium-range ballistic missiles.

The system interacts with other air defence missile complexes, air defence missile systems and air defence missile/gun complexes in a complicated tactical situation as well as with other S-400s.

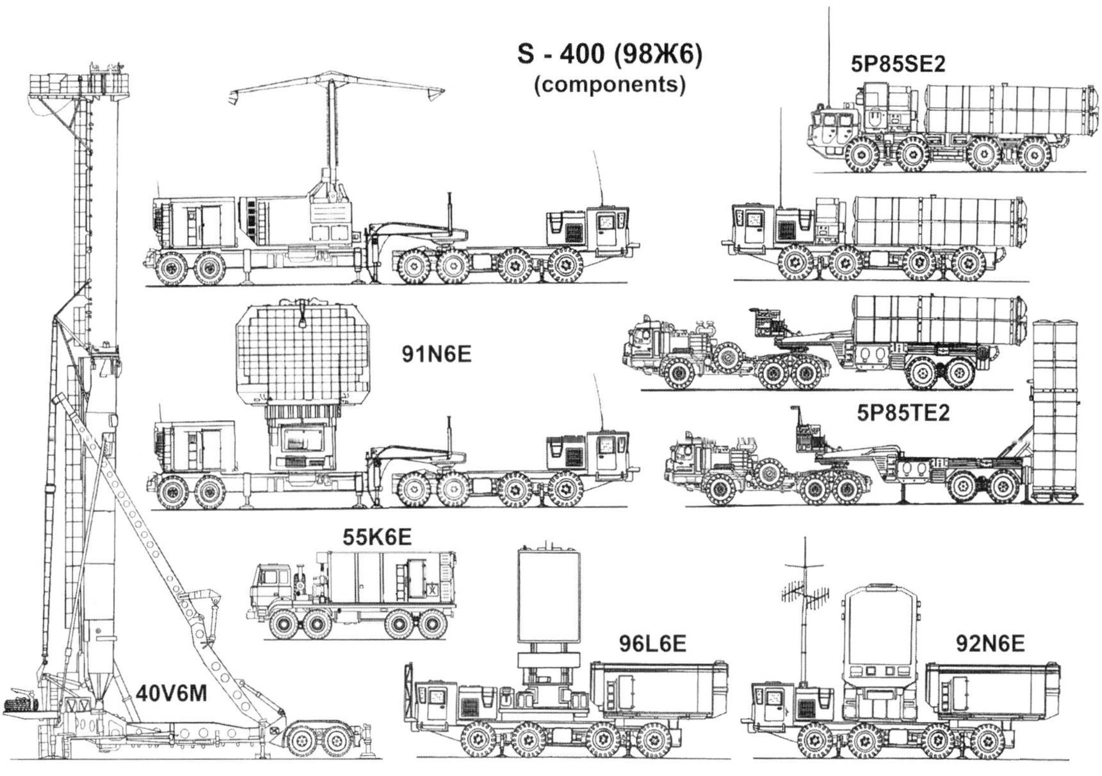

Figure 3-36: Typical S-400 components.

S-400 Triumf incorporates:

- 30K6E – an administration system which manages eight battalions.
- The 55K6E – a command and control centre based on the Ural-532301(Fig. 3-37).

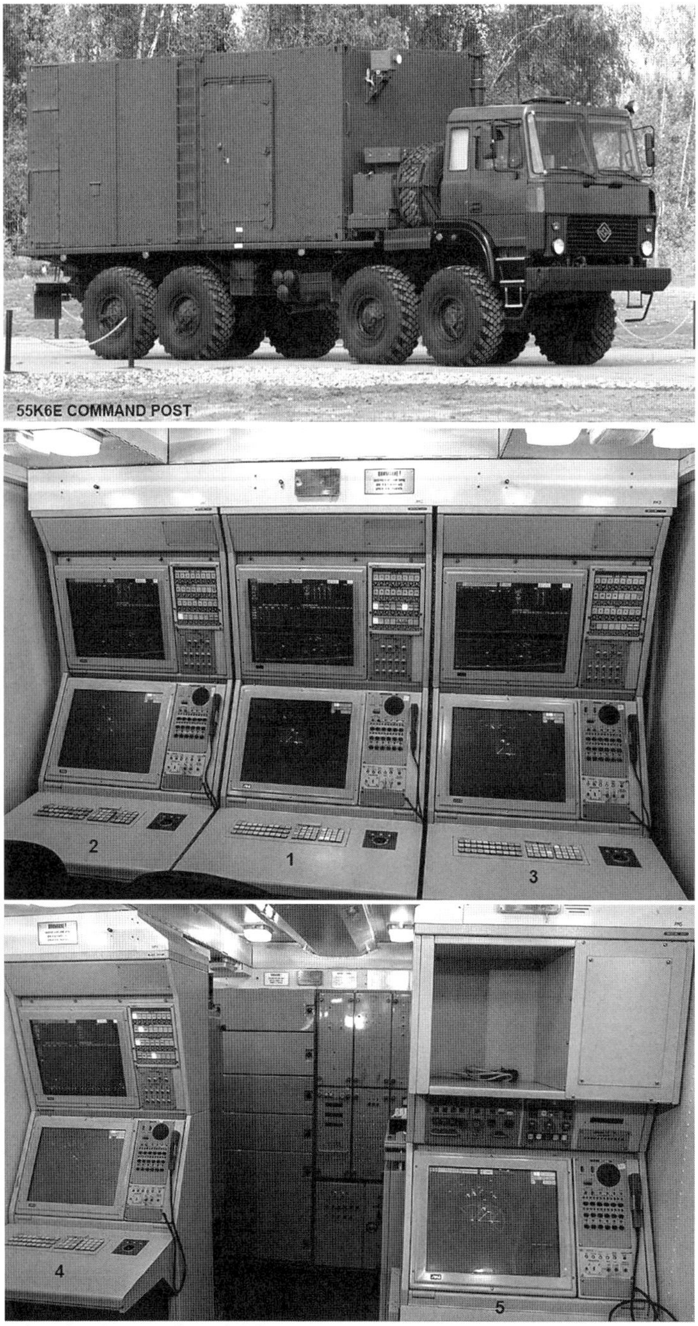

1 - regiment commander workstation
2 & 3 batallion (or other tactical unit) workstations
4 - airspace control workstation
5 - units condition control workstation

Figure 3-37: 55K6E.

Figure 3-38: 91N6E.

Figure 3-39: 92N6E (front) and 96L6E (back).

- The 91N6E – a panoramic radar detection system (range 600km) with protection against jamming which is mounted on an MZKT-7930. The S-band system can track 300 targets. Six battalions of 98ZH6E surface-to-air missile systems (an independent combat system) can track no more than six targets on their own, with an additional two battalions if they are within a 40km range (Fig. 3-38).
- The 92N6E (or 92N2E) – a multi-functional radar with 400km range which can track 100 targets (Fig. 3-39, 3-40).
- The 5P85TE2 launcher (Fig. 3-41) and the 5P85SE2 (Fig. 3-42) on a trailer (up to twelve launchers).
- The 48N6E, 48N6E2, 48N6E3, 48N6DM, 9M96E, 9M96E2 and the ultra-long-range 40N6E (Fig. 3-43).

Figure 3-40: 92N6E interior.

Figure 3-41: 5P85TE TEL.

Figure 3-42: 5P85SE TEL.

According to the Russian government, the S-400 uses an active electronically-scanned array. The first combat deployment of the system was at the Khmeimim air base in Syria. Optional elements of the S-400 (98Z6E) include the 15I6ME-98ZH6E, with coverage of 30km, 60km and 90km beyond the 30K6E's coverage. The 96L6E has a 300km detection range. The 40B6M houses the 92N6E or 96L6E radar. The Protivnik-GE is an anti-stealth UHF radar with a 400km range. The Moscow-1 passive sensor is 2½ times more effective than the Protivnik, with a 400km range. The Orion for target-designation on the air defence system, and the Avtobaza-M and Orion+ Avtobaza, add high-precision detection. The 1RL220BE versions are reportedly used for jamming. In addition, the 200+km range S-200D Dubna (SA-5C) missiles and S-300 P-family radar systems can be utilised without additional command-and-control centres. S-300 system missiles can also be guided. A-50, A-50U and A-100 aircraft provide early warning and command-and-control target designation.

The 30K6E control system can be integrated with the S-400 Triumf's 98ZH6E system, the S-300PMU2 (through the 83M6E2 control system), the S-300PMU1 (through the 83M6E control system), the Tor-M1 through the Ranzhir-M battery-command post, and the Pantsir-S1 through the lead battery vehicle. The Protivnik-GE and Gamma-DE radars, integrated with the 92H6E radar system, enable communication between each battery with Baikal-E senior command posts and similar types, nearby 30K6E, 83M6E and 83M6E2 administration systems, the Polyana-D4M1 command post, fighter-aircraft command posts, and mobile long-range radars. The Nebo-M system is designed to hunt the F-35 Joint Strike Fighter. The system's VHF component provides sector search and tracking, with the X and L band components providing fine-tracking capability. Good placement of the radars relative to the threat axis enables the L- and X-band components to illuminate the incoming target from angles where its RCS is sub-optimal. Attempts to jam the Nebo-M would be problematic since all the radars have passive angle track capability against jammers; jamming permits passive triangulation of the target using three angle-track outputs. The RLM-S and RLM-D have better

Figure 3-43: 40N6E, 48N6E2, 9M96E2 and 9M96E1.

elevation-tracking accuracy than the RLM-M, and the Nebo M should be capable of producing high-quality tracks suitable for mid-course guidance of modern SAMs and trajectory guidance of legacy SAMs. Typical S-400 battery integration is shown in Fig. 3-44.

The Gamma-C1E SHF mobile radar station has a detection range of 300km. The Nebo VHF mobile radar station and the Resonance-NE radar station have a detection range of 1,200km and 65km to an altitude of 500m. All Nebo-family locators are doubled for army air defence. During the 1970s, the long-range mobile UHF 5H87 and SHF 5H69 low-altitude locators were used. A goal in the 1980s was detection at a

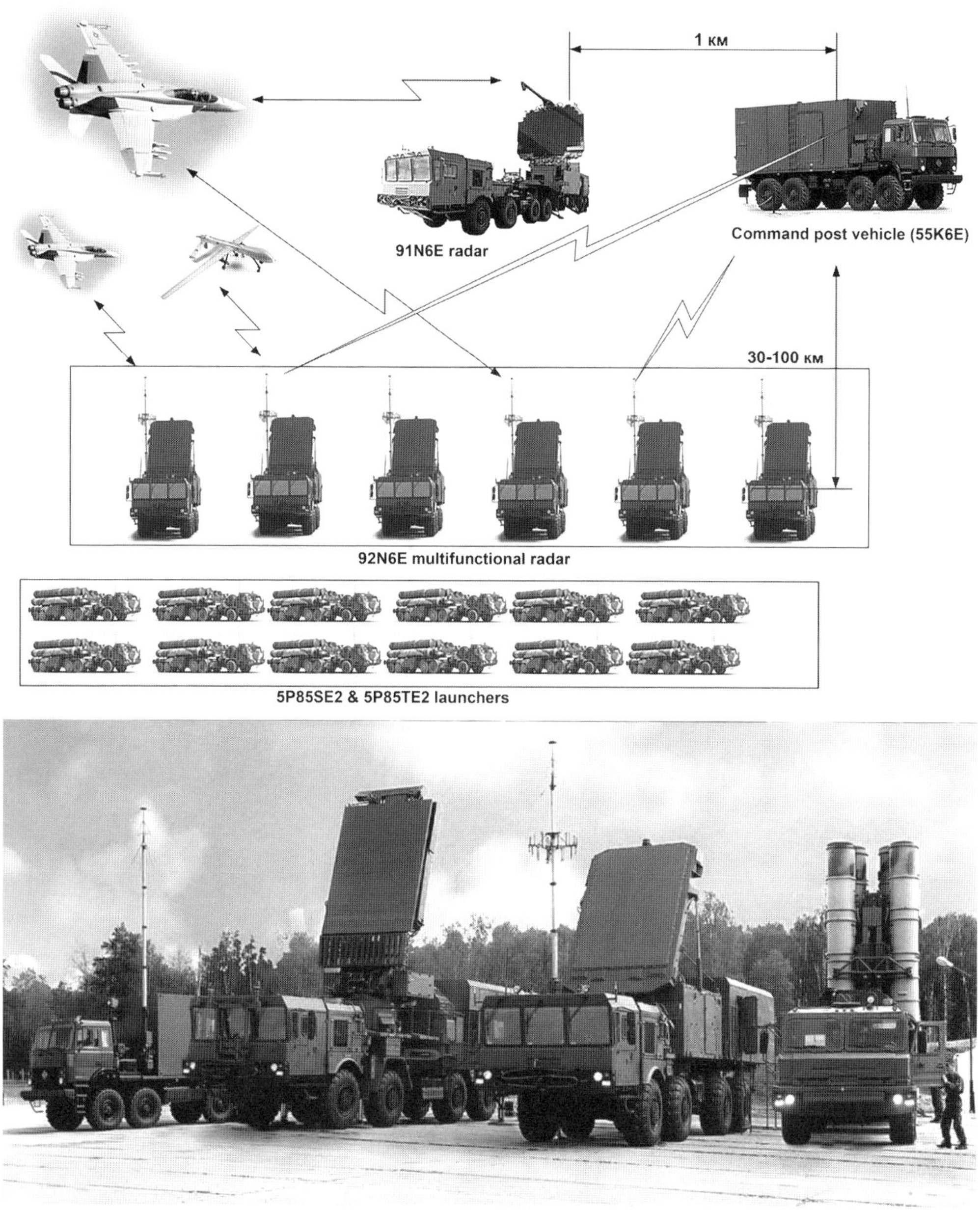

Figure 3-44: S-400 battery components and interaction.

height of 10m at a distance of 40km. For export to foreign customers, with the purpose of integrating their existing air defence systems, additional work on improvement of the 30K6E administration system is in progress at the time of writing.

Additional equipment includes external power supply facilities, group SPTA sets, training/operating missiles, towers for the antennas of the multifunction radars, 96L6E radar to improve detection of low-altitude targets, a maintenance complex incorporating an air-conditioner, a unified compressor station, a mobile vehicle-mounted repair workshop and other equipment.

One system, comprising up to eight battalions, can control up to seventy-two launchers, with a maximum of 384 missiles. The missiles are fired by a gas system from the launch tubes up to 30m into the air before the rocket motor ignites, which increases the maximum and decreases the minimum range. In April 2015 a successful test firing of the missile was conducted at an airborne target at a range of 400km. TELs carrying the long-range 40N6 may only be able to hold two missiles instead of the typical four due to its larger size. Another test recorded a 9M96 missile using an active radar-homing head reaching a height of 56km. All the missiles are equipped with a directed-explosion warhead, which increases the probability of the complete destruction of targets.

In 2016, Russian anti-aircraft missile troops received new guided missiles for S-300 and S-400 defence systems. An anti-aircraft missile system designed to destroy aircraft, cruise and ballistic missiles, it can also be used against ground targets. The S-400 is able to intercept cruise missiles out to a range of about 40km due to their low-altitude flightpaths.

S-400 ammunition includes 48N6E3 and 48N6E2 surface-to-air missiles. The 48N6E may be also used. The 48N6E and 48N6E2 missiles are similar to those the Favorit air defence missile system employs. A new 48N6E3 SAM has been developed by upgrading the 48N6E2. Upgrade of the engine by using a solid propellant grain with higher energetic characteristics offered an opportunity to expand the engagement zone at the outer boundary and to increase the engagement zones against ballistic missiles.

Figure 3-45: S-400 at Khmeimim in Syria.

Upgrade of the missile payload, i.e. a radio fuze for the controlled warhead, has enhanced its effectiveness against high-speed, small, manoeuvring targets, also providing for high probability of initiation of the high-explosive payload of ballistic targets, including medium-range ballistic missiles flying at up to 4,800m/s.

In November 2015 the deployment of S-400 was reported in Syria, along with a contingent of Russian troops and other military hardware in the air campaign conducted by Russian forces on the side of the Syrian government. The first S-400 system was reportedly installed at the Khmeimim Air Base in Latakia Governorate (Fig. 3-45). Between April and July 2017, a second S-400 system was deployed 13km north-west of Masyaf, in Hama Governorate.

In the war in Ukraine, a Russian S-400 was able to engage and shoot down a Ukrainian Su-27 fighter at the distance of 150+km (launched from the territory of Belarus and hitting the target over Kiev) which is the system's the first combat engagement. Also, it was also engaged in Crimea downing Ukrainian UAVs. At the time of writing, these results have not been disclosed by the authorities.

Defending the Fleet – Naval S-300F

The S-300F system was designed using the scientific and technical background of the 'Kvant' anti-aircraft missile system for arming large (5,000+ tons displacement) warships. The preliminary design was completed in 1966.

The complex is designed to protect ships from attacks by advanced modern aircraft, cruise missiles and other means of air attack, including those manoeuvring and flying at extremely low altitudes above the water.

The main task of the S-300F system is to destroy carriers of anti-ship and anti-radar missiles, jammers, etc. at long ranges, outside the self-defence zone of target ships. At the same time, multi-channel capability, a wide range of ranges and heights of target engagement, a short reaction time and a high rate of fire allow the complex to participate in repelling large-scale air raids up to the near line of defence.

The S-300F receives target designations from the means available on the ship through an interface device, which is part of the control system. The complex is also connected through the interface device with the ship's pitch and roll angle sensors, heading and speed. In the autonomous search mode, the complex surveys the space and detects targets in a given sector of responsibility.

The multifunctional radar, which is part of the control system (codename 'Fort'), provides high accuracy in tracking targets and guiding missiles despite active and passive interference. A phased antenna array is installed on a rotary post, which allows engaging targets in almost any direction. The rigidity of the antenna post design and the electronic stabilisation of the antenna beam ensures the operation of the complex while the ship is pitching without loss of missile-guidance accuracy.

Initially, the S-300F complexes were supposed to equip the nuclear anti-submarine cruisers of Project 1144 'Orlan' (reclassified as Project 1144 patrol ships, work on which

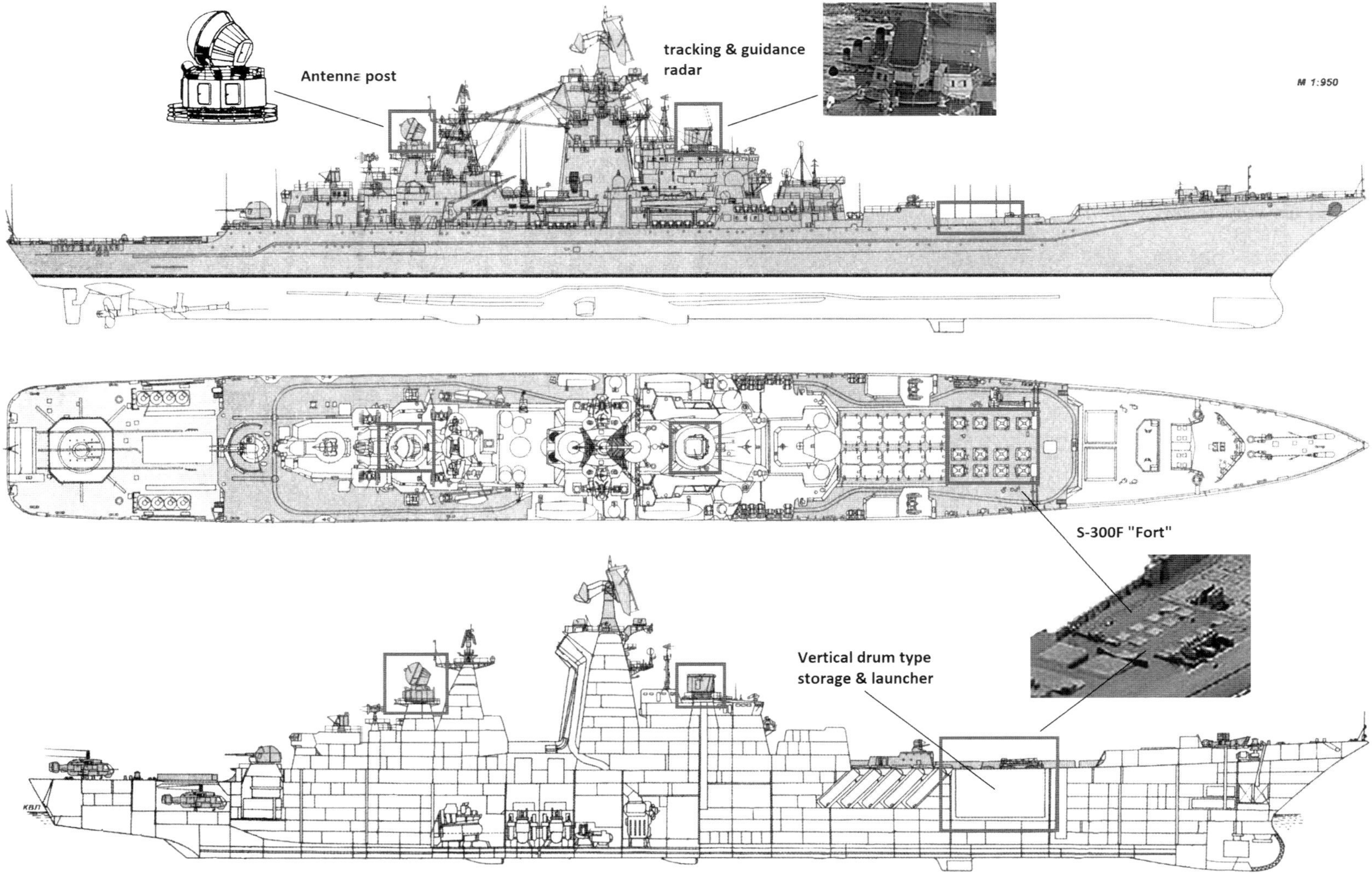

Figure 3-46: Project 11442 nuclear cruiser *Pyotr Veliky* (*Peter the Great*).

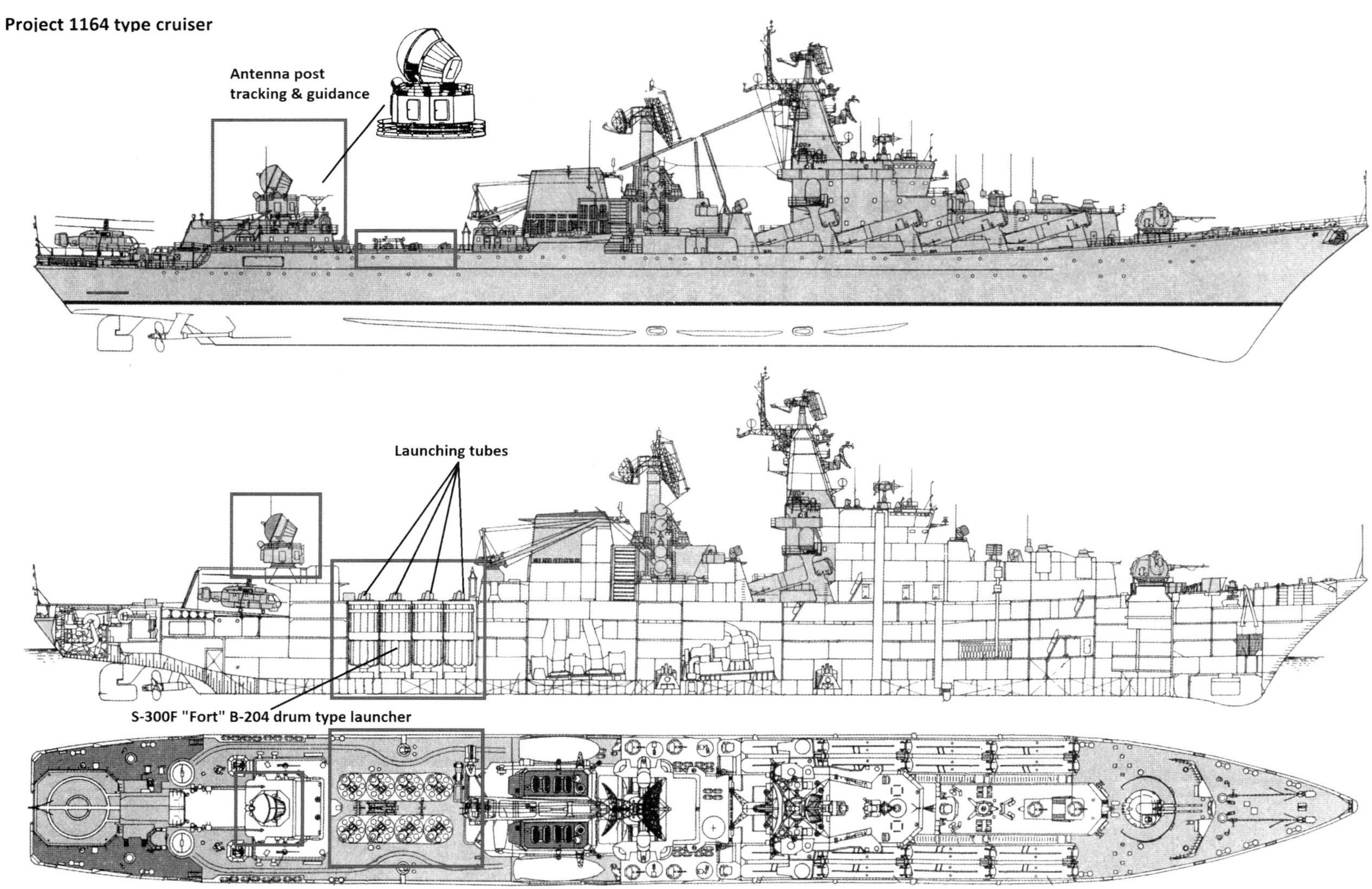

Figure 3-47: Project 1164 *Slava* class cruiser.

began at the beginning of the 1960s) and nuclear missile cruisers of Project 1165 'Fugas'. By a decree of the Council of Ministers of the USSR, adopted in August 1971, both projects were combined, and then the Northern Design Bureau designed a nuclear anti-submarine cruiser with strike missile weapons for finalising the experimental version of the complex and improving it. Tests of the complex were completed on another ship – the nuclear-powered missile cruiser *Kirov* in 1983. After being put into service in 1984, the complex was installed on the nuclear-powered heavy missile cruisers of the *Kirov* class (Project 1144 and 11442 [Fig. 3-46], four units were built by 1997) and on missile cruisers of the *Slava* class (Project 1164, Fig. 3-47, three units built).

The main purpose of the complex is to engage aircraft armed with anti-ship missiles and anti-ship missiles themselves flying at low altitudes, and electronic warfare and jammer aircraft, which is made possible by use of the 5V55RM missile unified with the S-300P complex (a modification of the 5V55R missile, which differs in equipment associated with the container).

The complex includes an under-deck drum-type launcher. Missile launch is from below decks, vertical from the transport-launch container with the start of the sustainer motor after the missile exits, which ensures the safety of the bay from fire or explosion. The missile is launched from the container located under the launch hatch. After the launch, the drum turns, bringing the next TPK into line to launch.

The launchers for the S-300F complex were developed by the design bureau of the Bolshevik plant. The reloading of the drum launchers is carried out using a deck charger, and there is some difference in the placement of under-deck drum launchers and the stock of missiles on ships of various projects. When developing the Project 1144 and 1164 ships, options were considered for placing missiles in individual bays or in drums in a common bay – the second proposal was chosen.

Project 1164 ships have a B-204 under-deck drum launcher with eight drum devices for eight TPKs, and all Project 1144 and 11442 ships have twelve drum launchers as part of the B-203A launcher with a total ammunition load of ninety-six missiles.

The launcher includes a loading device that delivers transport-launch containers with missiles from the deck of the ship to the bay and installs them on the drum guides. The operation of loading missiles into the bay is almost completely automated and on Project 1144 (development of TsKB-52, which since 1966 received the name SPKB, chief designer B. Kupensky) and Project 1164 ships, one loading device was installed, on the Project 1134BF ship the loading device was not installed and the cruiser *Admiral Nakhimov* (Project 11442, the third ship in the series) was fitted with an improved version of the complex with a type 48N6E missile, which was planned to be installed on subsequent ships, and on the cruiser *Pyotr Veliky*, in addition to the S-300F aft complex partially modernised for the use of 48N6 missiles, a bow complex with a new antenna post.

According to advertising and information brochures for export deliveries, a variant of the S-300F complex is proposed – the Rif complex with the 48N6E missile.

To place the equipment of the S-300F and Rif complexes on ships, a compartment with an area of 196m^2 is required. With an ammunition load of forty-eight missiles, the area occupied by drum launchers is 120m^2, with an ammunition load of sixty-four missiles, 166m^2. Power consumption of the complex is 480 kW.

The S-300F complex received the codename SA-N-6 'Grumble' in the West.

S-500 Triumfator

The S-500 Prometheus/55R6M Triumfator-M is a new Russian surface-to-air missile system for which a development of the S-400 system is used. In comparison to the S-400, it is designed for intercepting and destroying intercontinental ballistic missiles, as well as hypersonic cruise missiles and aircraft, and for air defence against airborne early warning and control and jamming aircraft. With a planned range of 600km for anti-ballistic missile (ABM) engagements and 400km for air defence, the S-500 would be able to detect and simultaneously engage up to ten ballistic targets flying at a speeds of 5,000m/s up to a limit of 7,000m/s (25,000km/h). It also aims at destroying hypersonic cruise missiles and other aerial targets at speeds of higher than Mach 5, as well as spacecraft. The declared altitude of a target engaged can be as high as 180–200km. It is effective against ballistic missiles with a launch range of 3,500km and the radar reaches a radius of 3,000km for an RCS of 0.1m^2. It has been announced that other targets include unmanned aerial vehicles, low earth orbit satellites, and space weapons launched from hypersonic aircraft, drones and hypersonic orbital platforms.

The system is highly mobile and has rapid deployability. Its capabilities can affect enemy intercontinental ballistic missiles at the middle and end portions of their flight. System developer Almaz-Antey declared that the external target-designation system (RLS Voronezh-DM and missile defence system A-135 radar Don-2N) was capable of mid-early flight-portion interceptions of enemy ballistic missiles, which is one of the final stages of the S-500 project.

In 2009 the system was under development at Almaz-Antey and had been planned to be completed in 2012. In February 2011 it was announced that the first S-500 systems would be in production by 2014. Two plants were developed to produce the S-500 by 2015. Under the State Armament Programme 2020 (GPV-2020), the plan is to purchase ten S-500 battalions for Russian Aerospace Defence (Vozdushno Kosmiceskaya Oborona).

The main components (Fig. 3-48) of the S-500 are:

- 77P6 launcher/transport vehicle (Fig. 3-49), based on the BAZ-69096 10x10 truck,
- 55K6MA and 85Zh6-2 command posts on BAZ-69092-12 6x6,
- 91N6A(M) acquisition and battle-management radar, a modification of the 91N6 ('Big Bird') towed by the BAZ-6403.01 8x8 tractor,
- 96L6-TsP acquisition radar, an upgraded version of the 96L6 ('Cheese Board') on a BAZ- 69096 10x10 (Fig. 3-49),
- 76T6 multi-mode engagement radar on a BAZ-6909-022 8x8,
- 77T6 ABM engagement radar on a BAZ-69096 10x10, and
- system response time for up to ten missiles, less than 4 seconds (compared to the S-400's 10 seconds).

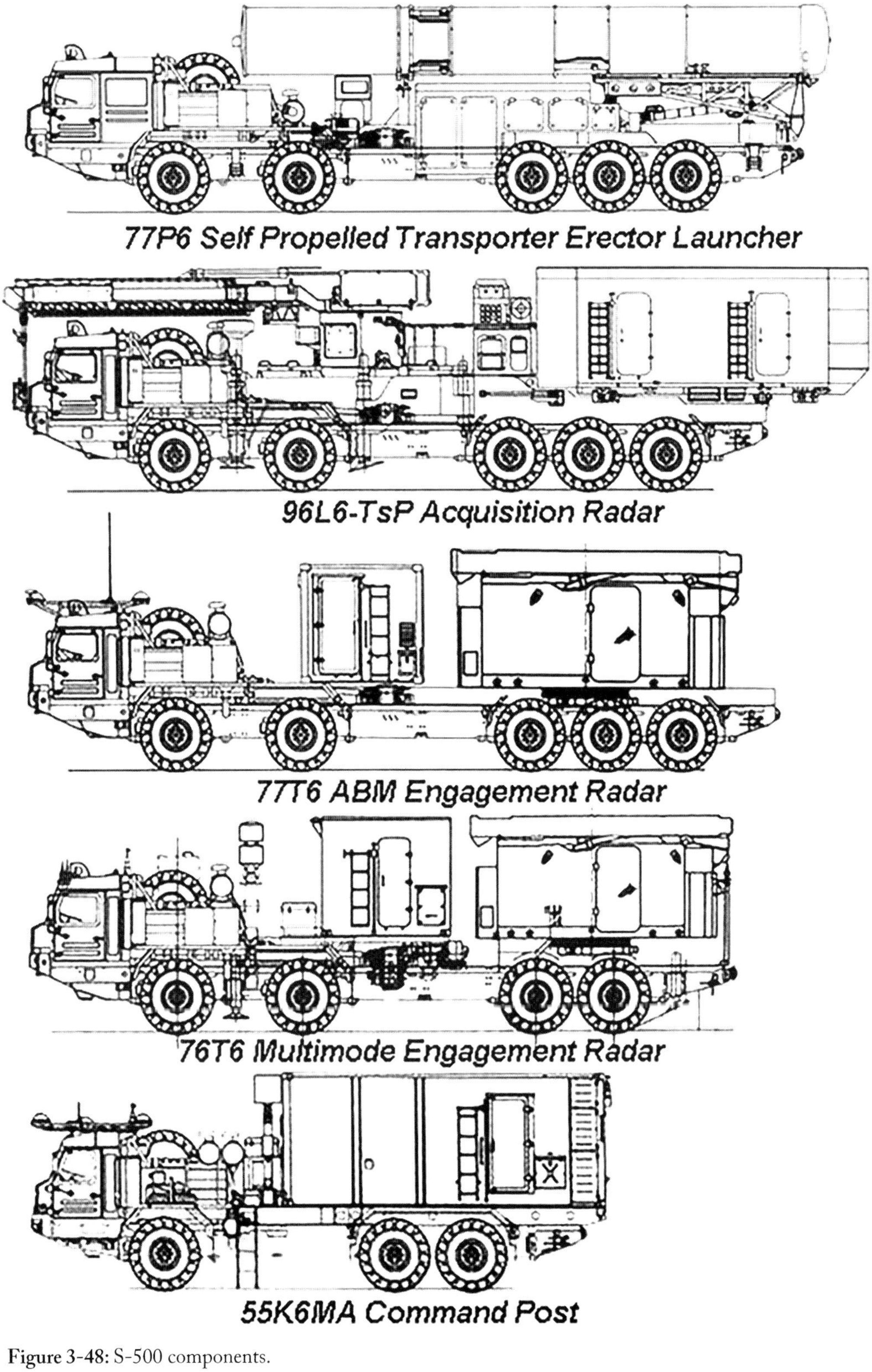

Figure 3-48: S-500 components.

Figure 3-49: 77P6 TEL.

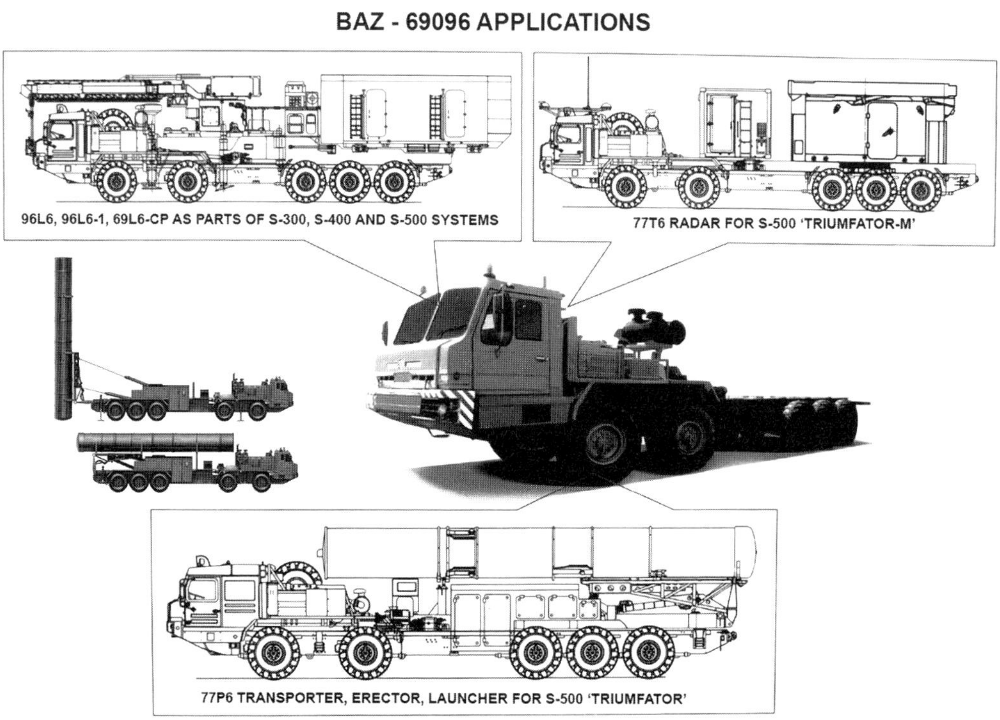

Figure 3-50: BAZ-69096 applications.

Although sharing a similar designation, the relationship between this new S-500 and the S-500U project of the 1960s is unclear. The S-500U multichannel anti-aircraft system was a 1968 initiative by the Soviet Air Defence Forces, Soviet Navy, Ministry of the Radio Industry (Ministerstvo Radio Promyshlennosti SSSR), and the Ministry of the Shipbuilding Industry, to create a unified complex for the National Air Defence Troops, Navy and Army. Missiles of the S-500U complex were supposed to engage enemy aircraft at a range of up to 100km. The S-500U project was rejected by the Soviet Army, which had a requirement to engage not only enemy aircraft but also short-range ballistic missiles. Consequently the S-300 family was developed instead.

Five batteries of S-500 missiles are planned to be in service by 2024. The S-500s will work with S-400s and are planned to together replace S-300 air defence missiles systems. The first units are planned to be deployed around Moscow and the country's central area. A naval version is the likely armament for the new *Lider*-class air defence destroyers due to enter service in 2023–5.

In November 2021 Russia announced a successful test of the new anti-satellite system. Substantive details about the system tested remain very limited and even contradictory. Previous reports have indicated that it was the new S-550, a further modification of the S-500. The new missile could be intended to engage a variety of targets at extremely high altitudes, including intercontinental ballistic missiles in the mid-course portions of their flights, as well as hypersonic weapons and satellites. At the time of writing, available information cannot be verified through independent sources.

S-350 Vityaz[7]

The S-350E Vityaz (50R6) is a new mobile SAM system designed, developed and manufactured by Almaz-Antey. Development began in the early 1990s. There was speculation that the system was mainly aimed at the export market, designed to complement the S-300/S-400 missile family. However, after successful trials, the Russian armed forces have adopted the new system. South Korea is developing a simplified version of the Vityaz called Cheolmae-2 with the help of the Almaz Central Design Bureau. The future of this project is questionable because of the sanctions against Russia. The Vityaz is expected to replace, at the time of writing, the older S-300PS systems. Vityaz has a more advanced radar and a launcher with sixteen missiles compared to only four on the S-300P/PS. The system was unveiled to the public for the first time at the MAKS air show in Moscow in August 2013. According to the developer, Vityaz could replace older SAMs like the venerable S-125 (operated by many countries) while adding multiple-target and anti-missile capabilities. It can be considered a 'budget' option instead of the S-300.

The system can be delivered in two configurations: a version optimised for protecting against high-precision weapons (cruise missiles, ARMs, smart bombs and tactical UAVs) able to simultaneously engage up to eight targets; or a multi-role version. In the former configuration the battery consists of a radar and up to four launchers with thirty-two

Figure 3-51: S-350 Vityaz 50P6 TEL.

'small' missiles each, while in the latter the heart of the battery is a mobile command post linked to one or two radars and up to eight launchers.

The S-350E Vityaz missile system is mounted on an 8x8 truck chassis, under the technical name of 50P6. It is a dual missile system whereby each of the standard

Figure 3-52: S-350 battery components.

containers can be replaced by a pack of four smaller and shorter weapons. The vertical launcher truck carries twelve tubular containers, in two lines of six (Fig. 3-51).

Each complete S-350E Vityaz combat unit typically includes (Fig. 3-52):

- Two to four 50P6 launchers.
- 50N6A fire-control system with target and surveillance radar.
- 50K6 command and control vehicle.
- 96L6-TsP acquisition radar (Fig. 3-53).
- Passive radar 96L6-VP (Fig. 3-53).
- Communication relay station.
- Technical and maintenance vehicles.

Each S-350 system is equipped with and active/passive radar system combining 96L6-VP with 96L6 forming 96L6AP (Fig. 3-53).

The missile for the S-350E is the 9M96 which was originally developed for the S-400 system. This can be used against aerial and ballistic targets with a firing range from 1.5km to 120km and to an altitude from 10m to 30km. It features passive IR homing guidance and is a dual-role anti-missile and anti-aircraft missile. The S-350 can also fire 9M100 guided missiles to engage aircraft, UAVs and cruise missiles. This is a short-range IR-guided missile that has been mentioned as both a SAM and an AAM, with a maximum firing range of 10km. The 9M96E missile is 'hit-to-kill' designed for direct impact and uses canards and thrust vectoring to achieve extremely high G and angular rate capability. An inertial package is used with a datalink from the MFMTR X-band radar for midcourse guidance, with a radar homing seeker of an undisclosed type. The small 24kg blast fragmentation warhead is designed to produce a controlled fragment

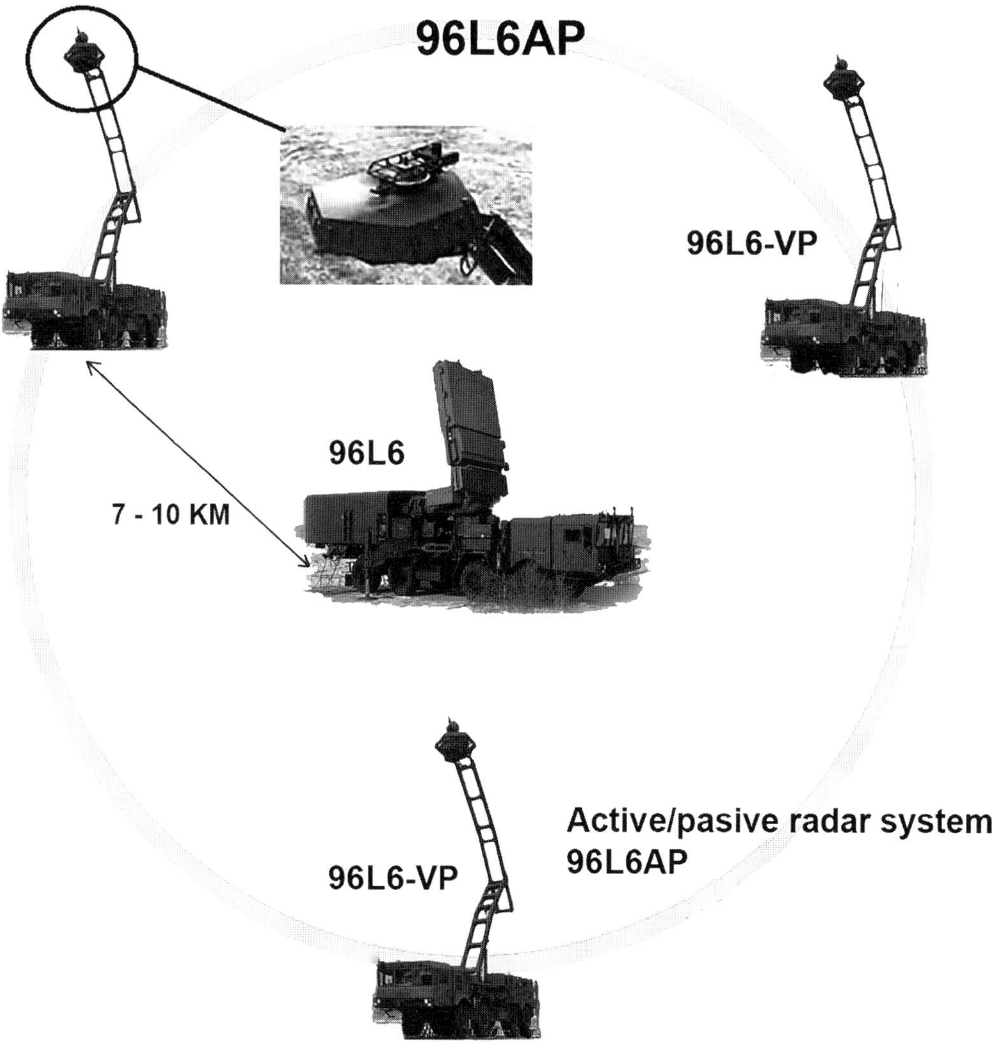

Figure 3-53: 96L6 active/passive radar.

pattern, using multiple initiators to shape the detonation wave through the explosive. A smart radar fuze is used to control the warhead timing and pattern.

A minimum-size S-350E Vityaz battery to perform combat duties may include a combat and control post, tracking and guidance radar, and one launcher. The basic missile load per full battery is forty-eight weapons. Each truck-mounted launcher assembly has two layers of six ready-to-fire missiles in their cylindrical container-launchers which, when in the traveling configuration, are horizontal. For cold launching they are swung into the vertical position at the rear of the vehicle and the missile is ejected to a height of about 30m where its main sustainer rocket motor ignites. All of the component system vehicles use four hydraulically-operated outriggers to stabilise themselves at the battery launch site. Each battery also has its own auxiliary power unit. The component vehicles

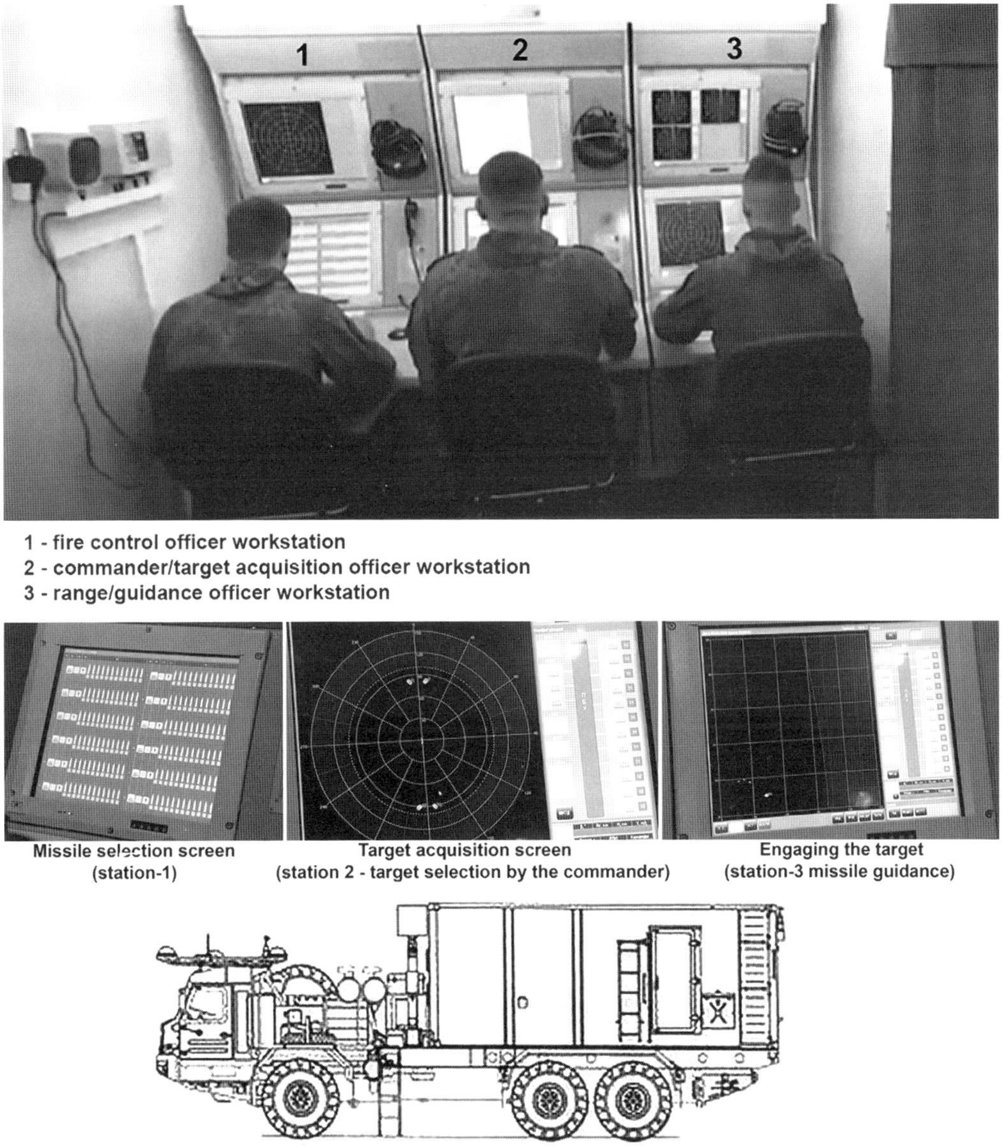

Figure 3-54: 50K6E combat control post.

use an inter-vehicle datalink to pass information back and forth with the fire-control system. Reload missiles in their container-launchers are loaded by crane.

The interior of the 50K6E is shown in Fig. 3-54.

Pantsir[8]

The Pantsir-S1 (SA-22 'Greyhound') is an air defence gun-missile system designed to protect vital small and large military areas, industrial targets and land-forces units and reinforce the air defence units responsible for the protection of troops and military

Figure 3-55: Pantsir-S1.

installations against precision-guided air attack from low and extremely low altitudes. The mobile version of the Pantsir-S1 system includes a combat vehicle (up to six vehicles in a battery), surface-to-air guided missiles, 30mm rounds, a transporter-loader vehicle (one per two combat vehicles), and maintenance and training facilities. The Pantsir-S1 is designed by the KBP Instrument Design Bureau of Tula, and is manufactured by the Ulyanovsk Mechanical Plant, Ulyanovsk (Fig.3-55, 3-57).

The armament of Pantsir-S1 consists of twelve 57E6 surface-to-air guided missiles and two 30mm 2A38M cannon developed from the two-barrelled 30mm GSh-30. It is provided with a multi-range radar capable of detecting aerial targets with an effective surface of dispersion of up to 2–3m^2 at a distance of more than 30km and tracking them down from a range of over 24km. With its missiles, the Pantsir-S1 can engage tactical aircraft at a maximum range of 20km and altitude of 10km, subsonic cruise missiles at a range of 12km and altitude of 6km, and high-speed air-to-ground missiles at a range of 7km and altitude of 6km. With its guns, it can destroy aerial targets at a maximum range of 4km and a maximum altitude of 3km (Fig. 3-56). The Pantsir-S1 can operate independently or in a formation (Fig. 3-58).

The missiles are arranged into two six-tube groups on the turret. The missile has a two-stage body in tandem configuration. The first stage is a booster, providing rapid acceleration within the first 2–3 seconds of flight after it is separated from the sustainer stage. The sustainer is the highly agile part of the missile and contains the high-explosive multiple continuous rods and fragmentation warhead, contact and proximity fuses as well as a radio transponder and a laser responder to be localised for guidance. The missile is not fitted with a seeker to keep target engagement costs low. Instead, high-precision target and missile tracking are provided via the system's multiband sensor system and guidance data is submitted via radio link for up to four missiles in flight (Fig. 3-58). Missiles can be fired in at up to four targets but also in salvos of two missiles at one

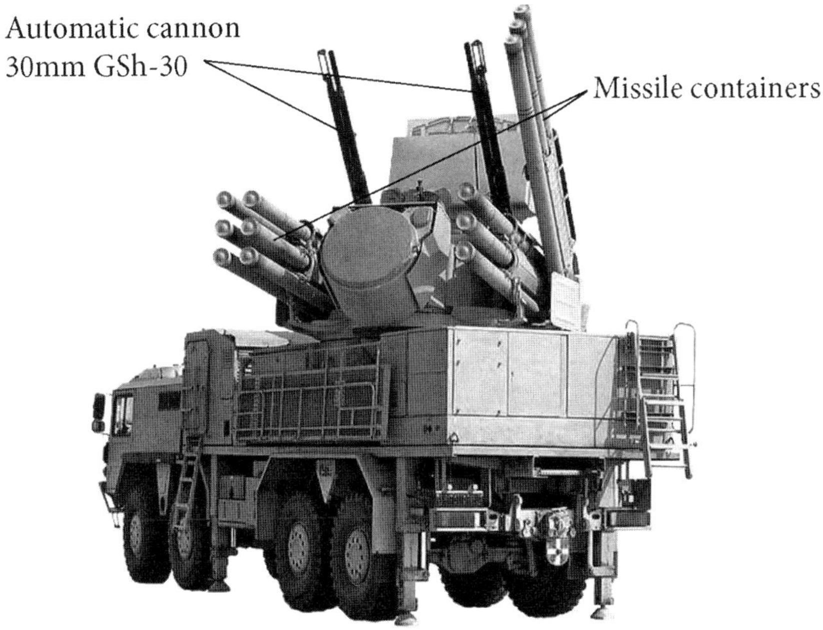

Combat vehicle 72V6

Guided missile 57Э6

Ammunition types

Type	**Characteristics**
High explosive fragmentation projectile ZUOF8 	General purpose round, used against aerial targets and ground targets such as troops and unarmoured targets.
Fragmentation tracer projectiles ZUOR6 	The same as ZUOF8 with the smaller explosive charge and fragmentation head. In addition, provides the tracing. Used together with ZUOF8.

Figure 3-56: Combat vehicle and munitions.

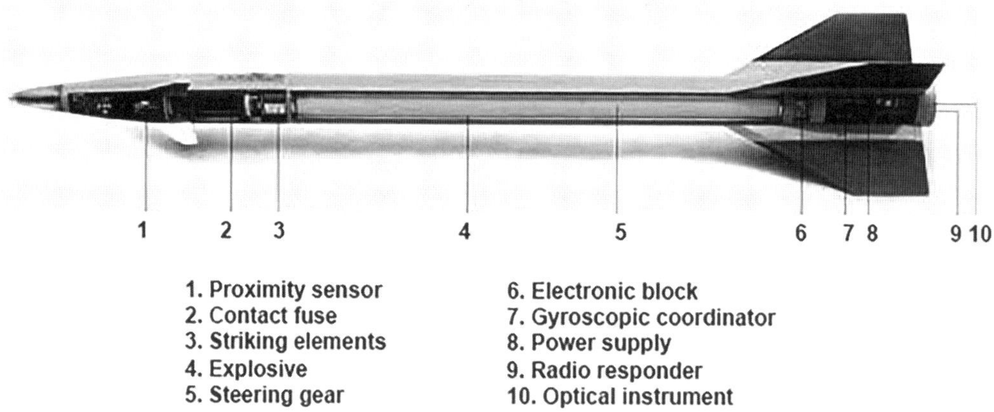

Figure 3-57: 57E6 marching stage.

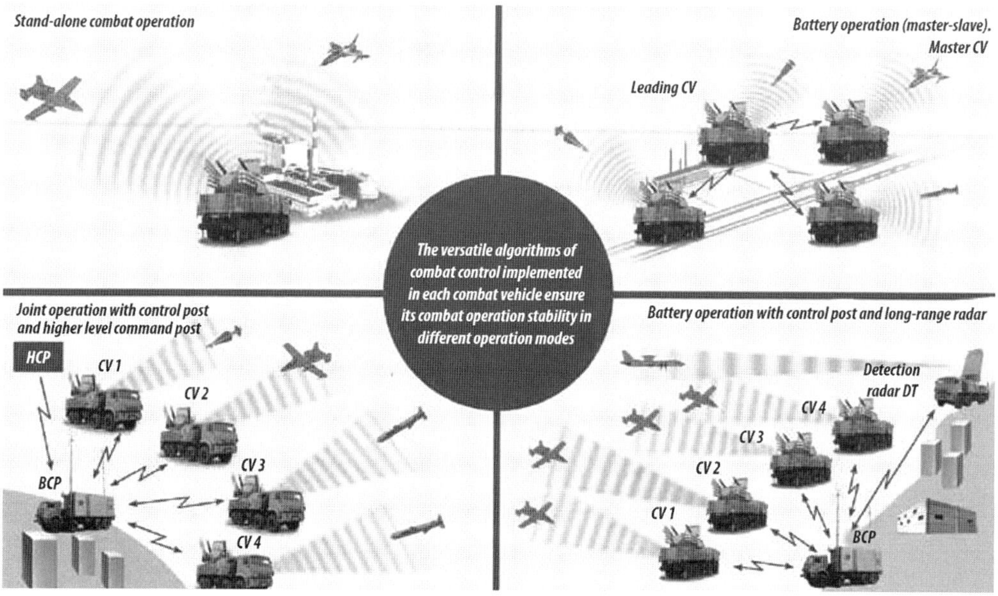

Figure 3-58: Combat operation mode.

target. The missile is believed to have a hit probability of 70–95 per cent and have a 15-year storage life in its sealed containers. Pantsir-S1 combat vehicles can fire missiles on the move (Fig. 3-56, 3-57).

The Pantsir-S1 can be mounted on a different truck chassis with a turret that houses the armament, laying drives, sensors, control equipment and crew. The turret is a modular design and can be installed on multiple platforms. For example, the Ural-5323 truck is four-axle, 8×8 all-wheel drive with single-tyre wheels. The first and second axle wheels are steerable. The engine is an air-cooled diesel Ural-74510 providing 290hp. The dual-plate mechanical clutch has a pneumatic booster and a three-range five-speed gearbox. In the Russian Army, the Pantsir-S1 weapon system is mounted on a Kamaz 6560 8x8 chassis (Fig. 3-59).

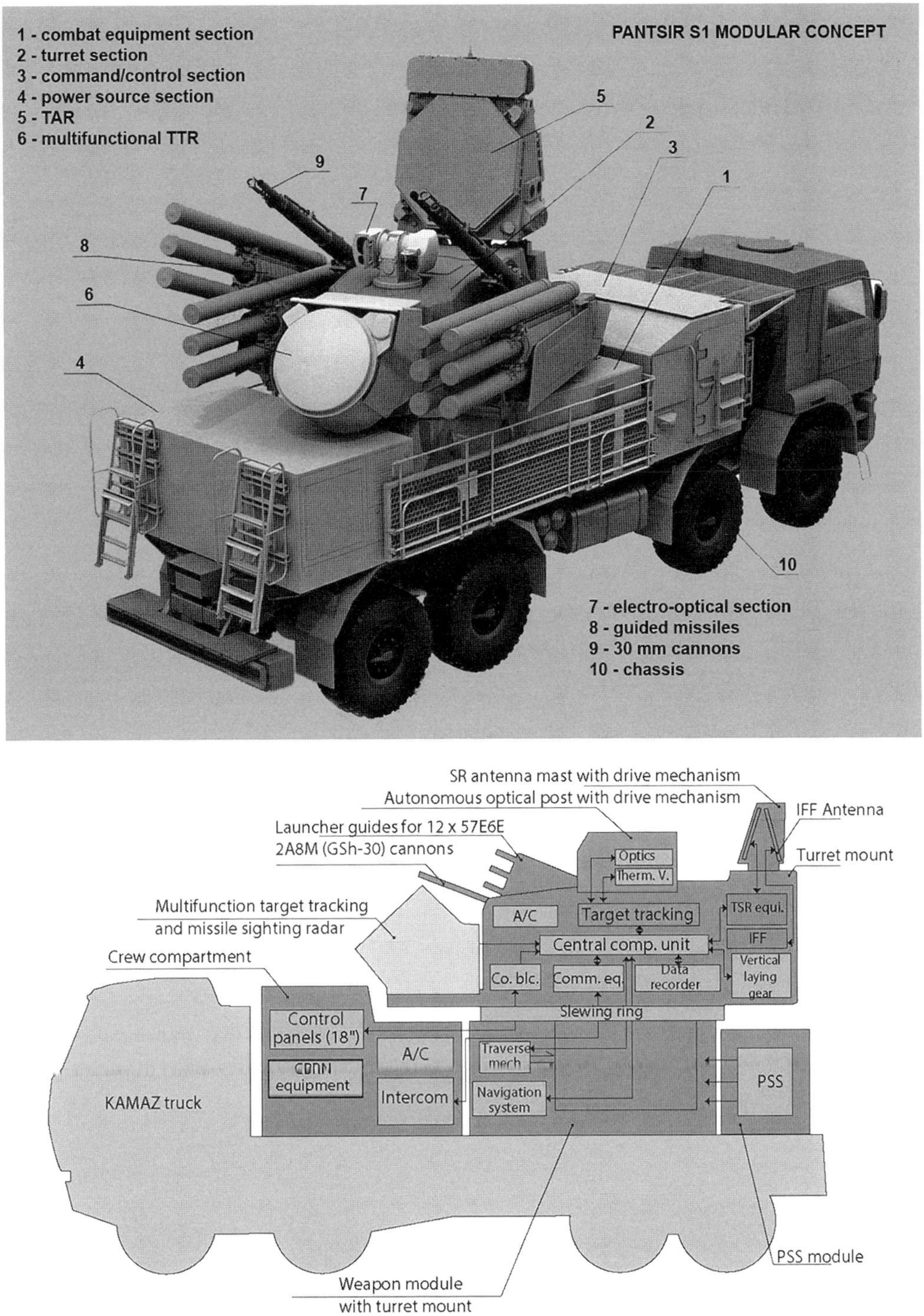

Figure 3-59: Modular concept.

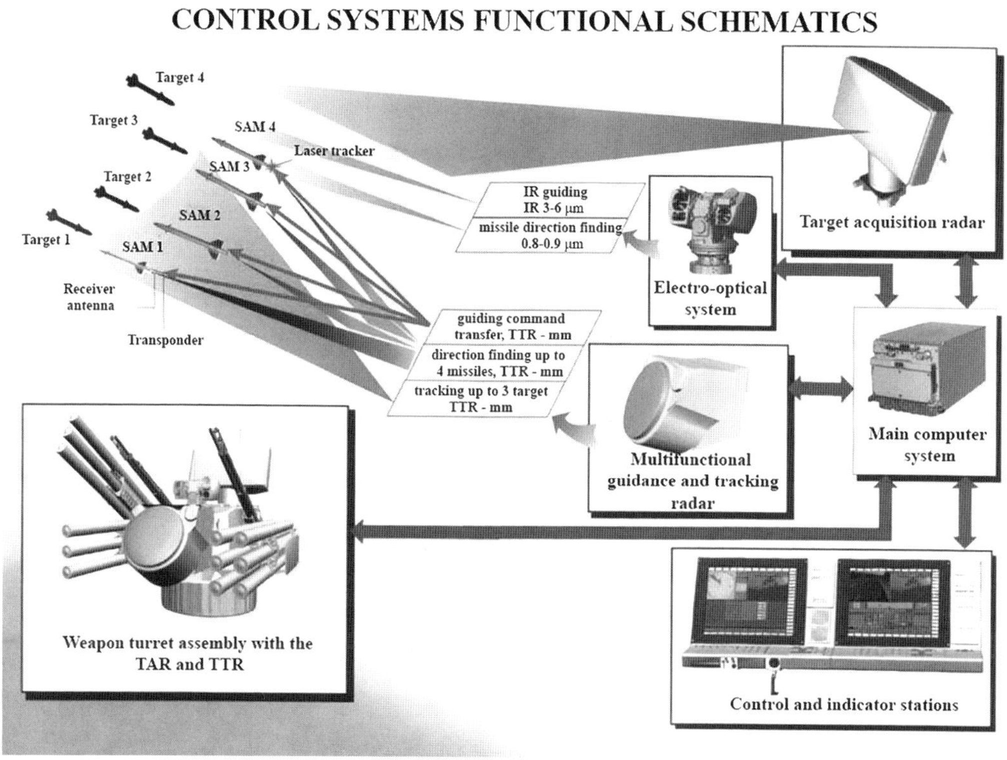

Figure 3-60: Control system.

The Pantsir-S1 fire-control system (Fig. 3-60) includes a target-acquisition radar and dual-waveband tracking radar (1RS2-1), which operates in the UHF and EHF wavebands. Its detection range is 32–36km. This radar tracks both targets and the SAM while in flight. The minimum target RCS for tracking is 2–3cm^2. The fire-control system has an electro-optic channel with a longwave thermal imager and an infrared direction finder, including digital signal processing and automatic target tracking. The two independent guidance channels – radar and electro-optic – allow two targets to be engaged simultaneously and four in more recent options. The maximum engagement rate is up to 10–12 targets per minute.

The specific feature of the Pantsir-S1 system is the combination of a multiple-band target acquisition and tracking system with a combined missile and gun armament, creating a continuous target-engagement zone from 5m height and 200m range up to 15km height and 20km range, even without any external support (Fig. 3-61, 3-62, 3-63, 3-64). By design and functionality, the compact combat control system, with its high level of automation, is very similar to the combat system of a fighter jet.

In the war in Ukraine, Pantsir-S units provide the vital AD for the advancing Russian troops. It is proven that one of the launchers downed seven Ukrainian drones and one helicopter.

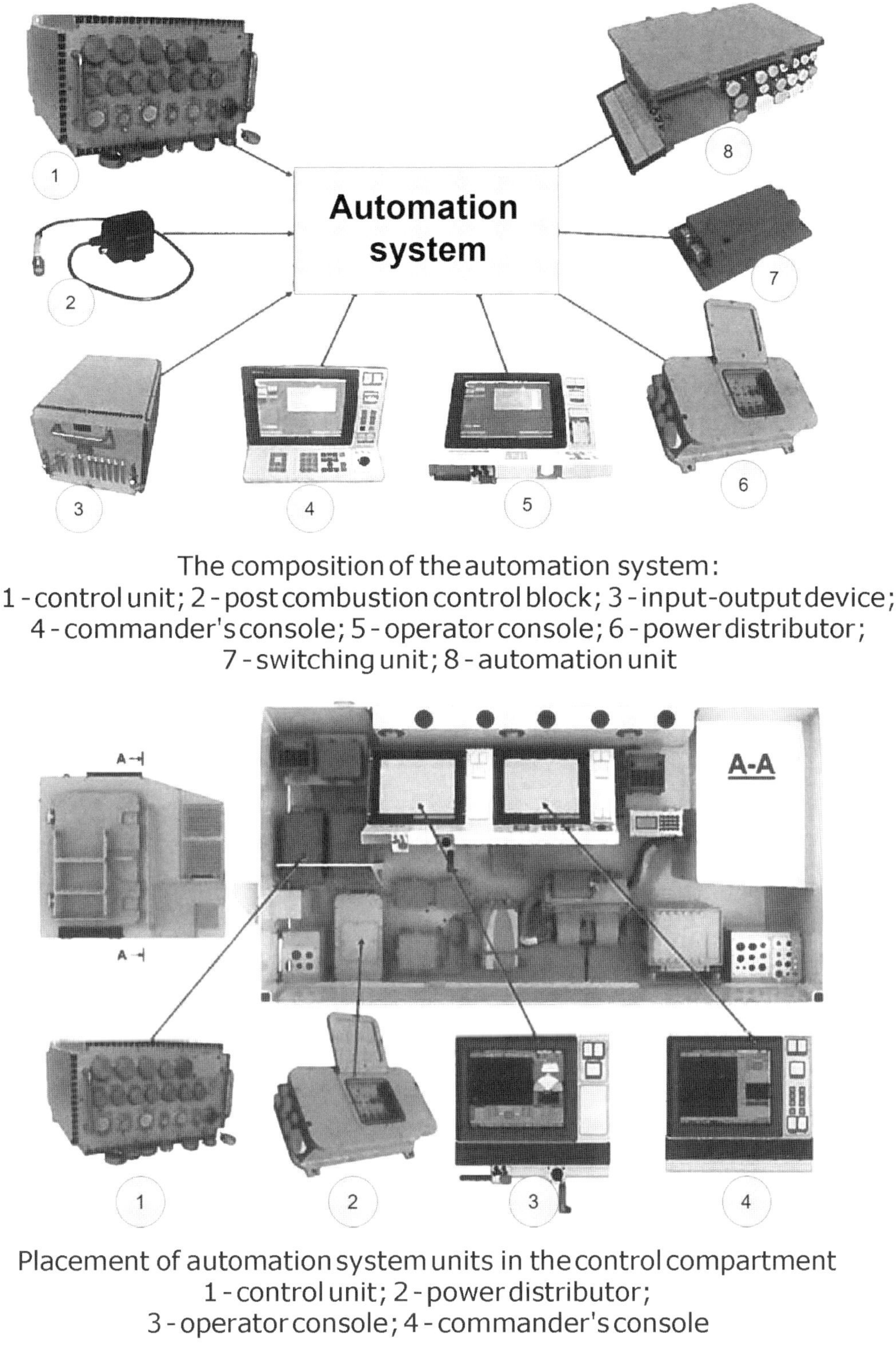

Figure 3-61: Automation system.

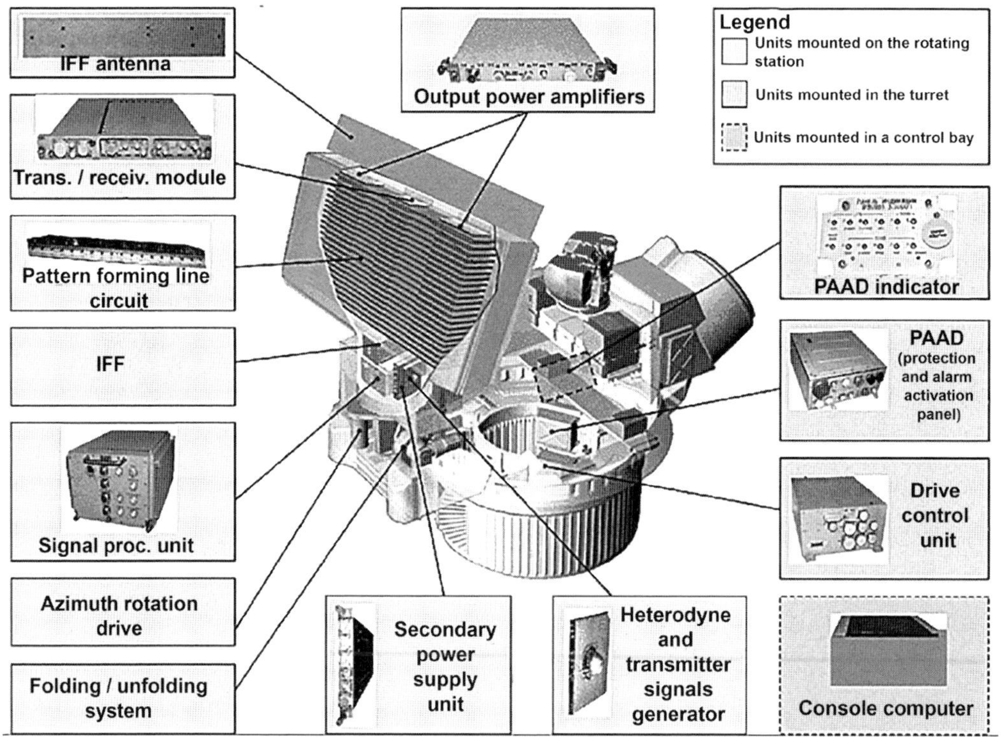

Figure 3-62: Target search/tracking radar components.

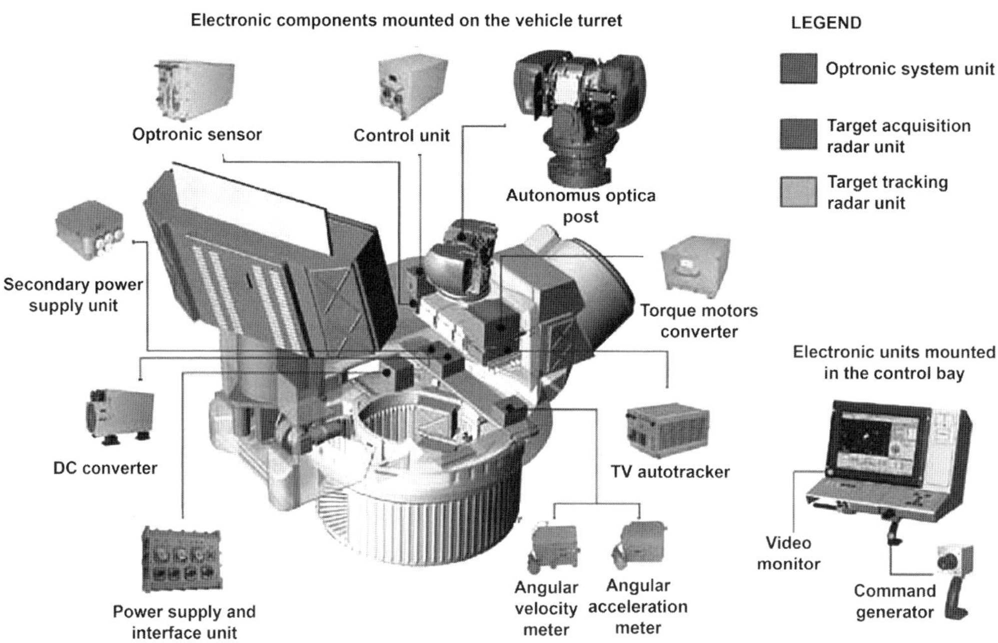

Figure 3-63: Vehicle turret electronic components.

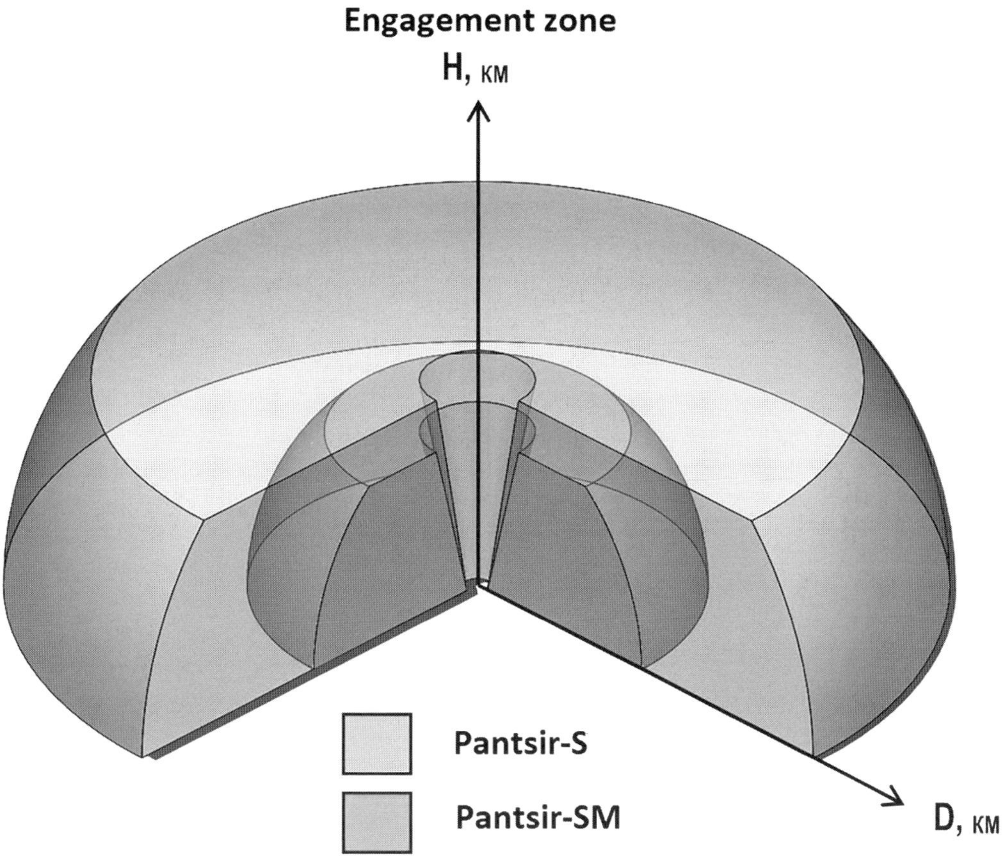

Figure 3-64: Engagement zones.

Prospective Systems: 42S6 Morfey

42S6 Morfey or Morfei with the 9M338K or RZV-MD missile, based on and derived from Tor-M2, is a short-range air defence system currently being developed for the Russian armed forces. It is a mobile system with a range of 5km. Development has been ongoing since 2007 and it was supposed to be introduced in 2015 but has been delayed. It is being developed by Almaz-Antey. It is reported to feature an omnidirectional cupola-type radar with an active electronically-scanned array.

This system is designated as a short-range air defence system to protect the S-400 missile system from various threats at their terminal phases, and will also act together with the S-350E as a supplement to the S-400. Together, these systems form part of the Aerospace Defence Forces.

The missile system consists of an omnidirectional 29YA6 radar, infrared sensors and thirty-six missiles. The missiles have up to 10km range and an altitude of up to 3,500m.

The concept has similarities with the Israeli Iron Dome regarding the position of the missile container. According to some reports, 42S6 is deployed at the Russian Khmeimim airbase in Syria but as of the time of writing this book, there is no concrete evidence.

The system consists of:

- Command post – BAZ or 'Tiger' vehicle chassis.
- 29YA6 multifunction radar (Fig. 3-65 and 3-66), created in the framework of the ROC 'Morpheus' on a 70N6 combat vehicle and according to unconfirmed reports is an annular phased-array radar with AFAR or dome lens (probably hemispherical phased array). The hemispherical phased array consists of 2,048 transceiver modules. It is likely that the SAM command control uses this radar.
- Launcher – with 29YA6 radar on BAZ chassis. Missiles are launched vertically from their containers. The first example of the BAZ-69092-024 chassis variant was shipped from Almaz-Antey in May 2010. According to unconfirmed reports the combat vehicles mounted 70N6 radar and the infrared guidance station; BAZ-69092-022 (2008 or earlier) and BAZ-69092-024 – with twelve or twenty-four missiles (most likely) and forty-eight missiles presumably mounted on BAZ-6909 chassis.
- 9M338K missile.

Figure 3-65: 29YA6.

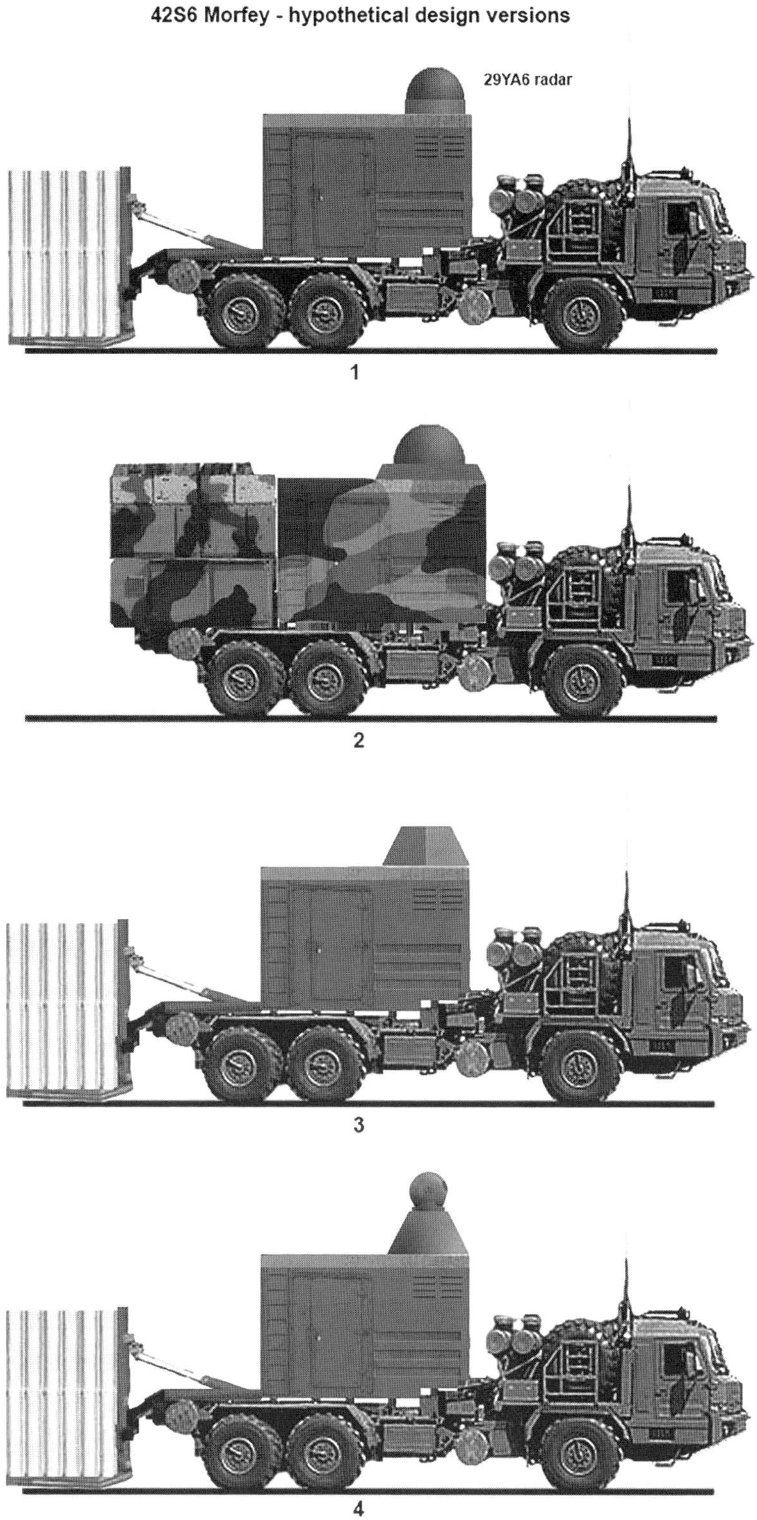

Figure 3-66: 42S6 launcher (design phase).

The Moscow Shield – Anti-Satellite Missiles

In the 1960s and 1970s, the A-35M strategic ballistic missile defence system was created as part of a separate missile defence corps. In the 1990s, the A-35M missile defence system exhausted its combat capabilities in the face of the enemy's use of means to overcome missile defence and was withdrawn from service in December 1990. In 1996, a more advanced A-135 system was adopted, which was subsequently modernised to improve its combat and operational characteristics, expanding defence zones, and solving

Figure 3-67: A-135M anti-ballistic and anti-satellite missile.

the tasks of intercepting existing and future targets (ballistic missiles and satellites) in the interests of aerospace defence.

At present, the A-135 missile defence system (Fig. 3-67), together with the air defence systems such as S-300, S-400 and S-500, forms the missile and air defence command of the Aerospace Defence Forces and performs the tasks of defending the city of Moscow and the Moscow industrial region.

It should be noted that the A-135 system includes the Don-2N multifunctional radar which, in addition to missile defence tasks, also serves in the early warning and the strategic ballistic missile roles. The system is designed taking in consideration new means of strategic attack. The modernisation potential laid down by the general designer makes it possible to consider the multifunctional radar as one of the main information means of the air defence and missile defence command in the long term.

The new A-235 system should replace the A-135. The two main differences will be that the A-235 will use conventional warheads and it will be mobile. The Russian military conducted an anti-satellite weapon test in November 2021 involving the destruction of a defunct Soviet intelligence satellite, which created a dangerous debris cloud in space.

Chapter 4

Ground Forces Air Defence

Tactical Air Defence

A tactical air defence system is a complex of functionally connected surface-to-air missile and artillery systems, surveillance, target detection, identification and designation systems, automated control systems, electronic warfare systems and other systems with the main task of defending combined-arms troops against air or ballistic-missile attacks.

A special feature that distinguishes the tactical AD system from the general AD systems used by other branches of the military is that the weaponry and equipment are situated in ground forces battle formations and can be used to secure tactical facilities and infrastructure during both defensive and offensive operations and on the march while approaching predetermined objectives and positions. These operations require the weapons to possess high mobility and the ability to withstand enemy attacks of any kind.

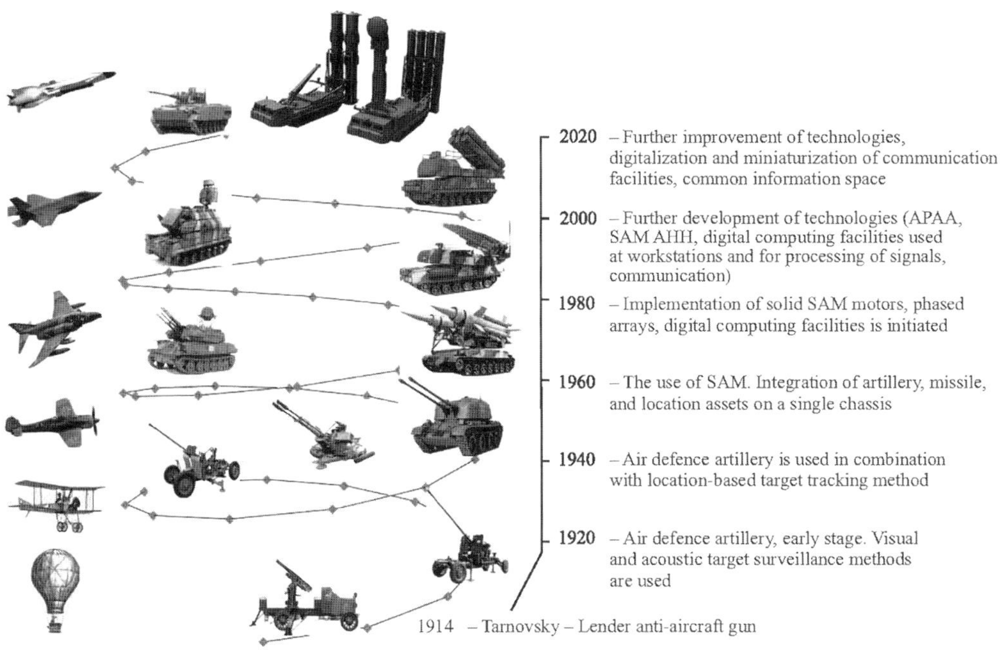

Progressive development of tactical air defence weapons (SAM AHH – active homing head of the surface-to-air missile; APAA – active phased antenna array)

Figure 4-1: Progressive development of tactical air defence.

The development of Russian tactical air defence weapon systems has been characterised by a dialectical confrontation between attack and defence (attack-deterrence) technologies (Fig. 4-1). Due to progressive development of both attack and defence weapon technologies, new weapons and means of their application are created that, on the one hand, reduce enemy armament efficiency, and on the other hand, force the enemy to react and develop more advanced armament.[1]

An enemy's ability to deliver massive strikes with the simultaneous use of numerous decoys, anti-radiation missiles, combat deceptions and dense jamming are increasing. Due to the increase in the amount of UAVs used, as well as the fact that manned aircraft can attack without having to enter the air defence area or only entering such an area for the short time required for the attack, the level of sensitivity to military losses decreases. It is expected that by 2025–30, mainly unmanned air vehicles will be engaged in military operations in the defence area throughout the entire range of altitudes and speeds. Practically all the weapons used against particular elements of air defence formations and defence troops will be high-precision types. These and other trends significantly raise the requirements for tactical AD systems in terms of their efficiency, jamming immunity, mobility and survivability, as well as the size of ready-to-engage SAM combat modules.

The following are the most important trends in the creation of tactical AD weapons and technologies that have been designed in recent years, are being developed at present, or may become mature in the immediate future. The progress of development of information and reconnaissance means, primarily radar equipment used for target acquisition and designation can be described as follows:

- The full range of active radar bands (X, C, S, L, UHF) used for timely detection of various attack platforms and precise determination of their coordinates has been studied. Integration of locator equipment operating in different bands within a single weapon system with the arrangement on a single chassis is in progress. The existing design technologies, related first of all to antennae, allow designing deployable antennae characterised by short up-time (from a few minutes to tens of minutes);
- technologies related to highly effective passive radar means, including small-sized units that can be integrated into a single weapon with active radar equipment, have been developed;
- implementation of the active phased and digital antenna array in the construction of antenna systems which results in qualitative improvement in radar systems in terms of their capability to detect and process signals, a considerable increase in the number of channels used, jamming immunity, operating range, and the accuracy and reliability of the systems; and
- a new technological level for optoelectronic devices (OED) is used for detection and highly-accurate target tracking under dense jamming conditions for radar equipment.

Technologies related to the construction of all functionally relevant components of SAMs have been improved significantly. There is an ongoing process of design and development of technologies for constructing high-potential active homing heads (AHH) with relatively small antenna curtain diameters, fuel-rich propellants for rocket engines with specific thrust pulses up to 2,500–2,800Ns/kg, and compact airborne navigation and computing facilities. Along with mastering of high-density mounting technology, it allows, for example, the mid-section of intermediate-range missiles (IRM) and long-range missiles (LRM) to be reduced to 20–30cm, thus making the missile capable of reaching velocities up to 2,000–3,000m/s when moving in the atmosphere.

Development of the hardware and technologies of EW equipment, including implementation of adaptive active phase antenna arrays (APAAs), ensures the possibility of mounting them on a single chassis, together with the weapon system's radar equipment, thus constructing a single integrated system which results in creation of a multi-capable weapon for target destruction/suppression.

Development of new technologies for the construction of anti-aircraft artillery weapons and equipping of missiles with a guidance system resulted in significant increases in accuracy; and the use of programmed or command-based projectile destruction with the formation of a cloud of damaging elements allows the creation of relatively cheap and effective weapons to deal with a new type of targets: mini- and micro-UAVs.

The progress of development of weapons and troop control facilities includes an ongoing process of design and development of technologies for constructing high-performance special-purpose and general-purpose computers, as well as the creation of effective information-processing algorithms aimed at solving a wide range of computational tasks: from real-time radar signal processing, target recognition and route initiation, to such issues as optimal allocation of fire and information resources in the dynamics of combat operations between warring sides.

Development of control facilities along with the development of communication and time-synchronisation facilities (coordinated time system) provides new ways of solving tasks related to organising the defence, target distribution and target designation, as well as making it possible to generate a unified information-management system, that results in substantial increase in terms of system jamming immunity and survivability and a qualitatively new level of information processing. Thus, joint processing of data received from various locating facilities enables the prompt generation of a single spatially-distributed locator performing tracking of targets, coherent processing of their signals and missile guidance.

The integration of data obtained from air defence facilities used in inter-branch (common) ACS at strategic, operational and tactical levels, along with more precise data on the position and capabilities of air defence facilities, allows the time required to make decisions to be reduced, and, in general, to increase combat effectiveness of the ground force formations.

Based on the organisational structure of the protected troops, the structure of tactical air defence weapon systems is traditionally hierarchical. Each level of the forces' hierarchy (strategic, operational, and tactical) is related to a particular air defence weapon system (a set of weapons, i.e. anti-aircraft missile systems [AAMS] and complexes [SAMC] of the corresponding level) most effective against the aerospace attack weapon (ASAW) used to attack the troops being protected (major units and subunits). The hierarchical principle of air defence weapons construction is also implemented in classification of weapons by their combat capabilities and control systems. This ensures proper responsiveness of the troops to commands and the organisation of the AD system within the framework of the general system of tasks to be solved by the troops, according to the integrated combat operations concept.

Strategic-level air defence weapons (LR AAMS), while dealing with the traditional tasks of countering the enemy's air control and reconnaissance systems by preventing air command posts (ACP) and airborne early warning and control (AEWC) and reconnaissance aircraft from leaving the radio horizon as well as defending vital facilities against attacks by intermediate-range ballistic missiles (IRBMs) and operational-tactical missiles (OTM), shall at the same time take part in repulsing massive strikes by weapons that are typical for IR SAM, the density of which will increase significantly in future wars.

Operational-level air defence weapons (IR AAMS), while dealing, among others, with such tasks as tactical air force and tactical missile (TM) destruction and repulsing of massive strikes of cruise-type missiles as well as other usual tasks, should be able to defend the troops against operational-tactical missiles, while simultaneously securing facilities and using self-shielding against small-scale unmanned aerial vehicles. The experience of air defence weapons use in combat conditions in the Syrian civil war, as well as the withdrawal of the US from the INF Treaty, leads to the conclusion that in the mid-term perspective (for the next 15 to 20 years) dealing with such tasks will be a typical scenario for IR AAMS in possible local wars.

This results in the need to ensure the possibility of weapon-system combinations, meaning full implementation of weapons attributed to IR AAMS as part of LR AAMS, and weapons attributed to LR AAMS and short-range (SR) AAMS as part of intermediate-range weapon systems. Such weapon combinations will be based on a unified intelligence-information-control field (unified air environment assessment algorithms and protocols of information exchange between weapon systems) of an air defence grouping. In addition, to provide direct cover of commonly controlled positioning areas, SR air defence weapons and anti-aircraft artillery will be used.

Fire-control radars will provide SAMs with data of the required accuracy to guide them on their targets and have capacity enough for simultaneous tracking of the targets and interaction with SAMs being guided onto them. High density of impacts by ASAW and the need for quick carry-over of the radar beam from one observed object to another within relatively wide coverage sectors for intermediate range and long-range SAM define the need to construct their radars on the basis of APAA and DAPAA. SR SAMs with smaller operational areas may include passive phased antenna array (PAA) and APAA. The accuracy characteristics of firing radars are ensured by the use of X and C-wavebands and wideband signals.

The design of SAMs will be based on minimising the mid-section of the missile, thus increasing their speed. The missile velocity, in turn, determines its operational area, available acceleration and ability to choose the miss distance, as well as the rate of fire of the complex. Reduction of SAM dimensions also results in increasing the ammunition capacity of the launcher. Reduction of the mid-section can, however, be limited due to the following: packing density of the airborne equipment, the diameter of airborne direction-finder antenna, and engine nozzle cross-section that sets up the required gas efflux rate.

IR and LR SAMs and especially anti-ballistic SAMs for target interception above the atmosphere will be provided with the ability for flexibly-programmable fuel consumption depending on the flight profile – to save fuel, dense layers of the atmosphere will be transited at relatively low speeds. At the same time, to increase the far boundary of the interception, the maximum value of average missile speed will be ensured.

The SAM set included in SAMCs (batteries) of various types together with launchers will be able to deal with the entire range of fire missions in defeating the raids (strikes) of aerial weapon types specified for SAMCs. For this purpose, the firing locator will ensure simultaneous guidance of missiles of various types. Consequently, the missile guidance system will be unified.

This unification can be achieved through the use of radio correction during the major part of the flight trajectory when controlling the flight. When such a control system is used, flight-control commands are generated by airborne facilities as per the data on the missile coordinates obtained from airborne inertial navigation, and corrective information on the current position of the missile and target is transmitted by a ground locator as a unified code for different types of missiles. Time interval of the corrective signals is adaptable and is determined by flight dynamics and current guidance errors. The SAM transponder will operate in the frequency band of the firing locator. Bearing in mind the fact that different types of locators may be used to guide the missiles, the above condition can be satisfied by using multi-range missile transponders or SAM sets, including several transponders set to the frequency of a certain locator.

In terms of design, the chassis of air defence weapons will be unified to the maximum possible extent with one another, with maintenance facilities (weapon repair and missile delivery facilities) and with the weapons within general groupings of troops to reduce their cost and increase maintainability. Based on the above, a wheeled chassis will be considered as the standard for brigade-level facilities. CP and TDF, being parts of AAMS, are placed on chassis similar to those used for SAMC facilities.

All ground forces SAM systems are mounted on tracked chassis in order to increase their mobility and cross-country capacity when positioning them in the areas of troops disposition. At that, due regard shall be given to the need for IR, SR and LR SAMs on wheeled chassis to be used by combined arms and armoured carrier (AC) units, as well as meeting the requirements in terms of buoyancy (when used by amphibious forces) and airborne infiltration (when used by airborne forces).

Shown in Fig. 4-2 is a possible option for a tactical air defence weapon system structure created on the basis of the principles given above and ensuring troops (forces) groupings organisation in the theatre of operations.

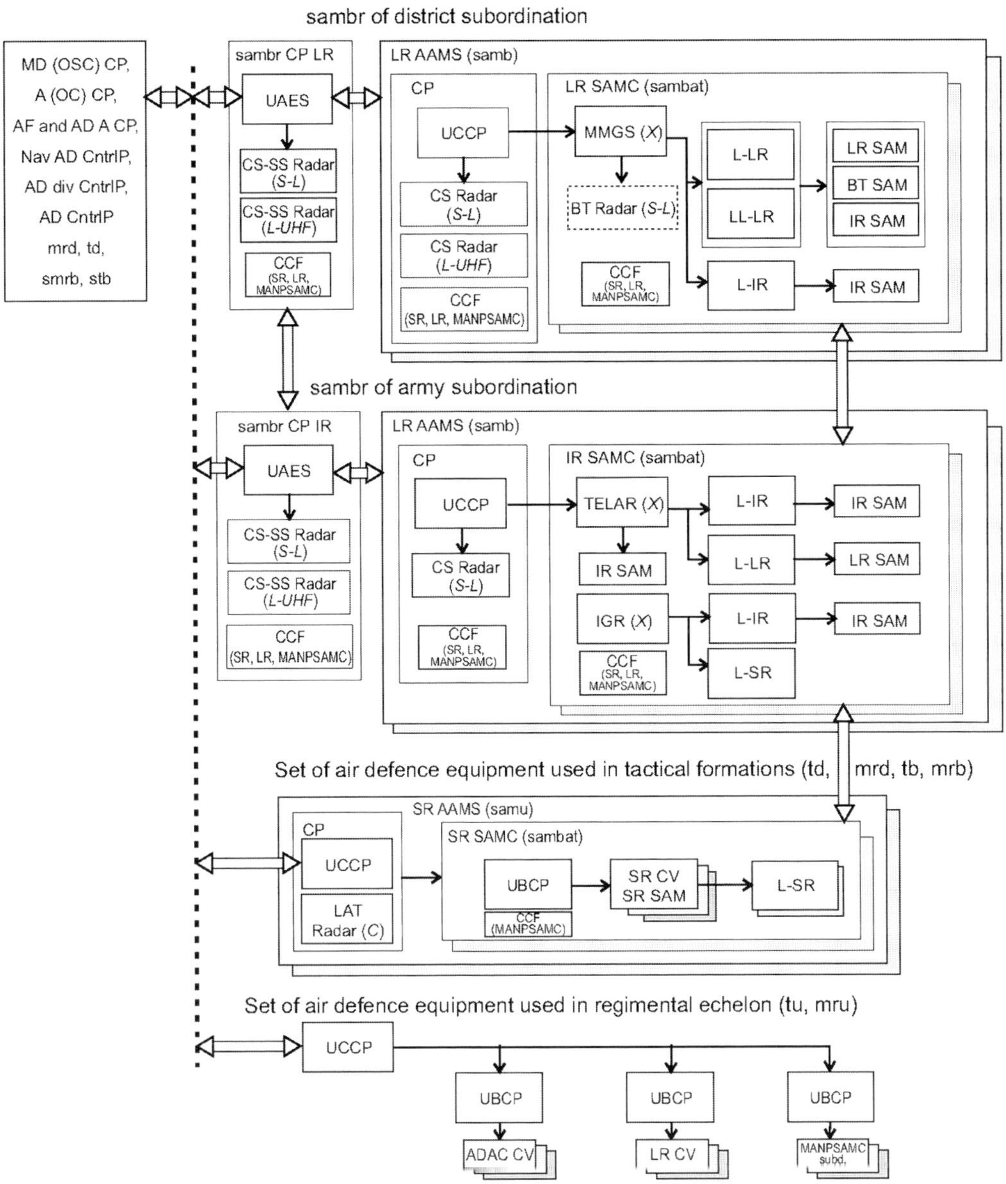

⇐ – network-centric information exchange within; MD – Military District; OSC – Operational-Strategic Command; A – Army; OC – Operational Command; AD CntrlP – AD Control Post; AD div CntrlP – AD Division Control Post; mrd – motorized rifle division; td – tank division; smrb – separate motorized rifle brigade; stb – separate tank brigade; sambr – surface-to-air missile brigade; sambat – surface-to-air missile battery; CS – Circular Scanning; SS – Sectoral Scanning; MMGS – Multifunctional Missile Guidance Station; CCF – Close-In Coverage Facilities; LL – Launcher and Loader; LAT – Low-Altitude Targets; CV – Combat Vehicle; ADAC – Air Defence Artillery Complex; MANPSAMC – Man-Portable Surface-to-Air Missile Complex

Possible option of prospective air defence weapon system structure used by troops (forces) groupings in the theatre of operations

Figure 4-2: Possible options for prospective tactical air defence.

In the structure diagram, the weapon system provides execution of air defence tasks at three levels: strategic, operational and tactical. According to this, three types of AAMS – LR, IR and SR – are shown in the diagram.

Universal control facilities are used at various levels of the hierarchy: universal automation equipment system (UAES), universal combat control post (UCCP), universal battery command post (UBCP), and universal radars of various types. The equipment and devices included in individual weapons are unified to the maximum possible extent in terms of their content.

The diagram reflects the possibility of information exchange among the entire scope of information resources of SAMCs and AAMSs on various levels and execution of tasks related to target search and tracking, target distribution and missile guidance within a single information field. Interaction between CPs of different brigades with the CPs of combined-arms formations of the corresponding levels, as well as joint interaction of air defence forces and facilities (interaction with air defence facilities of the Aerospace Forces and Naval Forces), is considered.

The principle of individual facilities' universalisation governing weapon-system creation allows the total cost required for this purpose to be reduced by distribution of development tasks related to various types of universal facilities among individual complex design and development works being carried out according to interrelated tactical and technical development tasks. A generalised list is shown in Fig. 4-3.

The process aimed at unification of the weapons' components is accompanied by unification of the technical support facilities (complex maintenance and repair – CM&R), including SAM delivery and loading, and by reduction of the number of spare-part sets being transported.

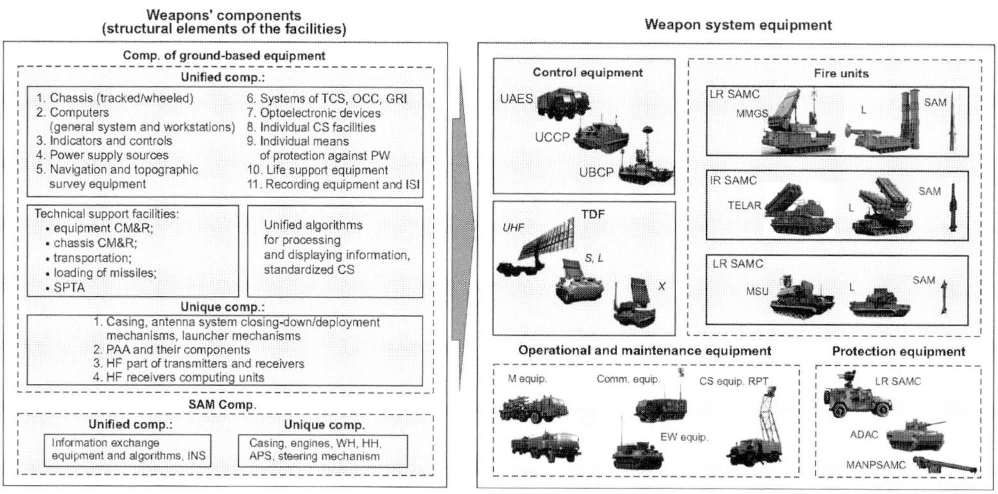

Design of a weapon system based on the principle of structural unification to the maximum possible extent (APS – (missile) airborne power source; Comp. – component, M – maintenance)

Figure 4-3: Generalised list of main components.

Based on the principle of maximum gain in weapon-system efficiency per unit of allocated funds, as well as considering the degree of readiness of available technologies, the weapons may be developed in accordance with the following order of precedence.

Battlefield Threat – Countering Drones

Russia has taken the recent developments in and combat results of drones and loitering munitions very seriously and has begun implementing countermeasures. Given the characteristics of medium-altitude long-endurance (MALE) UAVs and the tactics of their use, the fight against them will be the prerogative, first of all, of ground forces air defence systems. Considering the modern composition of equipment and air defence weapons, it is necessary to concentrate on the most effective facilities that are capable of effectively fighting hostile UAVs. Among them are TOR-M1/ M2 and Tor-2E, Buk-M2E and Buk-M3, Sosna, Morfey, Vityaz and Pantsir-S1.

The main problem that any air defence systems facing during an engagement with UAVs is their significantly smaller RCS due to:

- small overall dimensions,
- wide application of composite materials in the construction of UAVs,
- use of compact turboprop engines, and
- application of compact equipment and weapon loads – radar, optical devices, etc.

The Russian military is actively working to develop concepts, tactics, techniques and procedures against aerial drones. The Russian Ministry of Defence has invested heavily to defend its forces against the growing threat and proliferation of UAVs, large and small, from those manufactured by foreign states to those used by a growing number of non-state actors and terrorist organisations.

This investment comprises the development of technologies, incorporating the lessons learned from its own military and from other forces' combat experience, and continuing to refine its electronic warfare capabilities as a key element of counter-unmanned aerial system (c-UAS) tactics, techniques and procedures.

Concepts and Technology

In the Russian air defence forces, the ongoing efforts by non-state actors and terrorist organisations to improve their UAVs and their methods of use indicate that in the near future, the threats associated with the use of drones may increase not only in Syria but also in other countries.

Russia gained valuable experience in countering such drone attacks, and these skills and knowledge are now reflected in air defence combat manuals and are part of tactical, target selection and identification and reconnaissance training. In fact, the Russian Ministry of Defence notes that today all military districts across the country have units to counter enemy drones.

The Russian experience defending its Khmeimim base in Syria from UAV strikes has become the foundation of its military's c-UAS training programme. Starting in 2019, all major military exercises and drills include the defence against an adversary's massed drone attacks. The EW systems and technologies emerged as a key concept in this training. Across the Russian military services, in numerous drills, exercises and manoeuvres, EW training is regularly conducted against adversarial drones, and practically all c-UAS drills feature EW systems as a key element.

Such symbiotic pairing typically unfolds in drills where the 'adversary' forces use UAVs as key elements against Russian troops, vehicles and systems. Typically, the Russian military uses a combination of portable and wheeled EW systems. The Borisoglebsk and Zhitel systems are often tested in such drills; the EW specialists conduct electronic reconnaissance, then collect and analyse intelligence data, followed by conducting radio interference to 'drown' adversarial UAV control channels along with drones' communication channels with GPS navigation satellites.

In another typical c-UAS exercise that was conducted this year, the 'adversary' force used several UAVs to conduct reconnaissance and coordinate artillery strikes against Russian positions. The Southern Military District's mobile EW groups used an R-934BMV automated jamming station, the Silok-01 electronic warfare system and the Pole-21 advanced radio-suppression system to discover enemy UAVs in order to interfere with their communications and suppress their control channels, rendering them useless.

In Syria, the MoD confirms that a combination of hand-held and stationary systems are used to suppress and jam drones that continue to harass and attack Russian positions. These allow the Russian military to directly influence UAVs' control and navigation channel receivers. The EW troops intercept control channels, and the operator monitors the position of the UAV and proceeds to take control of it, giving it a command to land.

In Russia, military forces started using Stilet and Stupor portable c-UAS rifles, along with the newest Krasukha-C4 EW complex designed to identify adversarial strike aircraft and to suppress their communications and navigation. In a recent Black Sea drill, the EW detachments used the Krasukha system to target and disable multiple drones flying at low and medium altitudes.

Looking Ahead

Today, the Russian military is making c-UAS training mandatory across its services. In July 2018, the MoD announced that all ground forces, marines and airborne troops will have to learn how to shoot down drones with assault rifles, machine guns, sniper rifles and automatic weapons. This concept of c-UAS operations was developed taking into account Russian military experience in Syria. This experience and lessons learned are widely used to counter UAVs and loitering munitions in the 'special operation' in Ukraine.

There is also evidence that the Russian MoD is eager to expand its c-UAS training and field activity beyond countering small low-flying drones. In 2018, Russian EW systems jammed American drones operating in Syria, providing the MoD with valuable data and experience in countering more advanced adversarial UAVs.

The Russian military is also making sure its c-UAS systems and concept of operations involve the latest technologies, such as artificial intelligence, for the greatest advantage against the growing sophistication of the global drone force. New counter-drone radars and UAVs capable of targeting other drones are in development by Russian military-industrial enterprises.

As the UAV threat will persist, the efforts of the Russian MoD will be directed at the continuing refinement of its c-UAS practices, while seeking to introduce technology capable of offering protection against adversaries' drone developments.

Legacy Systems

The Air Defence Troops are an arm of the Russian ground forces, intended to protect troops and facilities air attack during combined-arms operations (combat actions), regroupings (marches) and being on site. They are assigned to fulfil the following main tasks:

- air defence combat duties,
- reconnaissance and surveillance,
- enemy forces engagement and destruction in flight, and
- ballistic and tactical missile defence in theatres of operations.

The Soviet experience in the Second World War (1941–5) confirmed that air defence had become one of principal components of combined-arms battle (deep-battle operations). As a result, on 16 August 1958, the Air Defence Troops were instituted as an integral part of the land forces. Later they formed the mainstay of army air defence of the Armed Forces of the Russian Federation.

As the land forces' air defence troops emerged as a new combat arm in 1958, immediately the need arose to develop highly mobile and effective SAM systems that would feature short deployment time (5–10 minutes) and operate either under the direction of some authority or autonomously. In the first case, they would be provided with their own all-around scanning target-acquisition radars in addition to target-tracking and missile-guidance radars. All elements of the SAM system (target-acquisition radar, guidance radar, and missile launchers with missiles) had to be mobile, so they were mounted primarily on tracked chassis. They had to be outfitted with navigation, survey and relative orientation equipment, coded radio communication equipment for tactical and technical information exchange, and autonomous power-supply units. Moreover, all the procedures involving their operational control, function test, setting up and closing down had to be automated to the maximum possible extent. For testing and repair of SAM systems in the field, highly mobile test and repair vehicles were required.

Equipped with new armament, the air defence system of the land forces looked like an assemblage of reconnaissance, command/control and firing assets operating in real-time. The methodology of rational air defence armament system substantiation was devised

for the air defence troops of the land forces by specialists of No. 3 Central Research Institute of the Defence Ministry of the Russian Federation. This methodology, plus the cost-effectiveness criterion, enabled the researchers to substantiate the most rational type of SAM and gun/missile systems blending organically into the structure of the land forces (front, army, division, regiment and battalion).

2K11 Krug (SA-4 Ganef)

2K12 Kub (SA-6 Gainful)

Figure 4-4: 2K11 Krug and 2K12 Kub.

9K31 Strela-1 (SA-9 Gaskin)

9K33 Osa (SA-8 Gecko)

Figure 4-5: 9K31 and 9K33.

ZSU 23/4 Shilka

9K32 Strela-2 (SA-7 grail)

Figure 4-6: Shilka and Strela-2.

P-15 (1RL13) 2D UHV radar (Flat Face) PRV-16 (Thin Skin) hight-finder radar

Figure 4-7: P-15 and PRV-16 radars.

Development of the first-generation armament systems of the air defence troops of the land forces was completed in the first half of the 1970s. It included: the Krug (Fig. 4-4), Kub (Fig. 4-4), Osa (Fig. 4-5), Strela-1 (Fig. 4-5), ZSU 23/4 Shilka, Strela-2 (Fig. 4-6) weapons systems; the P-15 (Fig. 4-7), P-18 (P-19), P-35 (Fig. 4-8) and P-40 (Fig. 4-9) target-acquisition radars; the PRV-16 height finder (Fig. 4-7); the K-1 control system; the Polyana-D1 automated battle-management system; and the PU-12 battle-management station.

This system was able to effectively counter the air attack weapons of the 1970s and early 1980s in all types of military operations and during troop movements. This was proved by military exercises and local wars and conflicts, where such weapons systems as Kub-Kvadrat, Strela-2, Shilka and Osa showed their worth. The Krug was the world's first highly mobile surface-to-air missile system, with all elements mounted on tracked chassis. The system's set-up/close-down time was only five minutes. It was the first SAM system in which the problem of compatibility of all electronic devices mounted on one tracked chassis was successfully resolved. This reduced the time necessary to prepare the system for operation and for engagement of low-flying targets. The Osa was the first system in which all functional elements such as radar and missiles were mounted on one self-propelled wheeled chassis. However, the first-generation armament system had some shortcomings, which were partly corrected in the process of modernisation. The most significant limitation of all these systems was their inability to defend troops against

Figure 4-8: P-35.

Figure 4-9: P-40. (Source: Vitaly Kuzmin)

Figure 4-10: S-300V4.

ballistic and cruise missiles. Consequently, a pressing need arose to take measures against ballistic and cruise missiles, AWACs and EW aircraft and so development of second-generation air defence armament systems began. Adopted for service in the 1970s and early 1980s, they included a range of weapon systems capable of engaging targets at different ranges and altitudes and operating on different frequency bands and physical principles, integrated into a single entity combatting the command/control, intelligence-gathering and electronic countermeasures subsystems. At that time, Soviet industry began producing the S-300V (Fig. 4-10, 4-11), Antey-2500, Buk, Buk-M1 (Fig. 4-13), Buk-M1-2 (Fig. 4-13), Tor, Tor-M1 (Fig. 4-14), Strela-10, Strela-10M and Strela-10M2(3) SAM systems; the Tunguska and Tunguska-M1 gun-missile systems; the Igla and Igla-1 man-portable SAM systems; the Obzor-3, Imbir, Nebo-SV and Kupol-M1 radars; and the Pori-P1 (Fig. 4-12), Pori-P2, Polyana-D4, Polyana-D4M, Polyana-D4M1, Ovod-M-SV, Sborka and Ranzhir automated battle-management systems.

The missions of the new armament system are:

- non-strategic ballistic missile defence (BMD) against theatre ballistic missiles (ThBMs), tactical ballistic missiles (TacBMs) and aeroballistic missiles (ABMs);
- defence against all types of aerodynamic targets, including strategic and tactical aircraft and cruise missiles. These missions are assigned to the S-300V, Antei-2500, Buk-M1 and Buk-M1-2 systems;
- defence against opto-electronically guided precision strike weapon carriers at ranges up to 12km (Tor and TorM1 SAM systems);

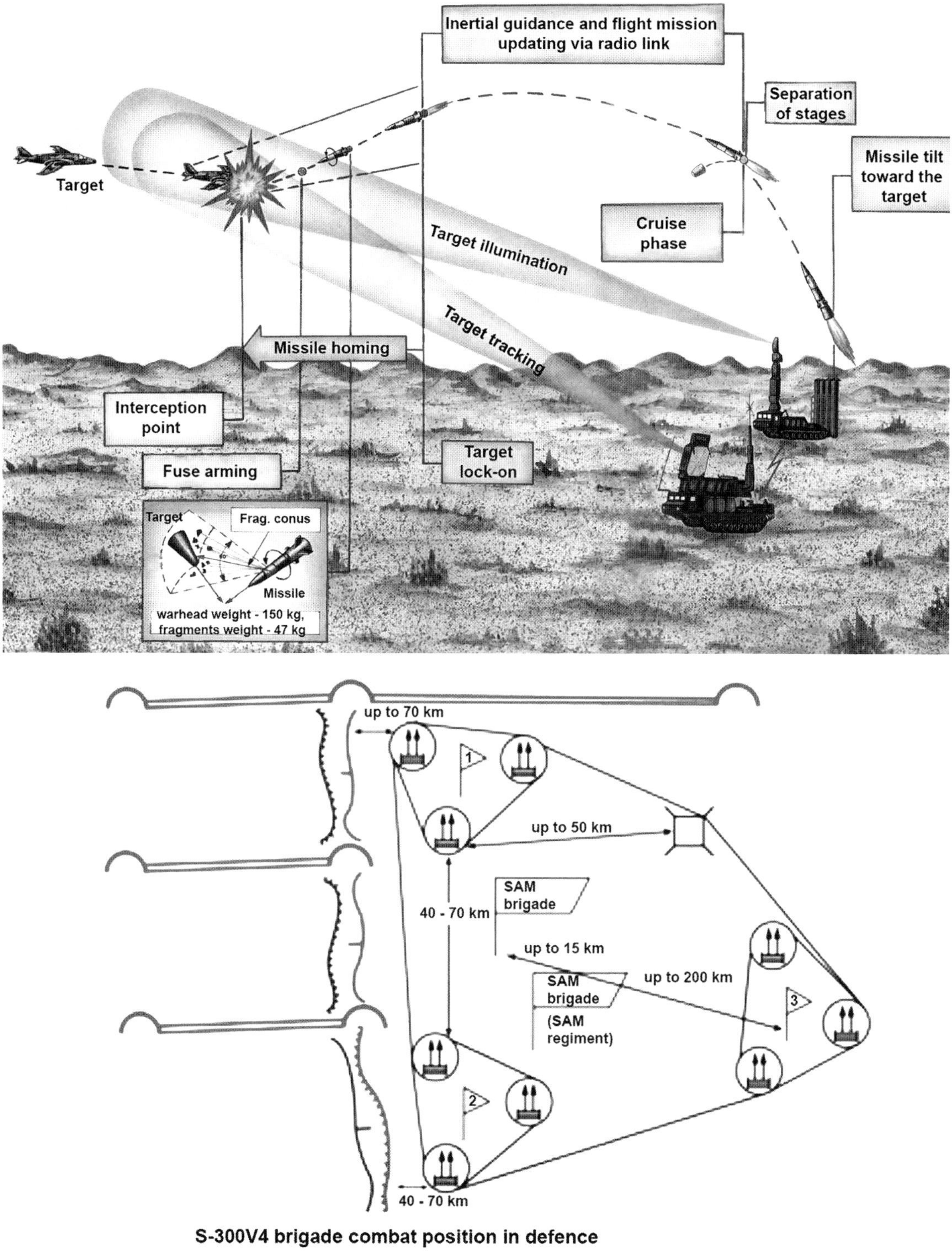

Figure 4-11: S-300V engagement.

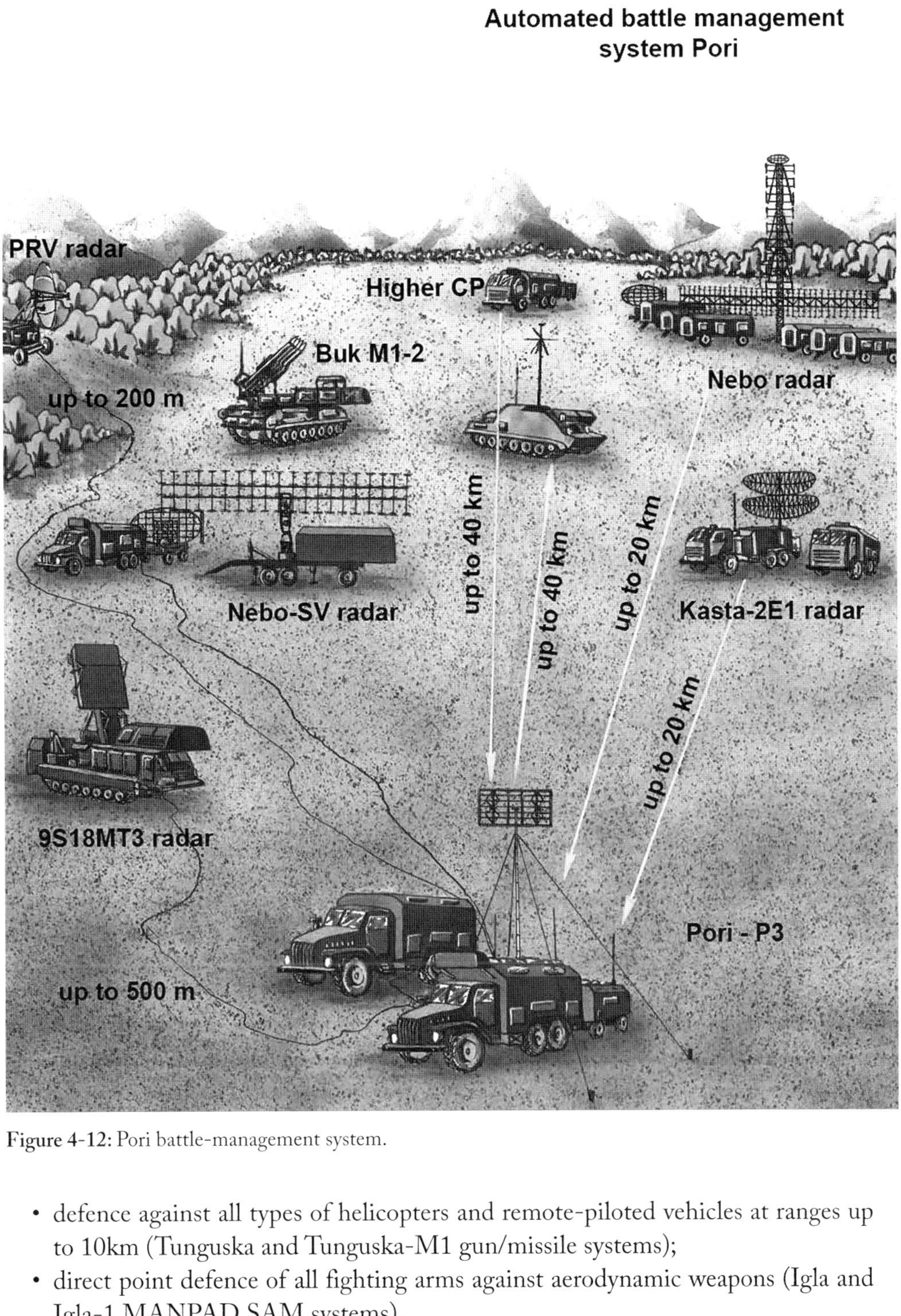

Figure 4-12: Pori battle-management system.

- defence against all types of helicopters and remote-piloted vehicles at ranges up to 10km (Tunguska and Tunguska-M1 gun/missile systems);
- direct point defence of all fighting arms against aerodynamic weapons (Igla and Igla-1 MANPAD SAM systems).

Figure 4-13: Buk-M1.

Figure 4-14: Tor-M1.

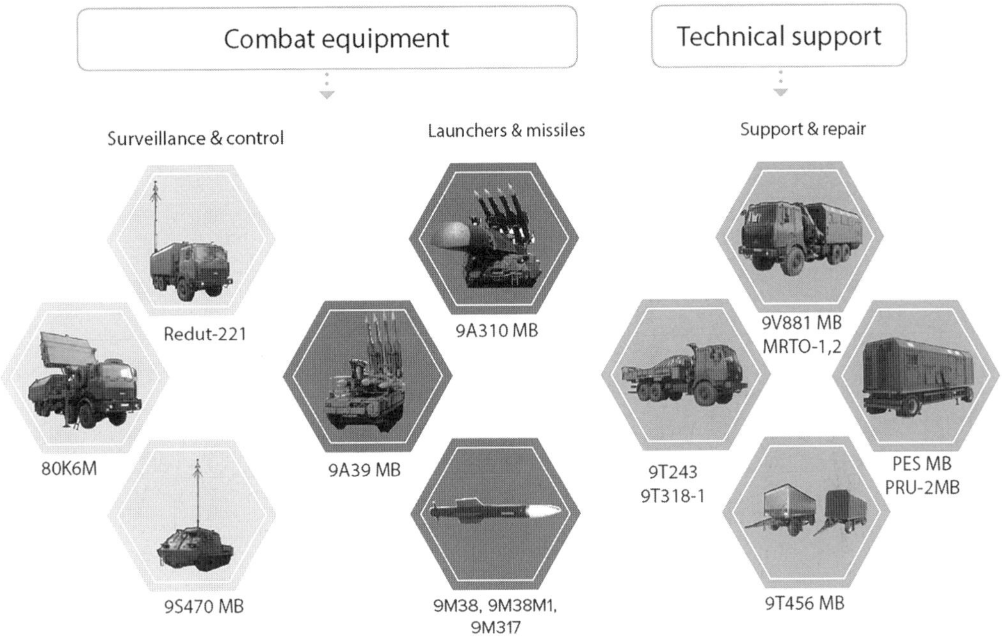

Figure 4-15: Typical Buk-M1 battery organisation.

The results of various military exercises have confirmed the correctness of the technical policy pursued in developing the second-generation air defence armament system for the land forces.

The S-300V was the world's first SAM system capable of defeating aerodynamic targets, as well as theatre, tactical and aeroballistic missiles. The Buk-M1 was the first mobile SAM system capable of defeating targets independently at a range of up to 35km. It is equipped with a self-propelled firing unit capable of detecting air targets and guide the missiles carried by it onto these targets autonomously (Fig. 4-13, 4-15). The Tor was the first SAM system, whose missiles were launched vertically from inside the self-propelled tracked chassis, which mounts all of the combat elements (Fig. 4-14). The Tunguska was the world's first air defence system combining gun and missile weapons on one platform to provide close/point defence.

Integration of air defence weapons of the land forces with electronic countermeasures assets enhances the operational effectiveness of such formations owing to:

- negation of the adversary's abilities to fly at extremely low altitudes (ELA) by jamming his airborne multi-functional radars (MFR) operating in low-altitude flight mode (LAFM);
- suppression of the adversary's multi-functional airborne radars operating in the air-surface mode to deny him the freedom to conduct aerial reconnaissance of military installations, including SAM system radars; and
- masking of SAM system radar emissions for protection against anti-radar missiles (ARM).

In the mid-1990s, modernisation programmes started to enhance the operational capabilities of existing air defence weapons and electronic countermeasures assets. Later in the decade, upgraded equipment was fielded. The high efficiency of the upgrades made to the weapons systems was proved during numerous field exercises and tests at firing ranges (Fig. 4-16, 4-17).

Today, the armament system of the air defence troops of the land forces includes weapons capable of defeating any type of threat and meets the requirements of the cost-

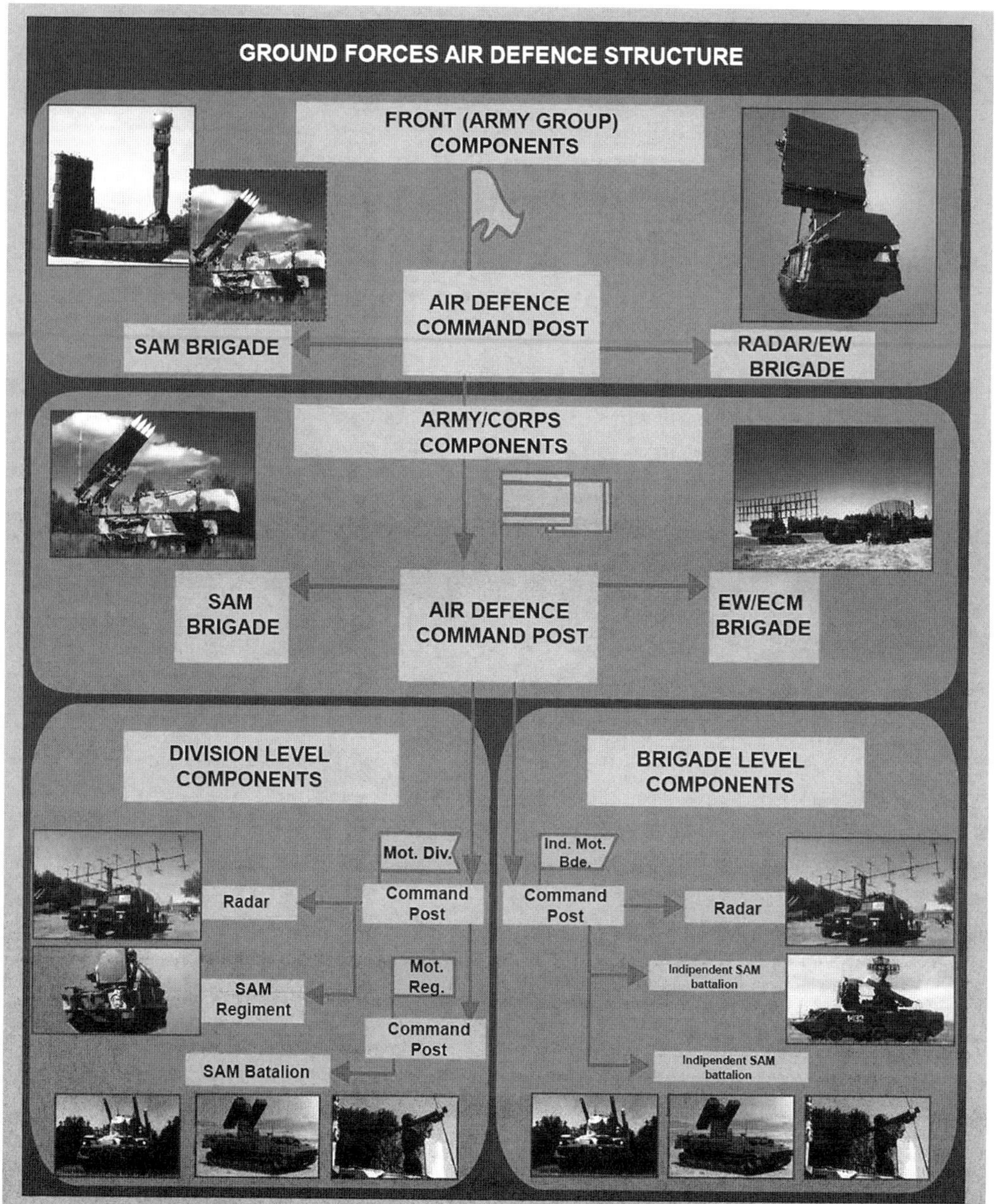

Figure 4-16: Ground forces air defence structure.

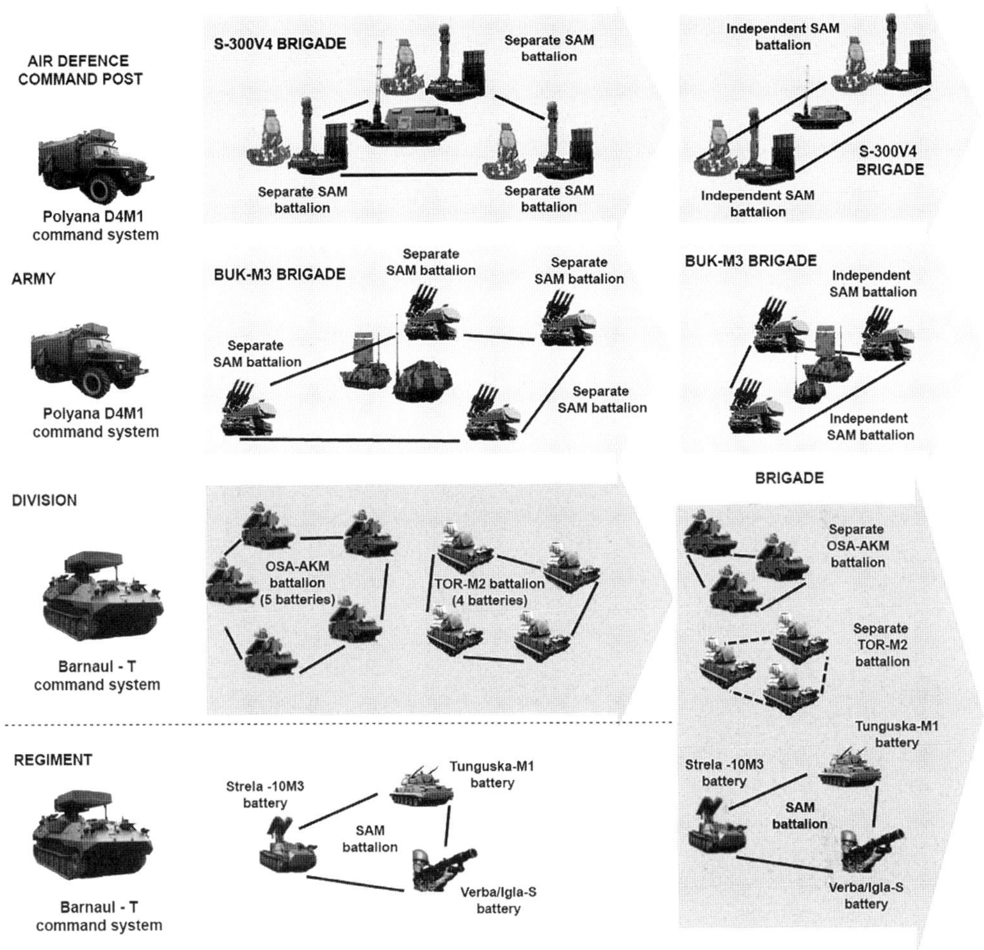

Figure 4-17: Ground forces air defence command and control levels.

effectiveness criterion. Some of the much-improved systems include S-300V4, Buk-M2, Buk-M3, Tor-M2 and Strela-10M3, and MANPADS such as Igla-1S and Verba. New automated battle-management and reconnaissance subsystems have been introduced. Generally, the new armament system is capable of defending troops and military installations in mobile forms of combat. If the reconnaissance assets, automated battle-management assets, weapons systems and electronic countermeasures assets are brought together, highly-effective mobile strike/reconnaissance formations can be organised within the structure of the land forces to counter aerodynamic threats, as well as theatre, tactical and aeroballistics missiles and PGMs.

To co-operate with the continually growing capabilities of air attack weapons, it is necessary to develop an advanced inter-service multi-functional air defence armament system built from separate modules and using the armament of different services.

Organisationally the ground forces air defence troops consist of army group components such as front, army or corps, AD command posts, missile brigades, regiments and

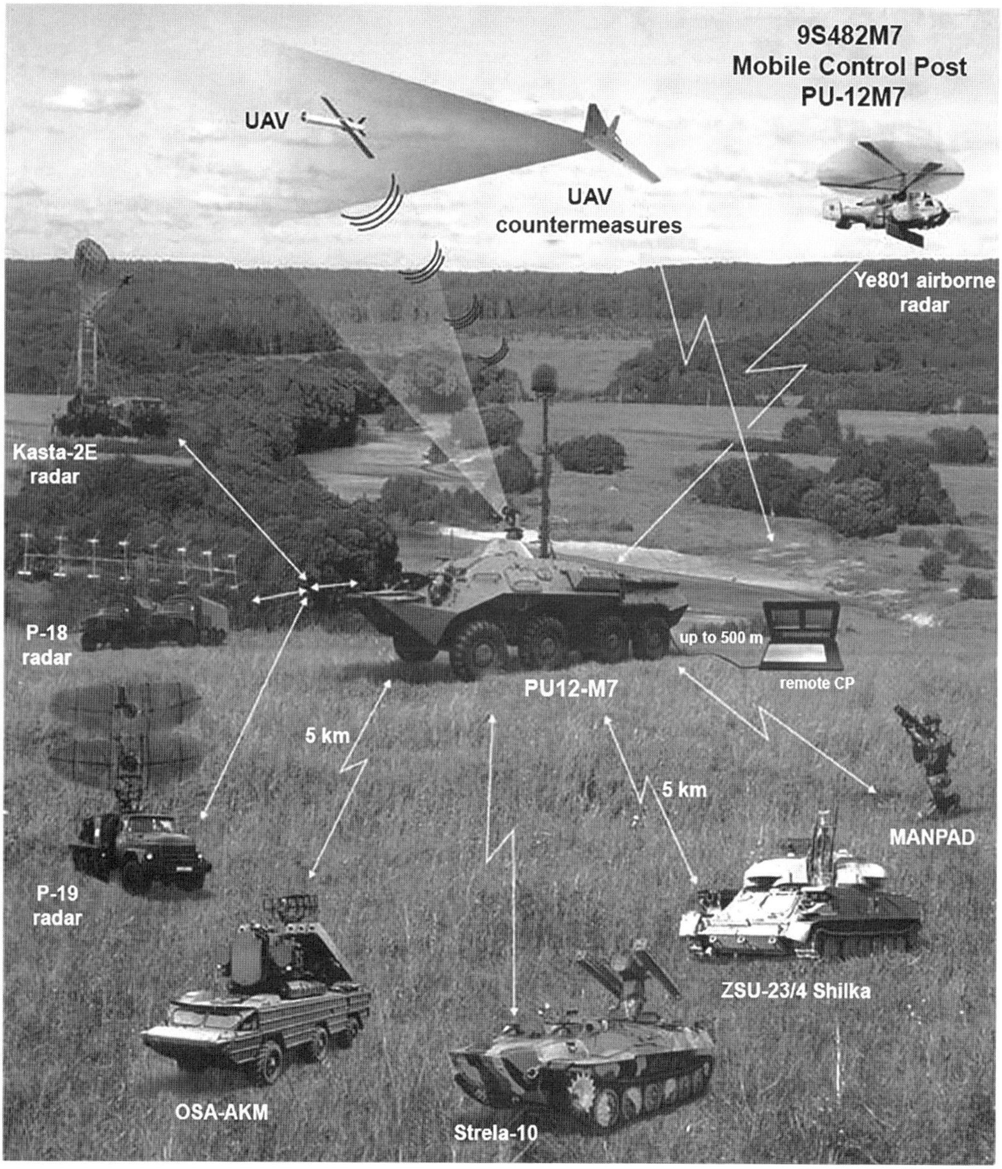

Figure 4-18: The 9S482M7 command post allows informational and technical interaction with a high-level command post and radio-location data sources, as well as controlling through automated control assets the following AD missile and short-range artillery systems: Tor-M1(M2E), Osa-AK (AKM), Strela-10M2 (10M3), Tunguska-M1 and their modifications, Shilka (modernised) and Igla MANPADS.

battalions, radar and electronic warfare formations, support units and subdivisions. They are capable of destroying enemy means of air attack throughout the range of altitudes (extremely low – up to 200m; low – from 200m to 1,000m; average – from 1,000m to 4,000m; high – from 4,000m to 12,000m, and in the stratosphere – more than 12,000m) and flight speeds (Fig. 4-16, 4-17).

Air defence formations, military units and subdivisions are equipped with anti-aircraft missiles, anti-aircraft artillery, anti-aircraft gun-and-missile systems and portable anti-

aircraft missile systems differing in range and altitude, guidance channel-ability and means of missile guidance. Depending on the range of destruction of aerial targets, they are divided into the systems of point or near range – up to 10km; short range – up to 30km; medium range – up to 100km; and long range – more than 100km.

Further development is carried out by improving mobility, survivability, covertness of operation, automation's degree, fire efficiency, expanding the parameters of the affected area, reducing the response time and the mass-dimensional characteristics of the guided missile (gun and missile) systems.

The use of UCAV and loitering munitions in recent wars puts additional pressure on point defence where the long and medium-range systems may be exposed to low RCS threats, emphasising the importance of short-range and point defence. The Russian military therefore developed a centralised command and control system for short-range and point defence (Fig. 4-18).

Chapter 5

S-300V (9K81) Long-Range Missile System

As previously mentioned, the S-300 family is made up of long-range air defence systems which share a very similar designation but are conceptually different because they are intended for two different military branches: Army or Ground Forces Air Defence and the Air Defence Branch of the Aerospace Forces.

Development of the S-300V air defence missile system, which was to supersede the 2K11 Krug, was begun by a Central Committee of the Communist Party and USSR Council of Ministers' Resolution of 27 May 1969. The S-300V system received NATO codenames SA-12A 'Gladiator' (with 9M83 'Type II' missiles) and SA-12B 'Giant' (with 9M82 'Type I' missiles).

The S-300V SAM system shares its earliest conceptual origins with the Almaz S-300P family, but the two product lines diverged dramatically very early in their development. As a result, they share the same technology base but are essentially unique designs, optimised respectively for the needs of the prime customers, the Army Air Defence (PVO-SV).

While both branches shared some static and semi-mobile radar systems, during the early 1960s the Army Air Defence deployed its unique inventory of fully-mobile SAM systems, reflecting its role of providing air defence cover for highly mobile Soviet tank and motorised infantry divisions. By the end of the 1960s, Army Air Defence had deployed a three-tier system: the 2K11 Krug (SA-4 'Ganef') system providing long-range area defence (medium by current standards); the quite effective 2K12 Kub/Kvadrat (SA-6 'Gainful') system providing medium-range area defence (these systems included cumbersome ramjet-powered command link-guided missiles); and short-range protection that included the 9K33 Osa/Romb (SA-8 'Gecko'), 9K31 Strela 1 (SA-9 'Gaskin'), and the ubiquitous ZSU-23/4 Shilka self-propelled anti-aircraft gun (SPAAG) providing low-altitude point defence.

The 'Antey' enterprise, under the leadership of general designer V.P. Efremov, was appointed as the new system's prime developer. It was also responsible for the command post, missile guidance station and programme scan radar. Viktor Epifanov was appointed chief designer. The development of both types of missiles was assigned to the OKB Novator Design Bureau led by L.V. Lyulev. Efremov and his team were a logical choice for the new project because they had previously created the 2K11 Krug mobile air defence system.

Conceptually, the S-300V, also named 'Antey-300V', is designed as a multi-channel mobile all-weather anti-aircraft missile system. It has to be equipped with two types of missiles. Following the requirements, this system was to be a battlefield air defence

weapon and engage ground- and air-launched ballistic missiles, cruise missiles, strategic and tactical aircraft, EW/ECM aircraft and attack helicopters, under conditions of their large-scale use, in a complex air and ECM environment, when the protected troops conduct mobile operations.

The main technical requirements in the creation of the system were determined by the tasks of missile defence, which in particular determined the use of the original missile guidance system. The missiles used by the complex are designed taking into consideration inertial guidance with mid-trajectory radio correction and semi-active homing in the final section of the trajectory. The use of missiles with a high-precision inertial control and radio correction system made it possible to use a radar seeker to intercept targets with an effective RCS scattering surface of $0.02m^2$ and more (Fig. 5-1).

Development of the S-300V was carried out in two stages. In the first the system was developed to counter aerodynamic targets, cruise and tactical ballistic missiles. A prototype system developed at this stage was tested from 1980 to 1981 and was adopted in 1983 under the designation S-300V1 (Fig. 5-2).

In the second stage, the system was modified to intercept ballistic missiles like the Pershing-1, aeroballistic missiles and ECM aircraft. Integrated tests of the system in the full configuration were conducted from 1985 to 1986. Then, in 1988, it entered service in full configuration (Fig. 5-3).

The S-300V system (designated 9K81 by GRAU) was officially adopted by the Soviet Ground Forces (Voiska) in 1984. The main components of the system include:

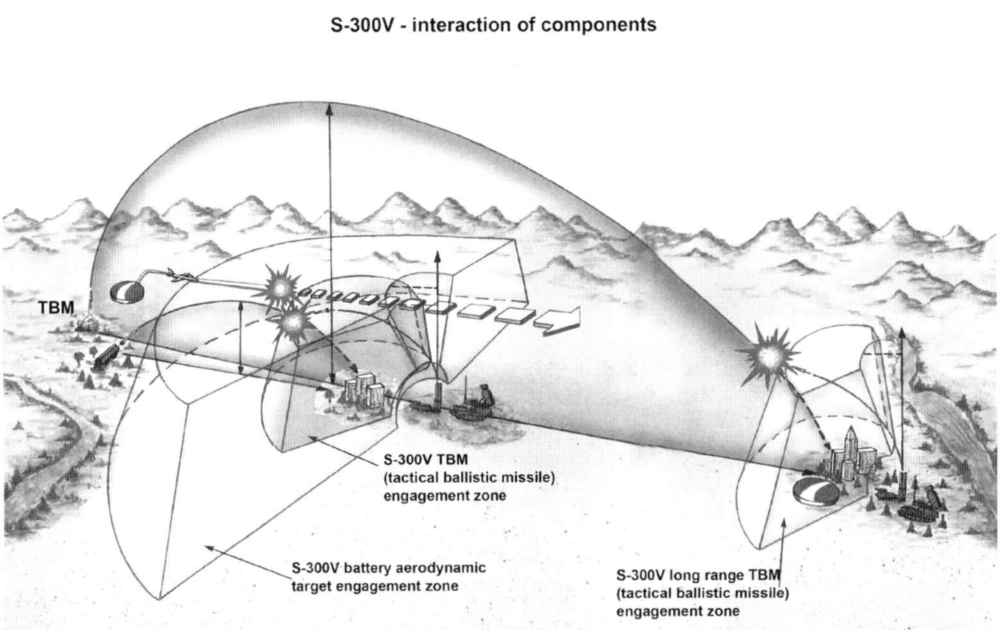

Figure 5-1: Interaction of S-300V components.

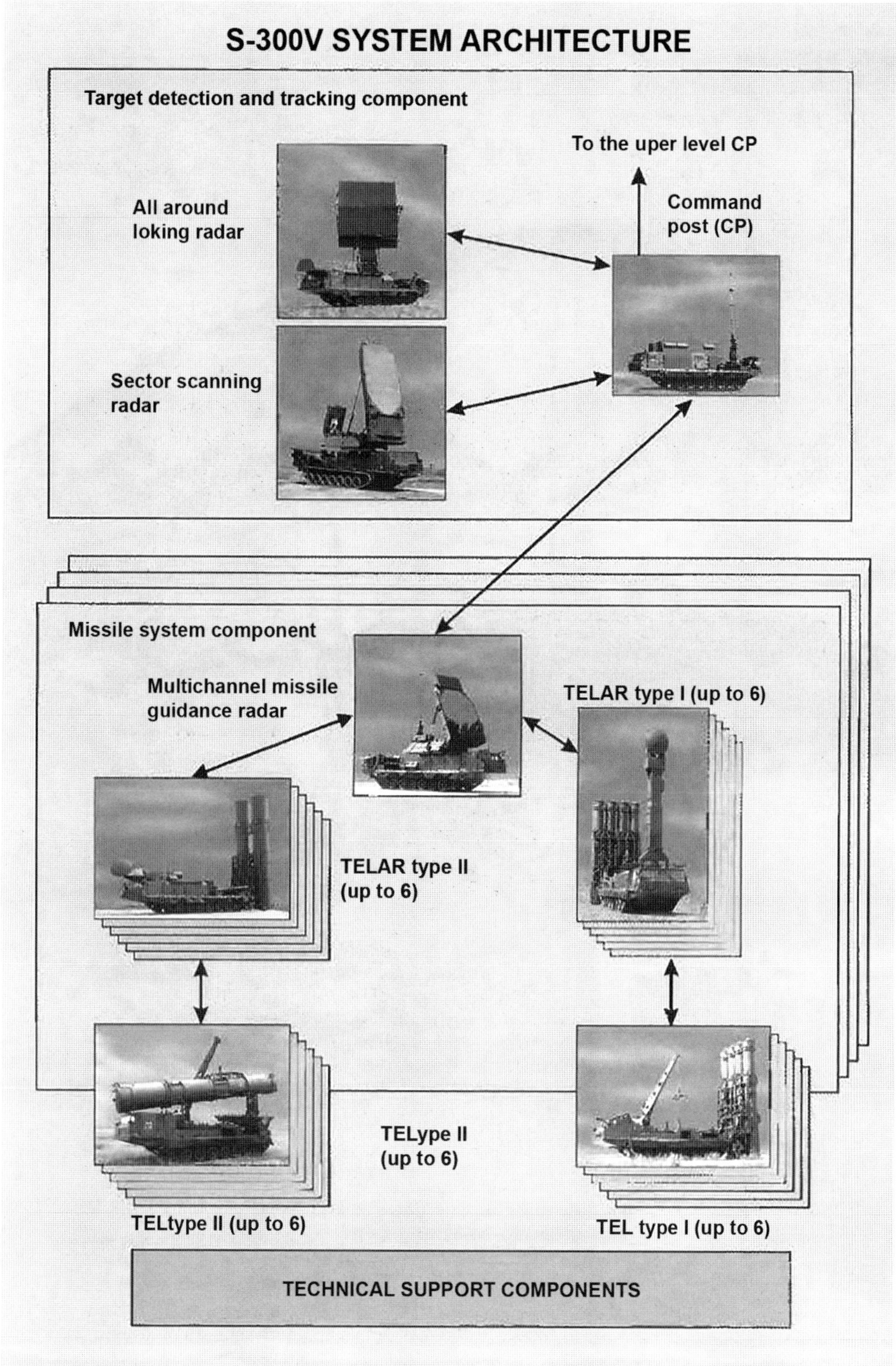

Figure 5-2: S-300V system architecture.

- 9S457-1 command post (Fig. 5-4),
- 9S15MT circular-scan radar (Fig. 5-6),
- 9S19M2 sector-view radar (Fig. 5-5), and
- four launcher batteries.

Figure 5-3: Two types of launchers and missile-guidance radar.

Figure 5-4: 9S457 battery command post.

Figure 5-5: 9S19M circular-scan 3D radar.

Each battery consists of the following systems:

- a 9S32-1 missile-guidance station (located within a radius of up to 10km from the system command post) (Fig. 5-8, 5-9),
- up to six 9A82 and 9A83-1 launchers (TELAR),
- up to six 9A84 and 9A85 (TEL) transporter-reloaders.

The full quantity of available 9M82 and 9M83 missiles per regiment, located on the launchers and loaders, can be from 96 to 192, depending on the configuration of the batteries combining launchers and missiles of various types.

The system was created specifically for operations in areas of intensive tactical aviation activity, which, along with the major task of providing constant all-round defence in the event of calculated combat losses of part of the equipment, required the use of an expanded outfit of radar equipment for surveillance, tracking and guidance.

The unique properties of the system make it possible for one launcher to protect an area of 500m^2 from a simultaneous strike by four Lance-type tactical ballistic missiles; an area

Figure 5-6: 9S15 circular-scan radar.

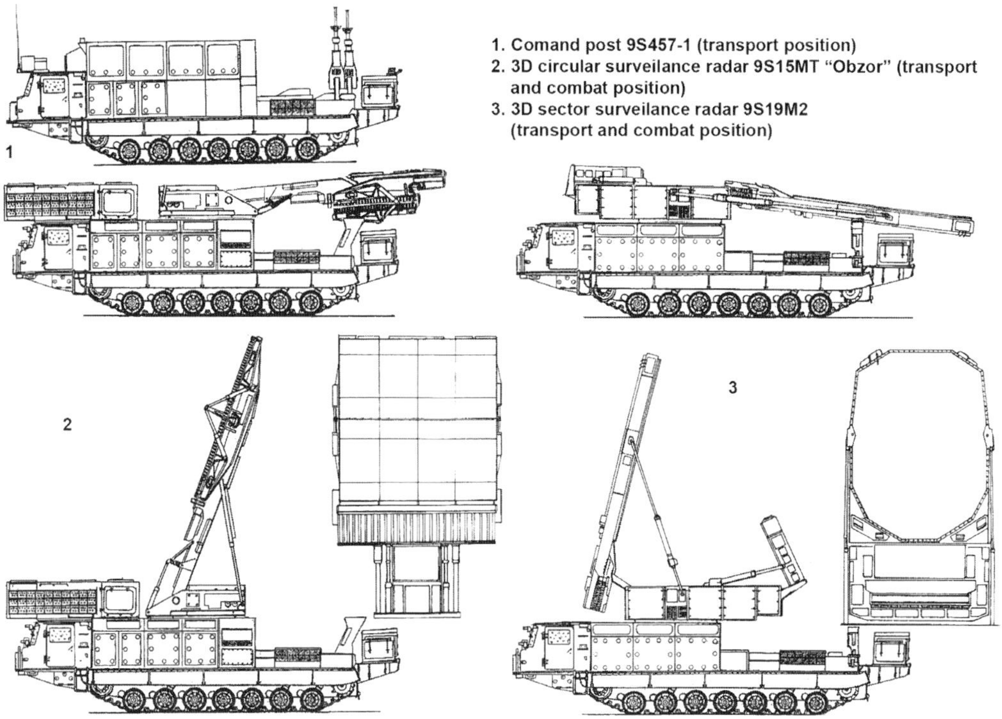

Figure 5-7: S-300V CP and surveillance radar.

Figure 5-8: 9S32-1 missile-guidance radar, 9A82 and 9A83 TELARs and 9A82 TEL.

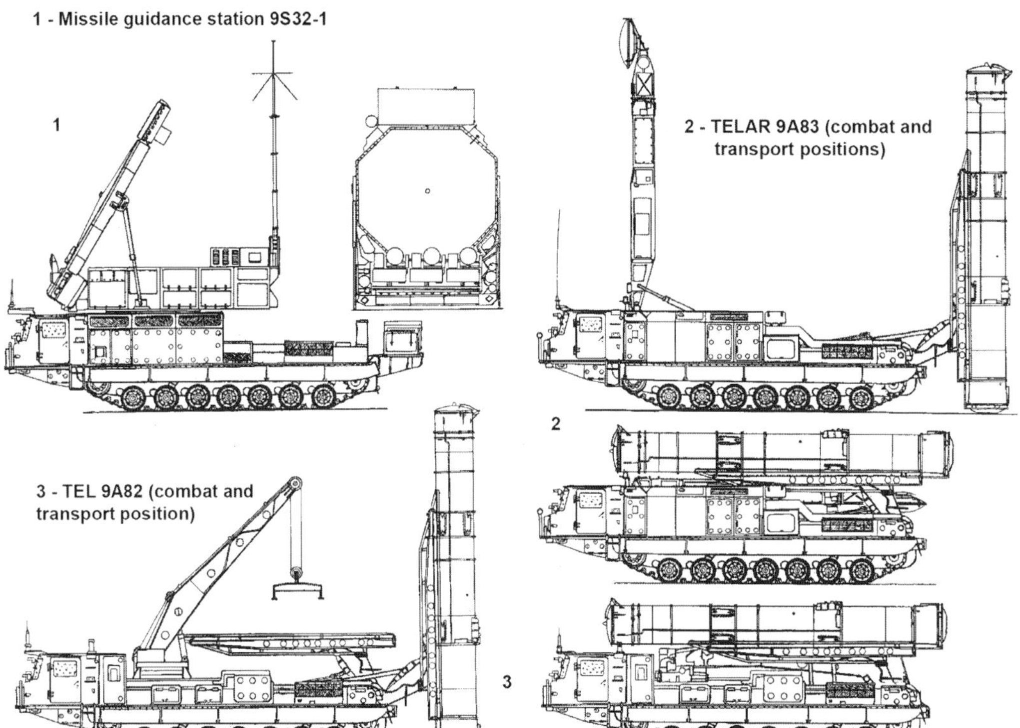

Figure 5-9: 9S32 missile-guidance radar.

up to 240km^2 from two Pershing 1 missiles; an area of up to 310km^2 from one Pershing 2 missile; or an area of up to 1,400km^2 from one 'Scud' type missile. All calculations were made taking into consideration the type of the ballistic missile warhead, and aircraft with an effective scattering surface of more than 0.02m^2.

The system is designed to be highly mobile, meaning that all combat equipment is optimised for off-road and rough-terrain movement. It was decided that all equipment would be mounted on the unified GM-830 tracked chassis (models 830 and model 835). This offered high manoeuvrability and cross-country capability, with autonomous power supply and radio communications. The S-300V system comprises no less than eight unique vehicles, the 9S457 mobile command post, the 9S15 ('Bill Board') acquisition radar, the 9S19 ('High Screen') anti-ballistic missile early-warning radar, the 9S32 ('Grill Pan') engagement radar, the 9A82 and 9A83 TELARs, and the 9A84 and 9A85 TEL/transloader vehicles.

The tracked chassis was designed by KB-3 (Design Bureau No. 3) of the Leningrad Kirov Plant (now SPETSMASH Joint Stock Company) under the leadership of chief designer N.S. Popov. The basis for the chassis was the well-developed self-propelled artillery chassis, which used the components and assemblies of the T-72 and T-80 tank chassis and V-46 or V-84 multi-fuel diesel engines. The engine and transmission compartment was moved to the rear of the vehicle. The dimensions of each of the means in marching configuration do not exceed 12.25m x 3.38m x 3.27m which is well within the sizes of the Russian roads and transportation means such as trailers, railways platforms and transport aircraft.

The system is designed to have the minimum reaction time between target detection and launching of the missile (Fig. 5-17).

The 9S457-1 mobile command post provides the battlefield control of the combat assets; performs analysis of the air situation, target distribution, and target designation to launchers (up to four in the system), as well as provides information in complex electronic warfare and intensive enemy jamming, and analyses the combat readiness and capability of combat vehicles. The centre of the search sector and its parameters are set relative to the position of the command post. It can track up to seventy targets and automatically distributes up to twenty-four of them to four missile-guidance stations.

The three-dimensional circular scan 9S15MT Obzor ('Bill Board') radar station (Fig. 5-6, 5-7), mounted on the model 832 tracked chassis, makes a regular scan of the space (at a rate of 5–10 revolutions per minute), detects up to 200 targets and transmits information about them to the system command post. The radar, manned by four operators, detects targets at ranges of 10–250km at a target elevation from 0–55°. It provides a tracking link, target trajectory and target identification. A phased wave-slit array antenna is used; mechanical scanning by azimuth and electronic scanning by elevation. The radar was developed at NIIIP. Currently, modernised 9S15MV3 and 9S15MT3 radars are being produced.

The 9S19M2 ('High Screen') three-dimensional sector surveillance anti-ballistic missile early-warning radar is designed primarily to search for enemy ballistic missiles in a designed sector of airspace. When viewing the space in the sector (+/-30⁰ in azimuth from a given direction, up to 75⁰ [80⁰] in elevation, detection range from 20km to 175km), targets are detected and their coordinates are determined with an accuracy of 200–300m in range and an angular error of 15'. The 9S19M2 radar makes a regular scan of the airspace, detects all air targets in the scanned sector, ties up to sixteen trajectories at ballistic targets, and transmits all information about the air situation to the system's CP. The combat crew of the station is four operators.

It is possible for radar stations to search for targets all-round and sectoral, reviewed by external instruction from the system CP and higher-level CPs.

The 9S32-1 ('Grill Pan') three-coordinate multi-channel missile-guidance station surveys the space in a 0°–42⁰ sector (perpendicular to the antenna plane). Rotating the antenna post provides the area scan by the azimuth in a 340⁰ sector. The guidance station of the 9S32-1 missiles measures the coordinates of the selected target, controls the operation of up to six launchers, and transmits to them all necessary information for launching and guiding missiles. It also automatically scans lower altitudes in which low-flying targets may appear. The antenna used is a phased array with electronic beam scanning. The combat crew of the station is six operators. When working in conditions of active interference by the enemy, the 'coordinate support' mode is used: the range to the target is determined using the detection radar (9S15 and 9S19), while the angular coordinates of the target are determined by the guidance radar of the 9S32-1.

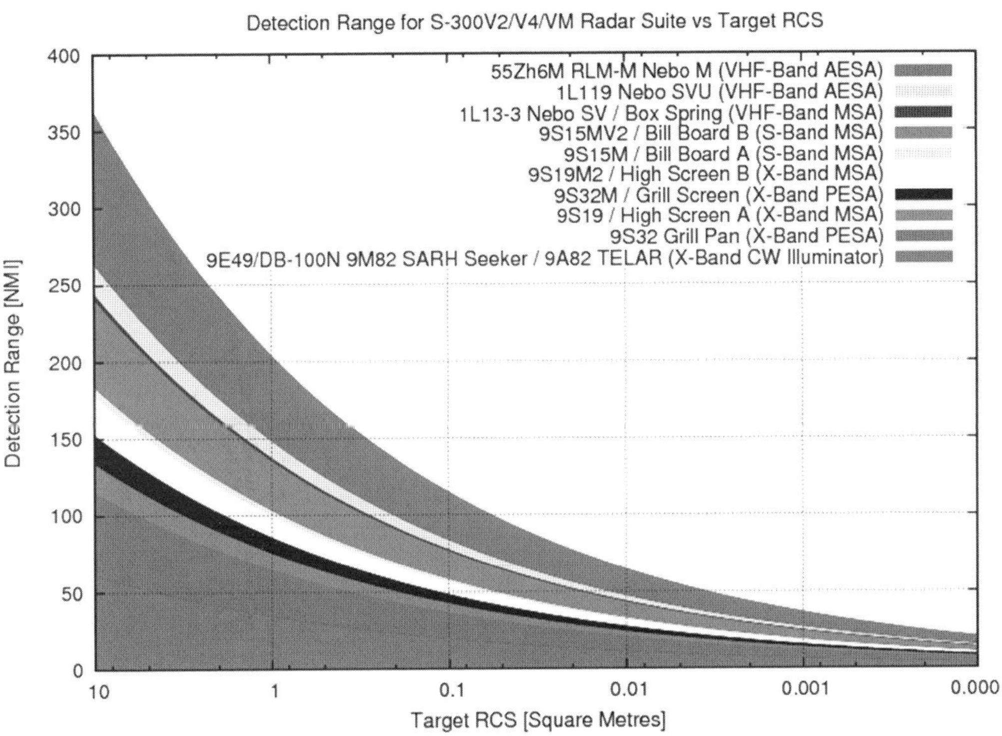

Figure 5-10: Target detection range vs target RCS for S-300V radars.

Like the 9S19, the 9S32 is a high power-aperture, coherent, X-band phased array but specialised for missile guidance, producing a main lobe of around 1° in width. The TWT-based transmitter is rated at 150 kW peak and 10–13 kW average power, with receiver sensitivity cited at 10–17 Watts. Cited detection ranges are about 148km for fighter-sized targets, 74km for SRAM class missiles, and up to 148km for larger IRBMs. The radar uses monopulse angle-tracking techniques, frequency hopping in all modes to provide high jam resistance, and chirped waveforms to provide a high compression ratio. Three auxiliary receiver channels are used for cancelling sidelobe jamming (Fig. 5-10).

Two basic operating modes are used. In the first, the 9S32 is controlled by the 9S457 command post and acquires targets within a narrow 5° x 6° field of view, alternately it can autonomously search and acquire targets within a 60° field. A telescoping mast datalink antenna is mounted aft of the array.

The paired acquisition radars are each optimised for their specific roles, with a limited overlap in capabilities, as the 9S15 has some ABM early-warning capability, and the 9S19 can acquire and track airborne targets. The 9S32 is more narrowly optimised as an engagement radar for missile guidance.

The 9S15 radar (Fig. 5-6, 5-7) has an interesting arrangement for stowing the array for transport. The top of the radar array first folds forward on the hinge at its centre to halve the height of the unit. The IFF array folds upwards across the lower front of this unit. The entire structure is then folded forward to a 45° angle from the vertical. At this point, the array unit rotates 90° in its aperture plane, reducing its width to match the vehicle width, and the structure continues to fold onto the roof of the vehicle. In this way, the erected array width can be twice the vehicle width, and the unfolded height can be somewhat greater than the array width. The entire process takes one minute and is carried out by hydraulic pistons with pushbutton control.[1]

The business end of this system against both operational-tactical ballistic missiles and aircraft is two types of missiles: 9M82 and 9M83, designed by the Novator SMKB (Yekaterinburg). The 9A82 TELAR carries two 9M82 long-range SAM/ABMs, and the 9A83 TELARs carry four 9M83 SAM/ABMs. Each TELAR is equipped with a steerable high-gain antenna used to transmit midcourse guidance commands to the missiles and provide continuous wave illumination of the target for the missiles' semi-active radar seekers during the terminal guidance phase – one source cites 10–12 kW of CW power rating.

The TELARs are controlled by the 9S32 radar using either cables or a bidirectional radio datalink, permitting the TELARs to return status information to the guidance radar. The 9A82 TELAR is optimised for engaging targets at higher altitudes and can slew its antenna through 180° in azimuth and 110° in elevation, while the 9A83 TELAR has an elevating and telescoping mast providing antenna coverage of the full upper hemisphere – this arrangement is intended to extend the engagement footprint against low-altitude targets (Fig. 5-11).

The TELARs are supplemented by the 9A84 and 9A85 TEL/transloaders, essentially dumb launchers which can be used only with guidance/illumination from a nearby

Figure 5-11: 9A83 (left) and 9A82 (right) TELARs.

TELAR and are equipped with hydraulic loading cranes instead of antenna booms (Fig. 5-12).

The 9M82 missile (or 'Type I') (Fig. 5-13 and 5-14) and 9M83 missile ('Type II') (Fig. 5-14, 5-15 and 5-16) are two-stage solid-fuel vertical-launch missiles, designed according to the 'bearing cone' aerodynamic scheme. The conical aerodynamic design and general configuration of both S-300V missiles are modelled on the earlier US Martin Marietta Sprint ABM which was similar in size to the 9M83 but had performance closer to the 9M82. Both Soviet missiles, intended to kill both aerial and ballistic targets, outrange the more specialised Sprint ABM. The missiles are largely common in design, the principal distinctions being different first-stage boosters, different control surface arrangements, and numerous detail differences. The missile is almost identical. The missiles are placed in reusable transport and launch containers 9Ya238 (9M82) and 9Ya240 (9M83) with lids opening before the launch.

At launch, the missile is ejected out of the container by the pressure of the combustion products of the gas generator and the aerodynamic control surfaces are then deployed. Pulsed motors provide a preliminary inclination of the rocket towards the launcher to prevent the shield covering the nozzle part of the launch stage from hitting and the gas jet of the launching rocket playing directly on the launcher structure. During the

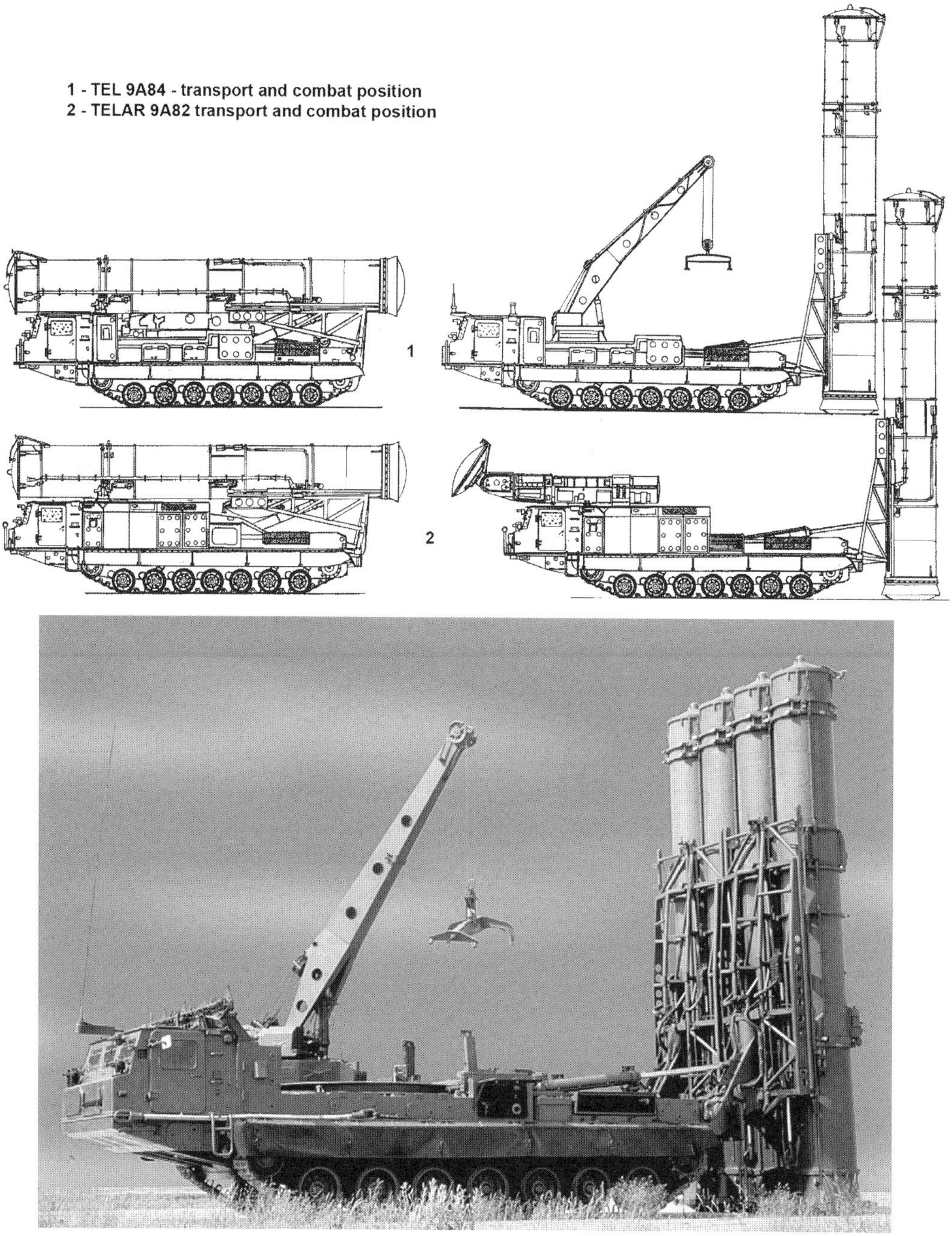

Figure 5-12: 9A84 TEL (top and bottom) and 9A82 TELAR (middle).

launch stage the thrust vector control system (four adjustable gas-bypass nozzles are located at the nozzle cut of the launch motor) ensures the guidance of the missile to the calculated meeting point with the target. After separating the main stage, in the event of a significant deviation of the missile from the planned interception point when firing at a manoeuvring target, the current coordinates of the target are transmitted to the missile

Figure 5-13: 9M82.

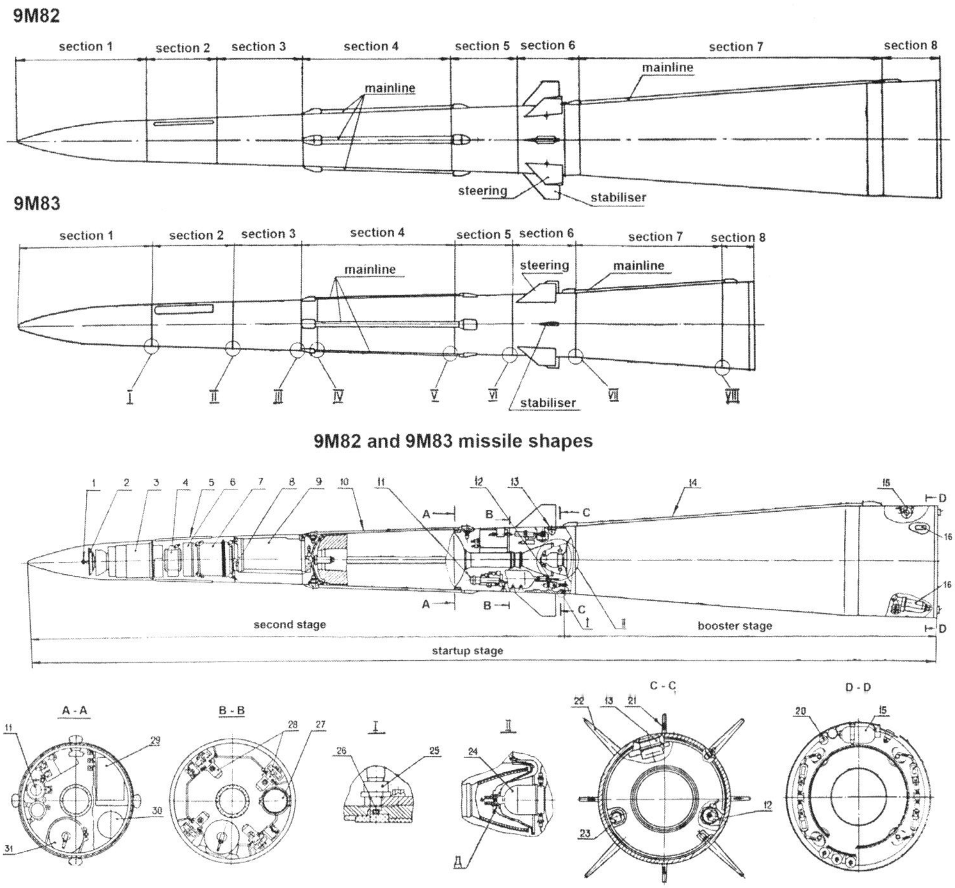

9M82 missile cutaway. 1 - proximity fuse antenna; 2 - seeker antenna; 3 - DB-100N seeker; 4 - proximity fuse RF module; 5 - proximity fuse antenna; 6 - computer; 7 - inertial guidance and navigation unit; 8 - safety device; 9 - warhead; 10 - cable duct; 11 - gas turbine module; 12 - connector; 13 - connector; 14 - cable duct; 15 - hydraulic power system; 16 - switch; 17 - gas generator; 18 - declination thruster; 19 - control actuator; 20 - compensator; 21 - stabiliser; 22 - aerodynamic control surface; 23 - selector switch; 24 - stage separation mechansim; 25 - electrical initiator; 26 - explosive charge; 27 - kill vehicle gas generator; 28 - control surface actuators; 29 - limit parameters block; 30 - hydraulic power unit; 31 - junction box

Figure 5-14: 9M82 and 9M83 plan and 9M82 cutaway.

9M82 launch tube & transport container

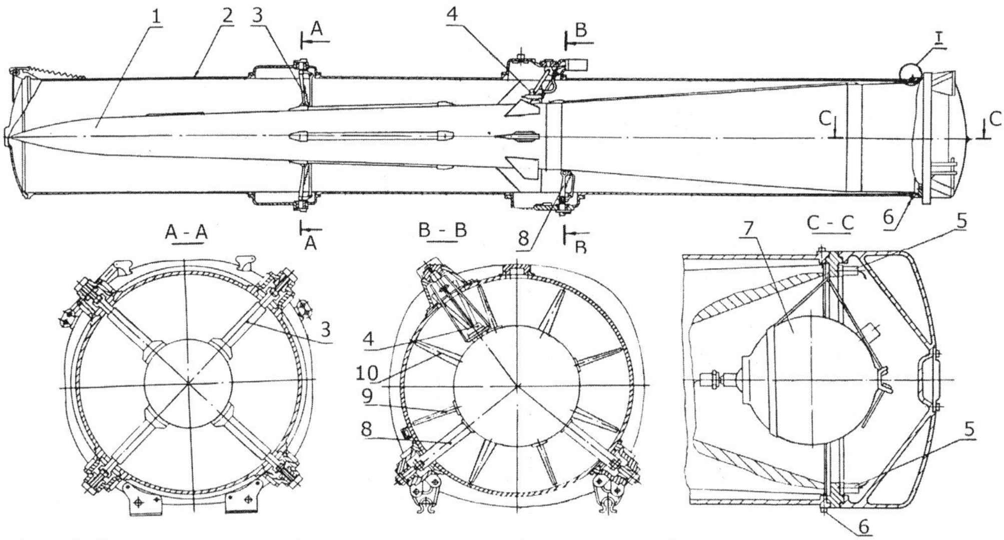

1 - missile; 2 - transport & launch container; 3 - front support (brace); 4 - connector; 5 - lock; 6 - stopper; 7 - gas generator; 8 - middle support (brace); 9 - stabilizer; 10 - aerodynamic surfaces (rudders/fins).

The spherical container (7) in the base of the launch tube is the high pressure gas generator pressure vessel for the cold launch system. The forward and centre missile fuselage is held in position in the tube by supporting braces (8)

9M83 launch tube & transport container

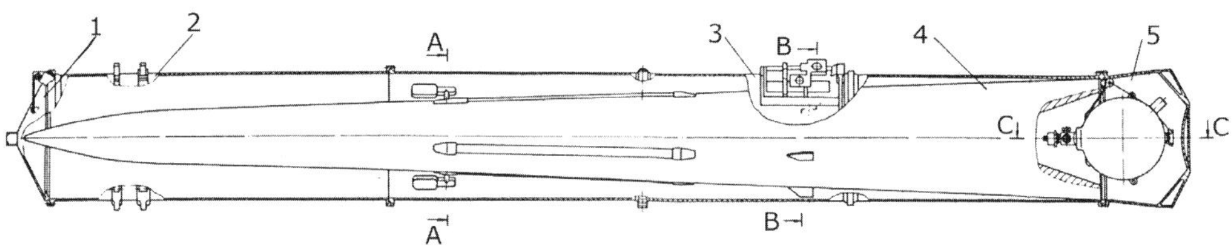

1 - lid/cover
2,3 - container
4 - missile
5 - bottom
6 - lock
7 - gas generator
8 - ring
9 - stabilizer
10 - aerodynamic control surfaces (rudders)
11 - connector
12 - support

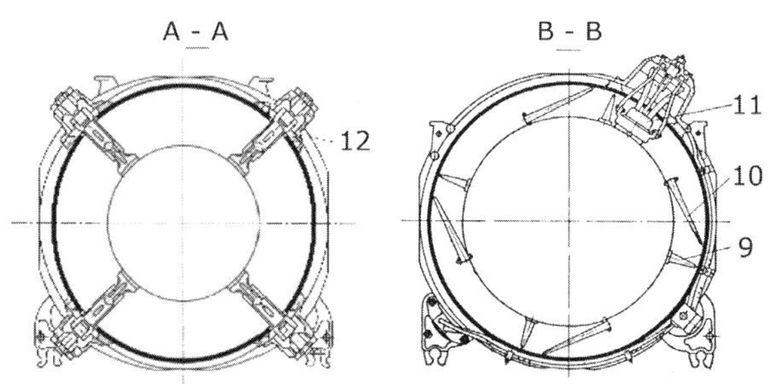

The control surfaces are folded before the missile clears the tube, the short span stabilisers are fixed in position

Figure 5-15: 9M82 and 9M83 missiles in TLC (TPK).

Figure 5-16: 9M82.

Figure 5-17: 9M82 launch.

from the launcher radar to introduce corrections to the onboard inertial guidance system. To optimise the flight parameters of the missile, the motor of the launch stage is turned on with some delay after the development and separation of the motor of the main stage.

A cold-start ejector is used to vertically eject the missile from the launch tube, using a spherical gas generator in the base of the tube. The 9D128 first stage then burns until exhausted, upon which the missile jettisons the spent first stage and transitions to its 9D126 midcourse sustainer powerplant. Immediately post-launch, once the missile has cleared the launch tube, the 9D124 'declination powerplant' is engaged. This is a short-burn thruster system which employs several exhaust ports on the lower rim of the first-stage nozzle. The purpose of this system is to affect a post-launch pitching manoeuvre to the intended target heading, and optimal elevation (pitch/yaw) angle for initiating the first-stage motor burn. Once the missile has been pointed in the desired direction, the first-stage motor is started and burns for 3.5 to 6.2 seconds in the 9M82, or 4.11 to 6.4 seconds in the 9M83.[2]

The method of guiding the missiles is a combined inertial output with semi-active homing in the final part of the flight. At the initial stage, the missile flies according to the data entered into the onboard computing device before launch. In the middle section of the trajectory, guidance is carried out according to radio correction commands. In the final one, the radar homing head takes over. When capturing a target with the homing head of the missile, control is carried out only on its commands.

During the midcourse flight, the missile employs inertial navigation. This is performed using the onboard 9B619 digital computer and a 9B627 inertial unit. Two midcourse guidance modes are employed:

- Inertial Guidance: in this mode target position and velocities are continuously updated by a datalink channel and the autopilot flies the missile using a P-nav algorithm, with vehicle position and velocities derived from the onboard inertial system, and
- Command Inertial Method (KIM): in this mode missile and target position and velocities are uploaded via a datalink channel.

In the former mode, the missile transitions to its semi-active homing seeker during the final 10 seconds of flight, in the latter 3 seconds before impact – a technique preferred in heavy jamming environments. The midcourse guidance system attempts to fly the most energy-efficient trajectory to maximise range. The datalink channel antennas are embedded in the cruciform tail surfaces.

The 9E49/DB-100N semi-active homing seeker will generate target angles and angle rates. A P-nav algorithm with lead bias is likely to be employed. The antenna is cued to the target pitch/yaw angles during endgame closure by the onboard computer.

Russian sources claim the dual-plane monopulse two-channel X-band semi-active seeker can lock on to a $0.05m^2$ RCS target from 30km. A two-channel radio proximity fuze is used to initiate the 9N127 class 'smart' warhead which has a controllable

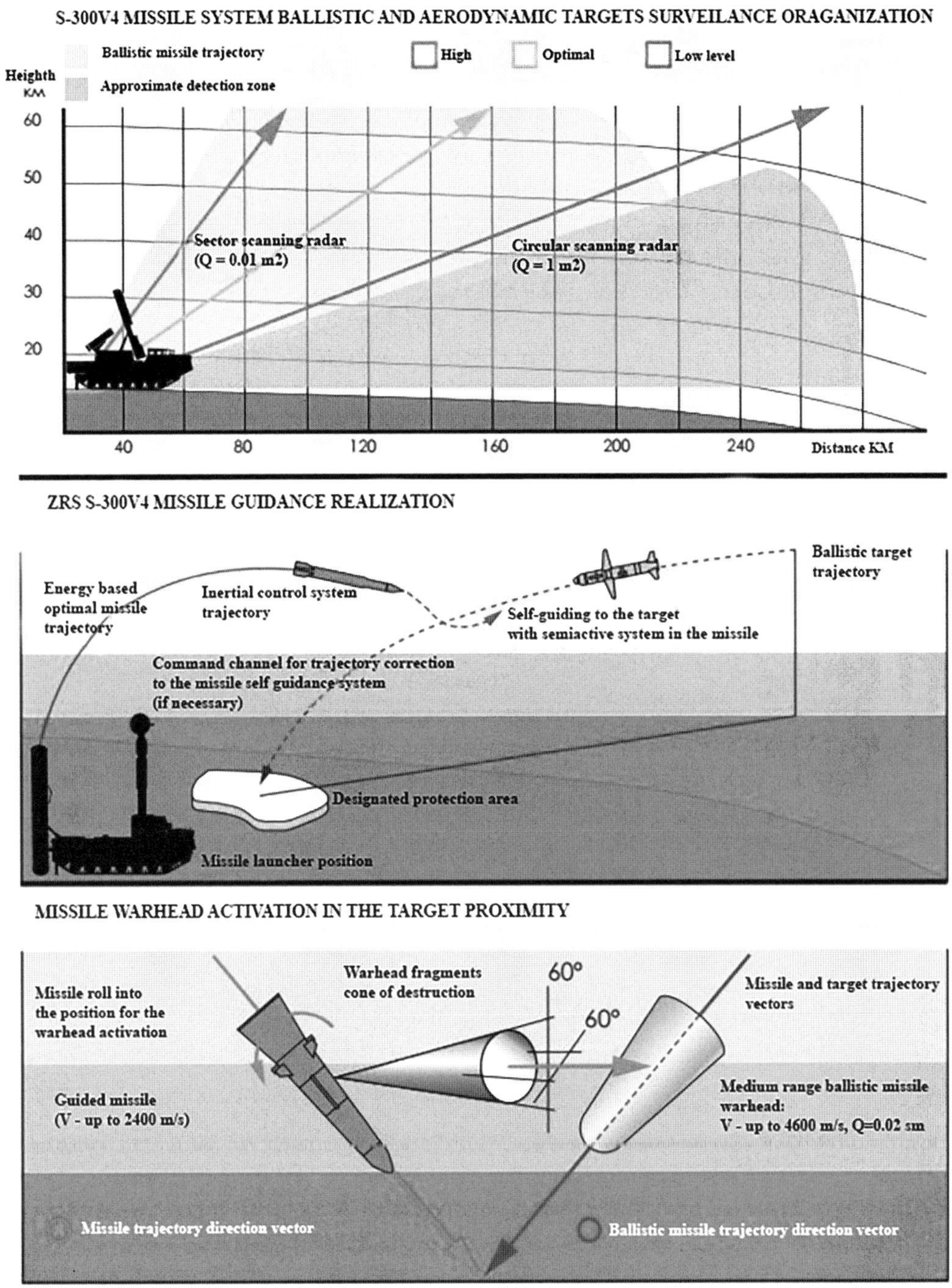

Figure 5-18: S-300V4 surveillance, guidance and warhead activation.

fragmentation pattern to maximise its effect. The missile is also equipped with a self-destruct system. As the missile approaches the target, it will perform a rolling manoeuvre to align the directional warhead with the plane of the target. The 9M82 'Giant' missile velocity entering the endgame is ~3.5 M (Fig. 5-18).

The engagement envelope of the baseline 9M83 'Gladiator' is 2.4–24km and range 5.9–74km, and the 9M82 'Giant' 0.9–30.5km and range 1–100km. The system can launch the missiles at 1.5-second intervals, and a battalion with four batteries can engage twenty-four targets simultaneously, with two missiles per target, and has a complement of between 96 and 192 missiles available for launch on TELAR/TELs. A TELAR can arm a missile for launch in 15 seconds, with a 40-second time to prepare a TELAR for an engagement, and 5-minute deploy and stow times – a genuine 'hide, shoot and scoot' capability.

The cited single-shot kill probabilities for the 'Gladiator' are 50–65 per cent against TBMs and 70–90 per cent against aircraft, and for the 'Giant' 40–60 per cent against IRBMs and 50–70 per cent against the AGM-69 SRAM – ballistic missiles with re-entry velocities of up to 3km/s can be engaged. Russian sources credit the missiles with endgame capability against 7–8G manoeuvring targets. The later 9M82M and 9M83M are credited with a 30G endgame capability.

The 150kg warhead (Fig. 5-19) is a high-explosive fragmentation-directed type. When approaching the target, an additional turn of the missile is made to roll for the appropriate orientation of the warhead and the destruction of the target by a dense

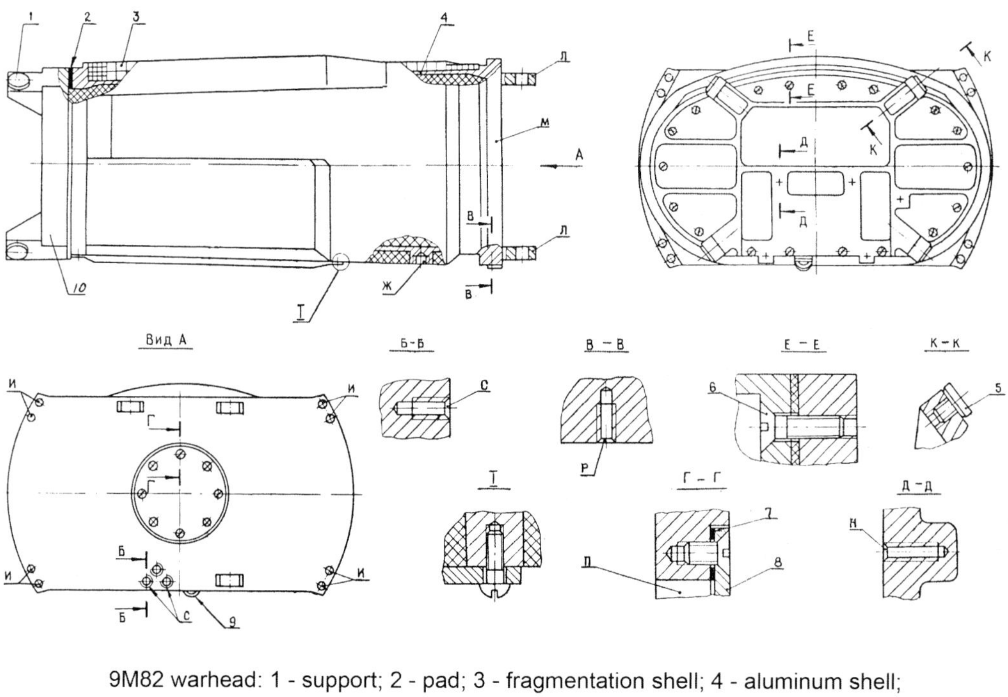

9M82 warhead: 1 - support; 2 - pad; 3 - fragmentation shell; 4 - aluminum shell; 5 - trust bearing; 6 - screw; 7 - pad; 8 - lid.

Figure 5-19: 9M82 warhead.

stream of heavy fragments (weighing 15g each). The detonation of the warhead is carried out based on the type of target: in the area of the warhead when firing at a ballistic missile (the target is neutralised with the explosion of its warhead or its removal from the calculated trajectory) and in the area of the centre of the airframe when firing at aircraft.[3] Up to two missiles with one launcher or up to four missiles with two launchers can be guided to each target at the same time.

Missiles are delivered directly from the plant in transport and launch containers and do not require preparation before combat use, with the exception of a 15-second pre-launch cycle (entering a flight task into the missile autopilot and checking the functioning of the on-board equipment).

The 9M82 missile is designed to defeat operational-tactical ballistic missiles at ranges up to 40km, aeroballistic missiles and aerodynamic targets, including active jamming aircraft at ranges up to 100km. The 9M83 missile is designed to defeat aerodynamic targets, including those manoeuvring with an overload of up to 7–8G, ballistic, aeroballistic and cruise missiles.

The 9A82 self-propelled launcher provides preparation for one or two 9M82 missiles mounted on it or on the 9A84 launcher/loader connected to it (with the same type of missiles), launches missiles, transmits radio correction information and illuminates the target. The self-propelled launcher is equipped with a target-illumination radar, which illuminates the target being fired only in the 'hemisphere' relative to the launcher.

The 9A83 self-propelled launcher provides preparation for one or two out of four 9M83 missiles mounted directly on the launcher or on the 9A85 launcher/transloader connected to it (with the same type of missile), launches the missiles, transmits information and radio corrections, and illuminates the target. The self-propelled launcher is equipped with a illumination radar raised on a special mast, which illuminates the target and transmits radio correction commands regardless of the target azimuth relative to the launcher. The total number of launchers of both types in the complex is up to six.

9A84 and 9A85 launcher-loaders (TELs) are interconnected with the same type (in terms of missile) of launchers, provide loading with a crane-beam, transportation and storage of missiles. Pre-launch control and launch of missiles are carried out. Launchers and missiles are manufactured at the Kalinin Plant (Yekaterinburg).

Deployment time from the march to combat-ready status in any area is 5 minutes, the disengagement time is 5 minutes. The time to transfer the system from standby mode to combat mode does not exceed 40 seconds. The total service life of the military equipment is 20 years. The complex can be transported by rail, air or water transport without restrictions on speed and distance. To transport combat vehicles of the S-300V system, heavy-duty semi-trailers towed by MAZ-537 tractors are used. For the delivery of missiles from arsenals and storage bases, KrAZ tractor-trailers and heavy-duty semi-trailers are used.

According to the press, during combat tests and exercises, more than sixty tactical and operational-tactical ballistic and aeroballistic missiles launched from 65km to 900km were hit. The missile warheads were covered with warhead fragments of the interceptor

Figure 5-20: 9A82 (right) and 9A83 (left) TELARs.

missiles and the ballistic missiles were diverted from the aiming point by a distance of up to 15km.

The unique properties of the anti-aircraft missile system allow it to deal with air targets that have an effective RCS of more than $0.02m^2$. Binding to a single coordinate system is provided by navigation equipment, and the orientation is provided on the combat vehicles.

In addition to the system radars, for long-range surveillance the 1L13-3 Nebo-SV mobile two-coordinate radar station of 360° view, designed and manufactured by the Nizhny Novgorod Television Plant (NITEL), is often attached. The radar station is designed to control the airspace, and detect and determine the coordinates (azimuth, range) of air targets at long ranges in conditions of intense radio countermeasures.

The Nebo-SV radar is distinguished by high efficiency of detection of air targets (including those featuring 'stealth' technology), high reliability, availability of automated diagnostic systems, continuous monitoring of operation, troubleshooting and localisation, data acquisition, the possibility of use as part of rapid deployment tools and as part of automated control systems, and easy maintenance. The dimensions of the main antenna are 16m x 3.24m. Main time before failure is 250 hours. The station and its equipment (complete set) are carried on three trucks and one trailer (Fig. 5-21).

The hardware module is mounted on the chassis of the Ural vehicle (total weight 12 tons). The hardware module includes: a transceiver, an operator's workstation, computer equipment, an information-processing computer, built-in equipment for monitoring and localising faults, an external telecode wire communication system, two

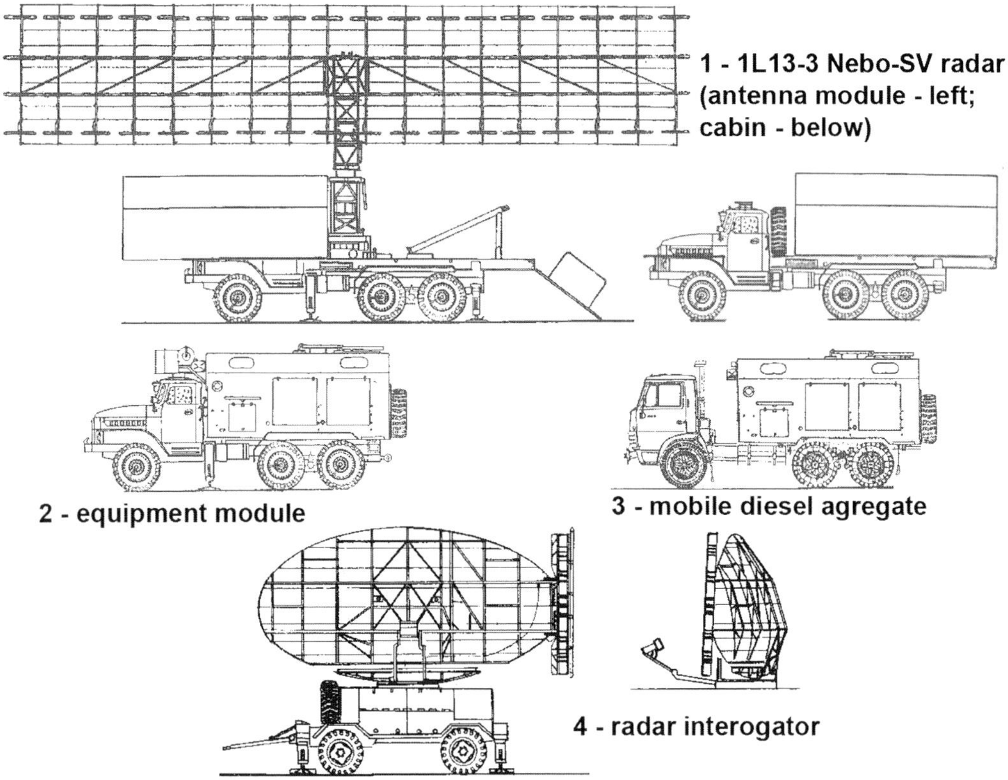

Figure 5-21: IL13-3 Nebo-SV radar.

external communication radio stations, a simulator and a IFF unit. Based on the KAMAZ chassis, a ED-2x30-TZOP-ZRA power plant consisting of two diesel generators is provided (when operating from a prepared position, it is possible to supply the station with power from the industrial network).

The main antenna module with cabin is located on the chassis of a Ural car, the total weight of the unit of equipment being 11.5 tons. The module consists of a flat antenna array, an electric drive with a support-turning device, a deployment mechanism from a marching position, a container with receiver equipment, and a moving protective casing.

The station is equipped with a ground-based radio-location requester (antenna synchronous tracking drive, and spare parts based on a low-bed trailer 2PN4M, total weight 5 tons). It is possible to augment the station with a remote-control post with two operator workstations, mounted in the body-van KAP. The road speed of the station complex is up to 75km/h. Transportation by rail, water and air is also possible.

The S-300V system can work in combination with the: Senezh (5S99M), Senezh-M (5S99M-1), 'Baikal' (73N6) and Baikal-1 air defence ACS. The ACS of the Polyana-D4 anti-aircraft missile brigade is designed for centralised automatic and automated combat control of the S-300V air defence system.

The chief designer of the detection radar included in the various modifications of S-300 systems was Yu.A. Kuznetsov (VNII RT).

When operating combat vehicles of the S-300V system, their maintenance is carried out by 98878-1 and 98879-1 vehicles. The 1P15 repair and maintenance unit is designed for maintenance and current repair of radio-electronic equipment. 98898-1, 1R16, and 9T447-1 units are used for equipment inspection, storage and transportation of spare parts. The S-300V system includes 9488 simulators for conducting complex training including the calculations of all combat vehicles when simulating the air situation.

In general, the development of the S-300V was a significant scientific and technical achievement, being far ahead of similar systems.

Known variants and subtypes include:

1. S-300V1: early production configuration.
2. S-300V2: block upgrade with improved ABM acquisition capability using paired optical cable-networked 9S19M2 radars instead of the 9S15M.

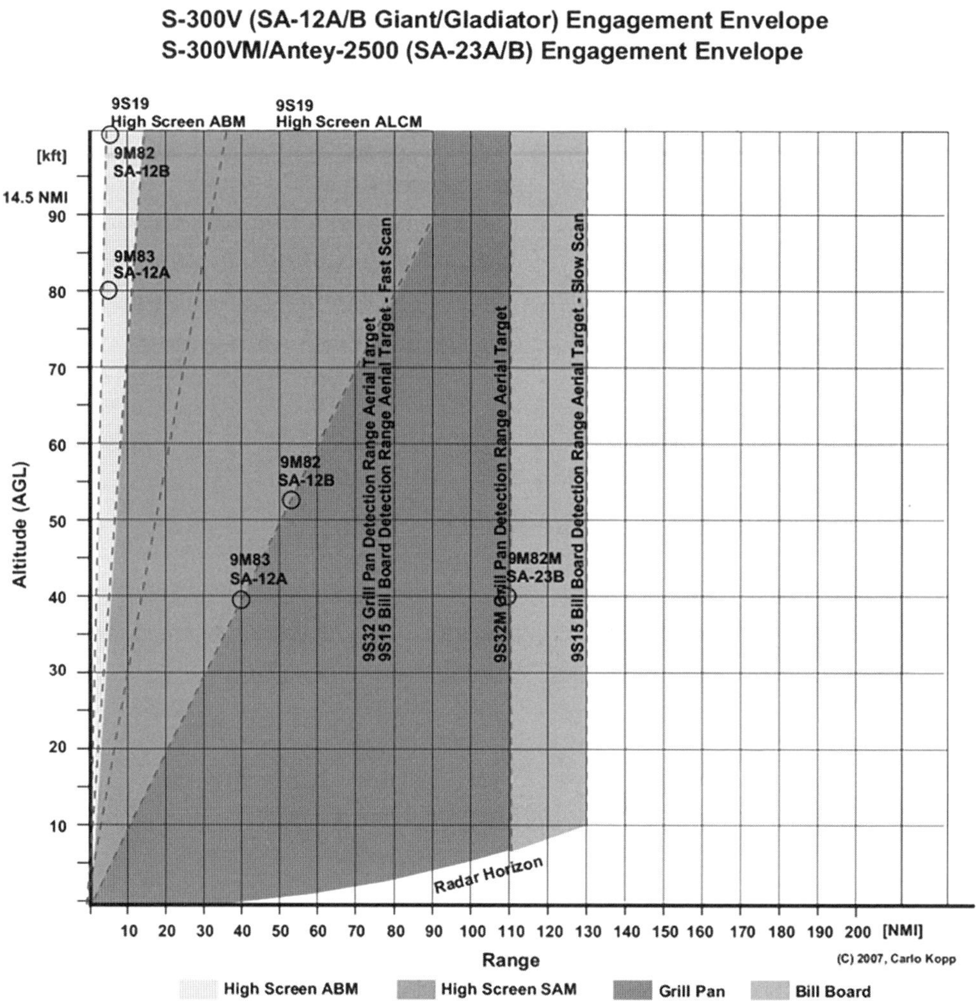

Figure 5-22: Engagement envelopes.

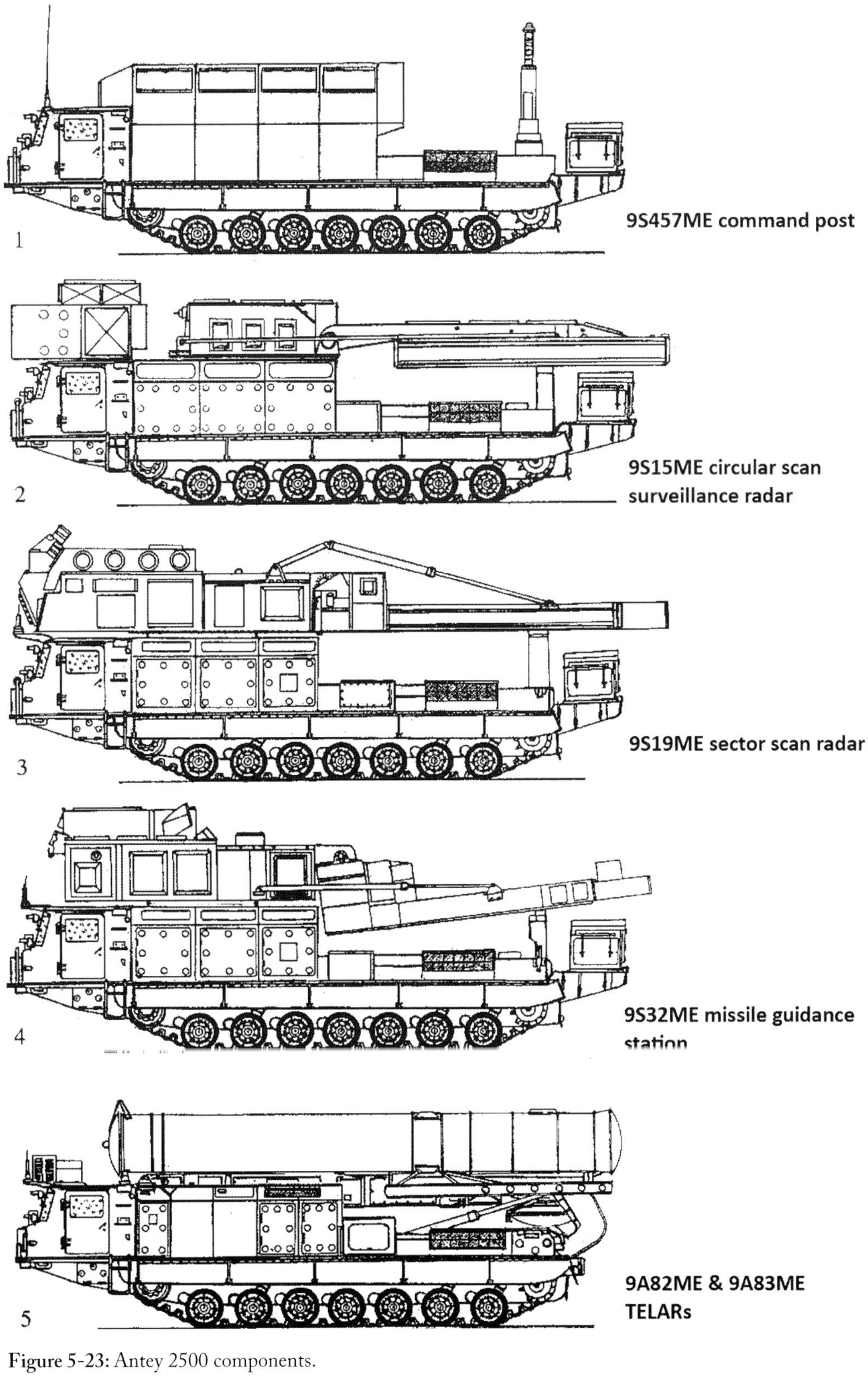

Figure 5-23: Antey 2500 components.

3. S-300V3: block upgrade with missiles with extended range, with a claimed doubling of range performance against aerial targets.
4. S-300V4: 'deep modernisation' with improvements over the S-300V3, providing '1.5–2.3 times the capability of earlier variants', intended for deployment with Russian Army units in 2011.

Figure 5-24: 9S32ME (top) and 9A82ME (bottom). (*Source: Almaz-Antey*)

Figure 5-25: 9S457ME (top) and 9S32ME (bottom) in combat position. (*Source: Almaz-Antey*)

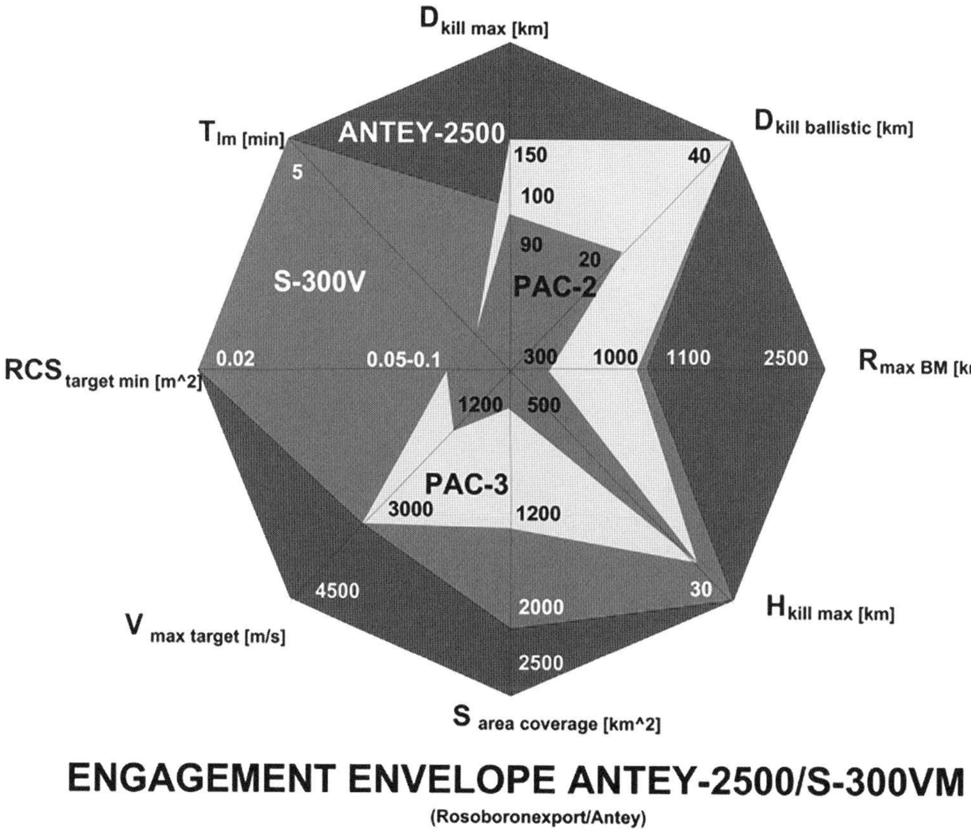

Figure 5-26: Comparison: Antey 2500 and Patriot PAC-3 engagement envelopes.

In the mid-1990s, the Antey-2500 ADMS was developed from the S-300V. It can intercept ballistic missiles with launch ranges up to 2,500km, while its maximum engagement range against aerodynamic targets has been extended to 250km (Fig. 5-23 to 5-26).

The first combat use of this system has been in Ukraine where it is engaged in intercepting the Ukrainian 9M79-1 ballistic missiles launched by the OTR-21 Tochka-U (SS-21 'Scarab'). According to the available information, S-300V was able to intercept almost all missiles. Based on its proven efficiency, there is consideration in Saudi Arabia to purchase this system because the performance of the US-supplied Patriot is not sufficient to stop attacks by Yemeni Houthis.

Chapter 6

Medium-Range Army Air Defence Systems

Legacy: 2A11 Krug (SA-4 'Ganef') and 2K12 Kub (SA-6 'Gainful') Missile Systems

During the 1950s the introduction of new main battle tanks and armoured personnel carriers with enhanced mobility and the development of tactics for the Soviet Army armoured and mechanised forces produced a new requirement for adequate protection against enemy aerial threats. The long-range air defence of armoured and mechanised divisions was provided by the 2K11 Krug (SA-4 'Ganef') missile system (Fig. 6-1). However, the question arose of what would happen if the long-range defence was unable to engage and stop all attacking aircraft, particularly those at low altitude. This situation dictated the new requirement: a need for a missile system that could engage low-level aircraft at medium and short ranges.

Figure 6-1: 2K11 Krug was the first Soviet Army mobile air defence missile system specifically designed for use by the land forces. (*Source: Wikipedia*)

Figure 6-2: 2K12 Kub concept: 2P25 missile launcher (top) and 1S91 central battery radar unit (bottom). (*Source: Author*)

The ambitious specifications and the use of immature technology, such as the CW semi-active homing missile seeker and solid propellant ramjet sustainer, resulted in a troublesome and protracted development process. Problems with the seeker and the powerplant resulted in numerous test failures, with the design only achieving certification in 1967–8, a decade after the commencement of the project.

Unlike the SA-4 complex, the SA-6 uses lighter chassis. One of the big differences is that all the radar equipment was placed not on two vehicles, as in the SA-4 system, but on one platform and the launcher carries three missiles instead of two (Fig. 6-2).

Very difficult tasks were also solved when designing the missile. The supersonic ramjet rocket motor ran not on liquid but solid propellant. This excluded the possibility of adjusting propellant consumption in accordance with the speed and altitude of the missile. In addition, the missile was made without a booster – the charge of the starting motor was placed in the afterburner of the ramjet motor. For the first time on an anti-aircraft missile of a mobile system, a semi-active Doppler radar homing head replaced the radio-control command equipment.

The design concept was for a single self-propelled 1S91 fully mobile engagement and fire-control radar system, with an integrated target-tracking and acquisition radar, controlling a group of four 2P25 series self-propelled TEL vehicles, each with three 3M9 series missiles mounted on a rotating platform. This generic battery structure would be supported by several 2T7 transloader/transporters, on the ZIL-157 truck reloader (Fig. 6-3).

Figure 6-3: 2K12 Kub in combat position.

The 2K12 (SA-6) export version, designated Kvadrat,[7] was supplied to the armed forces of more than twenty countries. The SA-6 complex has been successfully used in almost all military conflicts in the Middle East, Africa and the Civil War and NATO aggression in Yugoslavia and is still active in Yemen.

The SA-6 proved especially effective by destroying a sizable proportion of the Israeli Air Force's (IAF's) aircraft and indirectly by forcing Israeli aircraft into Arab AAA fire during the Yom Kippur War in 1973. The SAM's rapid speed and its new and changing frequencies were difficult to counter. The overconfidence of the Israelis, their neglect of ECM (at one point, the IAF stripped ECM from their aircraft for greater economy, speed and manoeuvrability), and US restrictions on ECM sales left the IAF in a serious bind. The result was that 'The IAF could go anywhere except near the Golan Heights and the Suez fronts, where it was needed most. As they had begun to do three years earlier, the Soviet missiles successfully redefined the nature of modern war.' In response, Israeli improvisation was speedy and effective, yet costly. During this war, Israeli pilots gave a notorious nickname to the system: 'Three Fingers of Death'. For them it was deadly – an estimate is that fifty-five Israeli pilots were killed and forty-four were able to eject. The high efficiency of the Kvadrat air defence missile system was also confirmed in the period from 8 March to 30 May 1974, when the launches of eight missiles destroyed six aircraft.

In the years that followed, countermeasures equipment and tactics were developed with the sole aim of dealing with the SA-6 menace. The Israelis learned a bitter lesson and thoroughly developed measures to suppress the SA-6. One of the greatest air defence suppression engagements after the Yom Kippur War was the Bekaa valley battle (Operation Mole Cricket 19), fought on 9 June 1982 between Syrian air defence and the IAF. The more modern and mobile Kub system was engaged, and this battle cemented the future of air suppression and air defence tactics for the wars to come. This is also the first engagement in which remotely piloted vehicles (RPVs) were used, later known as unmanned aerial vehicles (UAVs) or drones.

The Israeli Defence Force's (IDF's) attack against nineteen Syrian SA-6 sites was the execution of a highly orchestrated combined-arms plan that involved planning, intelligence, training, surprise, command, control and communications, and countless elements of electronic combat in a three-phase attack. These attacks were able to neutralise the Syrian SA-6 batteries in the Bekaa Valley but the concept of the highly mobile air defence system was proven as a necessity for any country. Although the basic system is obsolete nowadays, it is still in wide use in every conflict around the globe and still able to engage newer and more modern aircraft and drones. The Russian military phased out this system in the mid-1980s but its legacy is still clearly visible in modern medium-range mobile SAM systems.

Successor: 9K37 Buk (SA-11, SA-17) and 9K317M – Buk M3 Viking

9K37 Buk

Development of the 9K37 Buk (SA-11 'Gadfly' and SA-17 'Grizzly') self-propelled SAM system commenced in accordance with a Resolution of the Central Committee and USSR Council of Ministers dated 13 January 1972 and provided for cooperation between the main developers and manufacturers that had earlier developed the Kub system (Fig. 6-4).

The Buk missile system was designed to surpass the 2K12 Kub in all parameters. Its designers, including the chief designer Ardalion Rastov, visited Egypt in 1971 to see Kub in operation. As a result of this visit, the developers concluded that each Buk TEL should have its own fire-control radar, rather than being reliant on one central radar for the whole system as in Kub. The result of this move from TEL to TELAR was the development of a system able to engage multiple targets in multiple directions at the same time. Both Kub and Buk used self-propelled launchers developed by Ardalion Rastov.

In 1974 the developers determined that although the Buk missile system was the successor to Kub, both systems could share some interoperability. The result of this decision was the 9K37-1 Buk-1 system. Interoperability between the Buk TELAR and the Kub TEL meant an increase in the number of fire-control channels and missiles available for each system, as well as faster entry of Buk system components into service.

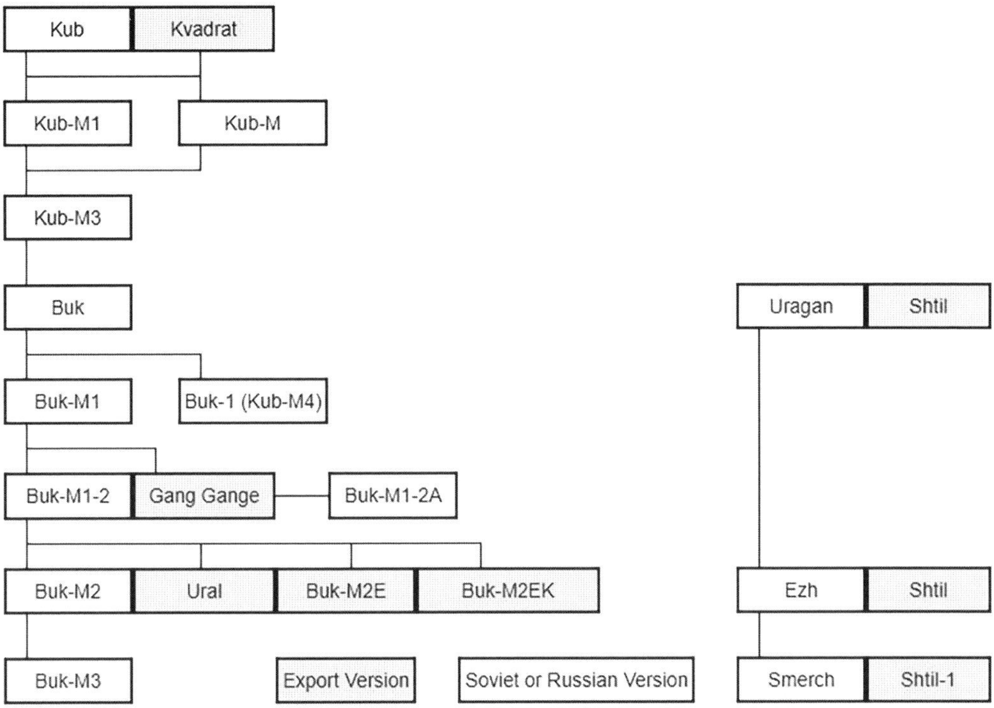

Figure 6-4: Kub and Buk system development. (*Source: Wikipedia*)

Figure 6-5: The 9K37 Buk-M1 TELAR (9A310) with 9M38M1 missiles is a further successful development of the 2K12 system.

The Buk-1 was adopted into service in 1978 following the completion of state trials, while the complete Buk missile system was accepted into service in 1980 after trials between 1977 and 1979 (Fig. 6-5).

Another modification to the Buk missile system was started in 1992 with work carried out between 1994 and 1997 to produce the 9K37M1-2 Buk-M1-2, which entered service in 1998. This modification introduced a new missile, the 9M317, which offered greater kinematic performance over the previous 9M38, and which could also be used by the Buk-M1 (Fig. 6-5) and Buk-M1-2 (Fig. 6-6 and 6-7).

Figure 6-6: 9A310M1-2 Buk M1-2/SA-17. This TELAR can use 9M38, M38M1 and 9M317 missiles. (*Source: Vitaly Kuzmin*)

Figure 6-7: 9K37 Buk-M1 radar (9S35 'Fire Dome'). The bulky dome was used to protect the radar and was the characteristic 'trademark' of the earlier Buk systems. (*Source: Author*)

Such sharing of the missile type caused a transition to a different GRAU (Russian Main Missile and Artillery Directorate) designation, 9K317, which has been used independently for all later systems. The previous 9K37 series name was also preserved for the complex, as was Buk. The new missile, as well as a variety of other modifications, allowed the system to engage ballistic missiles and surface targets, as well as enlarging the 'performance and engagement envelope' (zone of danger for potential attack) for more traditional targets like aircraft and helicopters. The 9K37M1-2 Buk-M1-2 received a new NATO reporting name distinguishing it from previous generations of the Buk system – SA-17 'Grizzly'. The export version of the 9K37M1-2 system is called 'Ural'; this name has also been applied to the M2, at least to early towed export versions.

Further developments include Buk-M2 (9K317) production of which started in 2008. The main visual difference between the M2 version and the previous one (comparing TELARs) is the flat dome that houses a phased-array radar (Fig. 6-8, 6-9).

The 9S35 tracking and illumination radar housed in the visually-distinguishing dome first emerged as part of the transitional SA-6 'Gainful' system, carried by the semi-autonomous 2P25MZ TELAR. The intent behind the design was to permit a larger number of concurrent engagements, by putting a tracking/illumination radar on every single TEL in the SA-6 battery to support engagements using the 3M9M3/9M9M3

Figure 6-8: 9A317 Buk M2/SA-17. The major visual difference between the Buk M1 and M1-2 is that the TELAR is equipped with new Tikhomirov NIIP 9S36 passive phased-array engagement radar, replacing 'Fire Dome'.

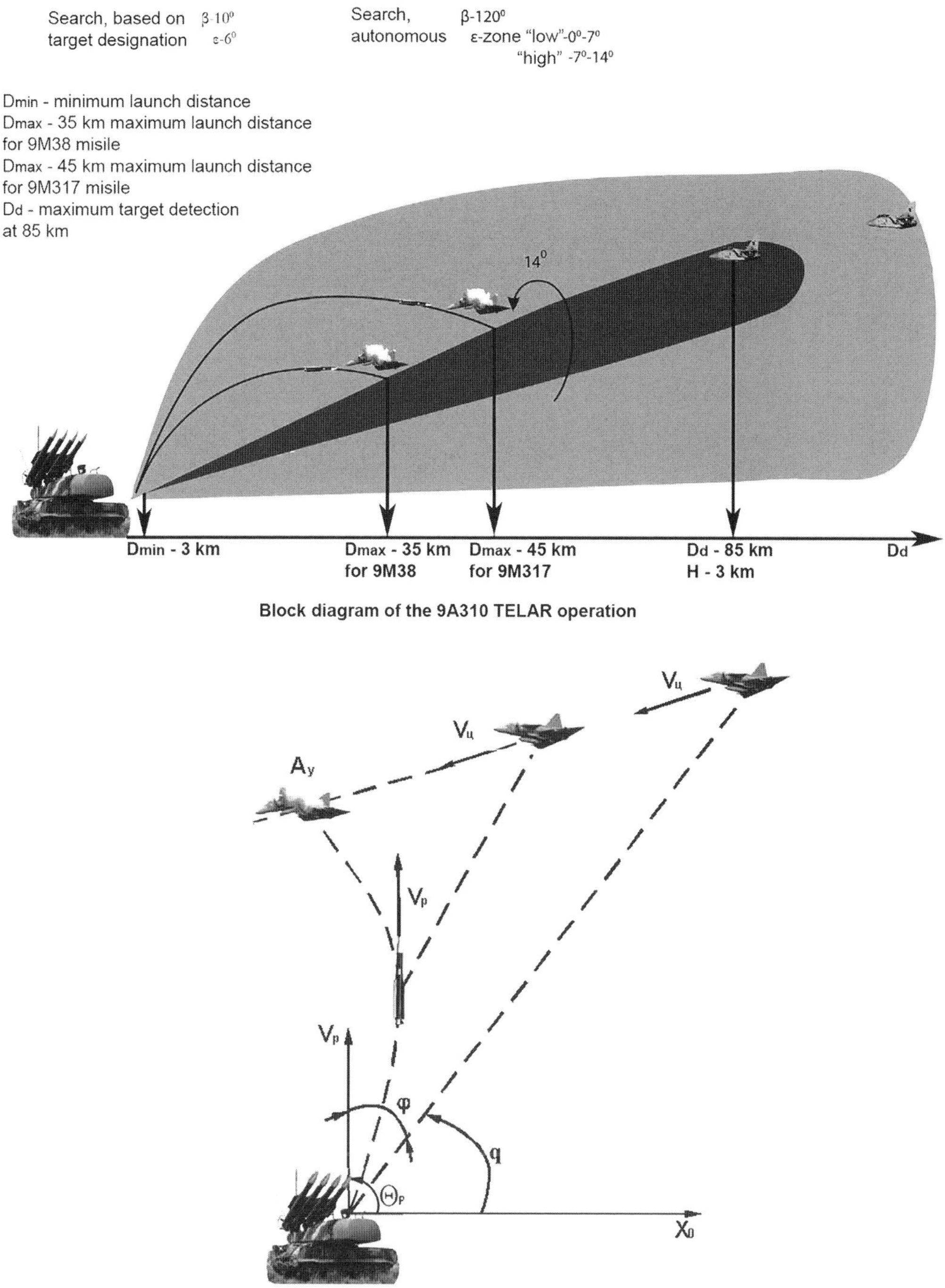

Figure 6-9: 9A310 TELAR interception capabilities (top) and missile proportional semi-active command guidance (bottom). (*Source: Buk manual, modified by author*)

SAM. With the advent of the new 9K37 Buk, the 9S35 was adapted for the new 9A38 TELAR and associated 9M38 SAs (Fig. 6-16, 6-17 and 6-28). The 9S35 is mounted on the front of the TELAR turret, the rear section containing the elevating launch rails for four SAMs.[8]

The 9S35 'Fire Dome' provides a limited search and acquisition capability, a tracking capability and CW illumination for terminal guidance of the semi-active homing SAM seekers. It incorporates an IFF interrogator, optical tracker and datalink, and is powered by the TELAR's gas-turbine generator. A shared antenna is employed for two X-band transmit/receive channels. These respectively provide a pulsed mode for search and track functions, with linear chirp for compression, and a CW mode for illumination. Monopulse angle tracking is employed for jam resistance. For target tracking the antenna and feed system provide a main lobe with 2.5° width in azimuth and 1.3° in elevation and for CW illumination the antenna a main lobe with 1.4° width in azimuth and 2.65° in elevation. Operating autonomously, the 9S35 will take 4 seconds to sweep a 120° sector, with an elevation of 6–7°. When cued to acquire and track, it will take 2 seconds to sweep a 10° x 7° azimuth/elevation angle. The range error is cited as 175m, the angular error at less than 1°. The radar can switch from standby to combat mode in 20 seconds (Fig. 6-9).[9]

9K317 Buk M2 introduced the new Tikhomirov NIIP 9S36 passive phased-array engagement radar (Fig. 6-8), replacing 'Fire Dome'. The beam-steering parameters cited by Russian sources are consistent with a tilted fixed passive phased array. The ESA element count, sidelobe performance, peak power and other cardinal design parameters have not been disclosed to date. The cited detection and tracking ranges for the 9S36 are not consistent with NIIP's airborne PESA design range performance, power densities and aperture sizes, and should therefore be treated with caution – NIIP have achieved considerably better range performance in the N-011M BARS and N-035 Irbis E airborne radars, with smaller apertures.[10]

The most interesting component of this design is the standalone mast-mounted 9S36 phased array, designed to provide extended low-altitude and surface coverage in air defence but also coastal defence applications. This design uses a 21m telescoping and elevating mast which mounts a radar head with the 9S36.

The principal tactical element of the Buk system capable of performing combat missions independently is the battalion. It includes a 9S470M command post (Fig. 6-12, 6-13, 6-14), 9S18M1 target-acquisition radar (Fig. 6-15), communications facilities, three missile batteries (two 9A319M1-2s and one or two 9A39M1s), a technical battery and maintenance and support units. The SAM regiment usually makes up part of a motorised infantry (tank) division (brigade) and the SAM battalion is included in an army's (corps') SAM brigade (four to six SAM battalions; command post, a technical battery and maintenance and support units).

The SAM battalion armed with the Buk SAM system is capable of performing air defence missions in the interests of combined-arms formations in all types of combat, protect high-value objectives (territories), simultaneously engage up to six aerodynamic

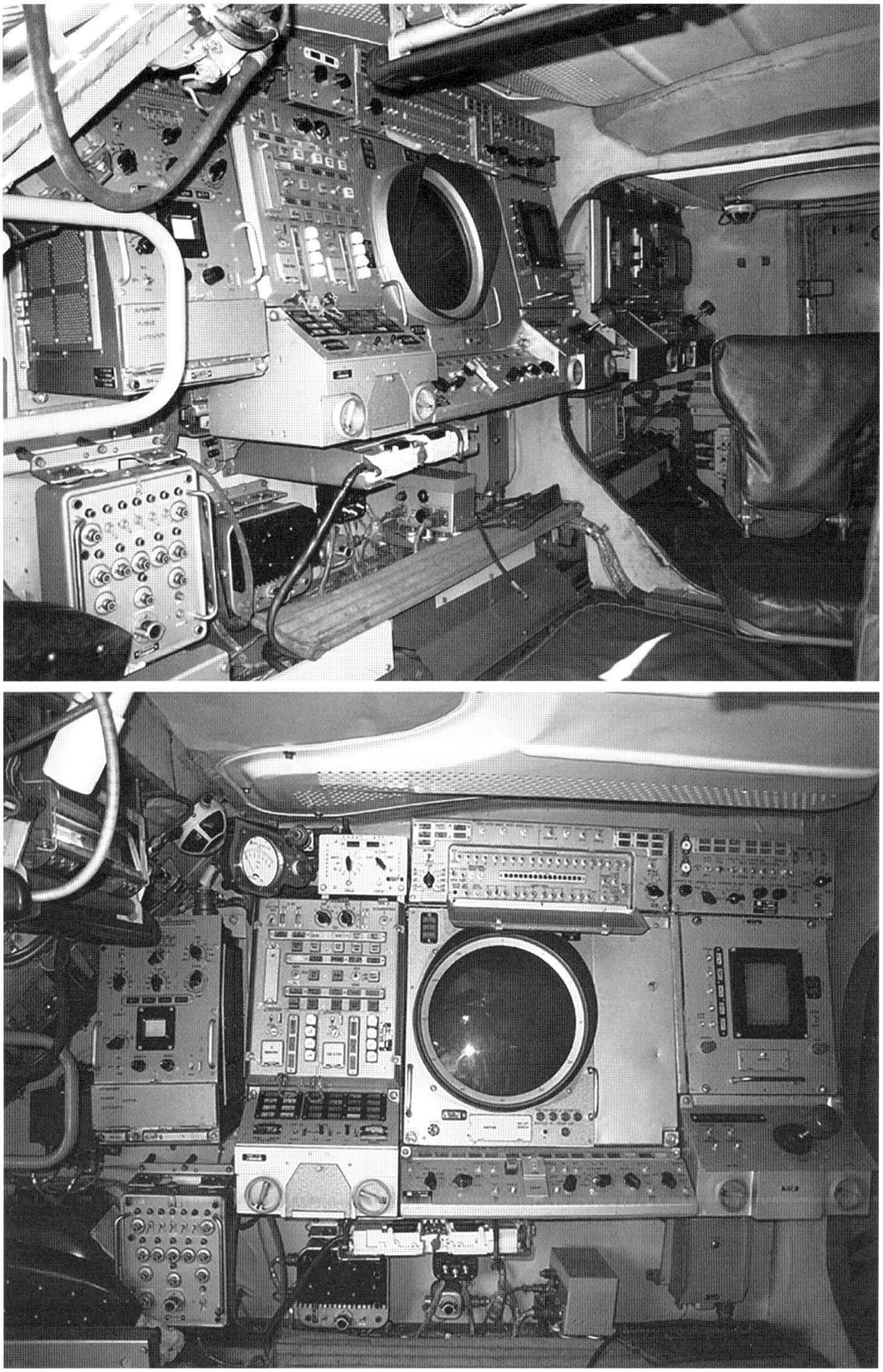

Figure 6-10: Top: Belarusian Buk-MN operator workstations front to back: commander, first operator (tracking) and second operator (fire control). The target-acquisition and tracking radar operator transfer the target to the precise tracking and illuminating radar which is actually a fire-control radar.
Bottom: Russian Buk-M1-2 commander (left console with the switches) and first operator station with large circular screen for target tracking. At the small rectangular indicator, the target blip is shown, and the precise coordinates can be determined by azimuth and distance.

Buk-MB operator consoles (left to right):
target acquisition and tracking - comander;
precise tracking (middle),
fire control operator station (right).

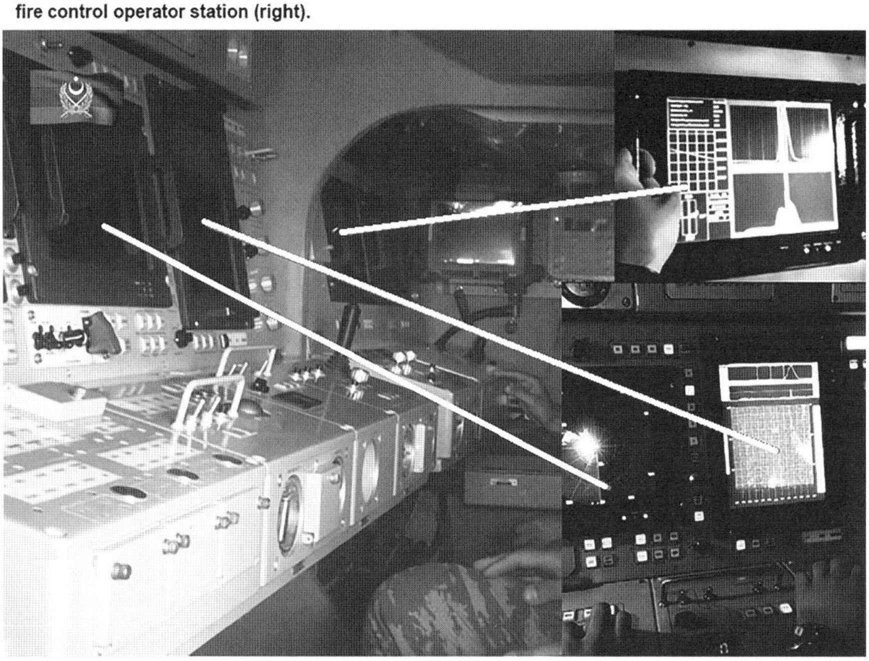

Buk-M1-2 operator consoles are slightly diferent but the functionality is the same (left to right):
target acquisition and tracking - comander;
precise tracking (middle),
fire control operator station (right).

Figure 6-11: Buk-MB (top) and Buk-M1-2 (bottom) operator consoles. Compared to Figure 6-10, it is evident how digital displays improve ergonomics and functionality.

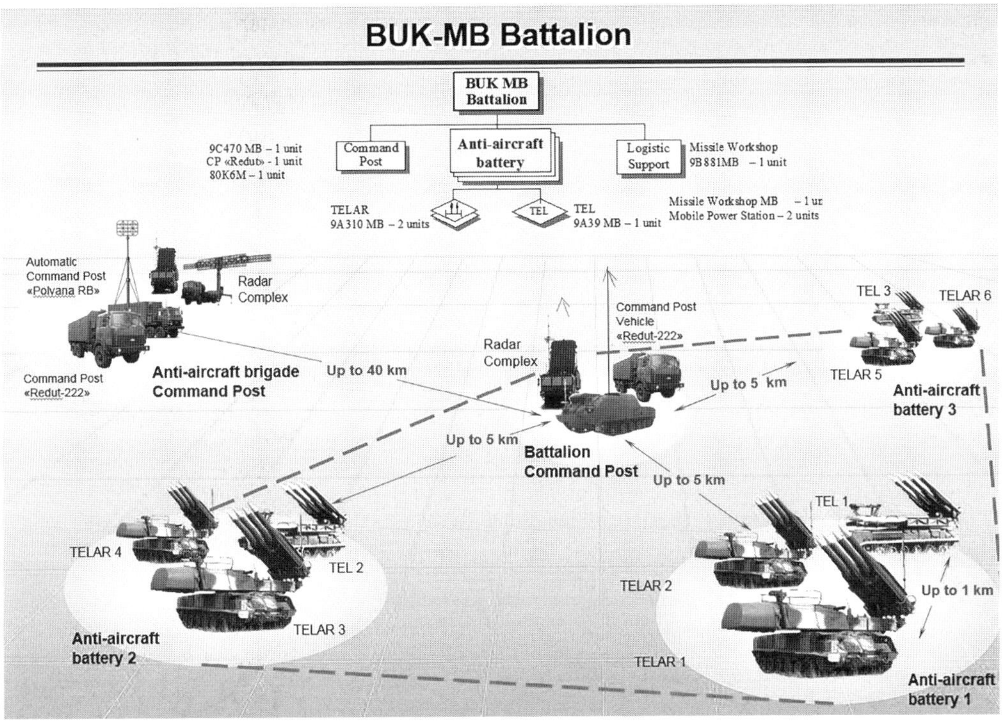

Figure 6-12: The Buk (all models) battalion is the most effective medium independent air defence unit. It consists of three to four batteries which cover each other. Combined, it has thirty-six missiles ready on the launchers.

Figure 6-13: Typical components of a Buk-M1 battery (left to right): 9S470 battery command post; 9S18 target-surveillance and tracking radar; 9A310 TELAR; 9A39 TEL; and 9T243 KrAZ-260 missile transport truck.

Figure 6-14: 9S470 battery command post.

Figure 6-15: 9S18M 3D radar.

targets or six ballistic missiles at a range of up to 140km, or attack six waterborne or ground targets. As a tactical BMD module, the SAM battalion (regiment) protects an area of about 800–1,200km.

The command post of the SAM brigade is equipped with the Polyana-D4M1 automated battle-management system. The Buk system has the 9S18M battery radar

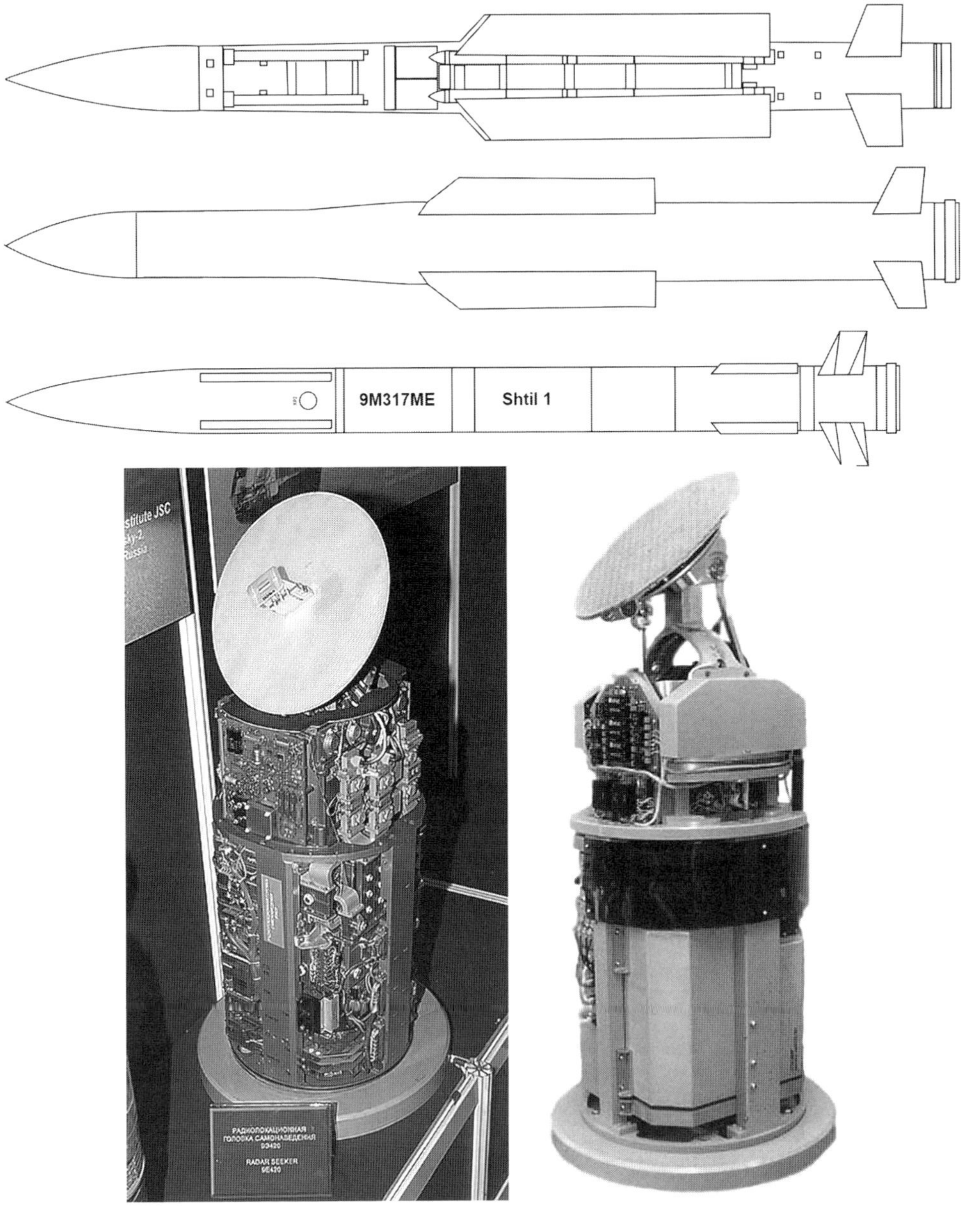

Figure 6-16: Drawings top to bottom: 9M38M1, 9M317 and 9M317ME Buk surface-to-air missiles comparison. Bottom left: Agat 9E420 digital CW dual plane monopulse semiactive radar-homing seeker for the 9M317 missile. The unique antenna arrangement is inherited from the 3M9/SA-6 series seekers; Bottom right: Agat ARGS Slanets monopulse active radar homing seeker for the 9M317 and 9M38M 'Gadfly' missiles. (*Agat*)

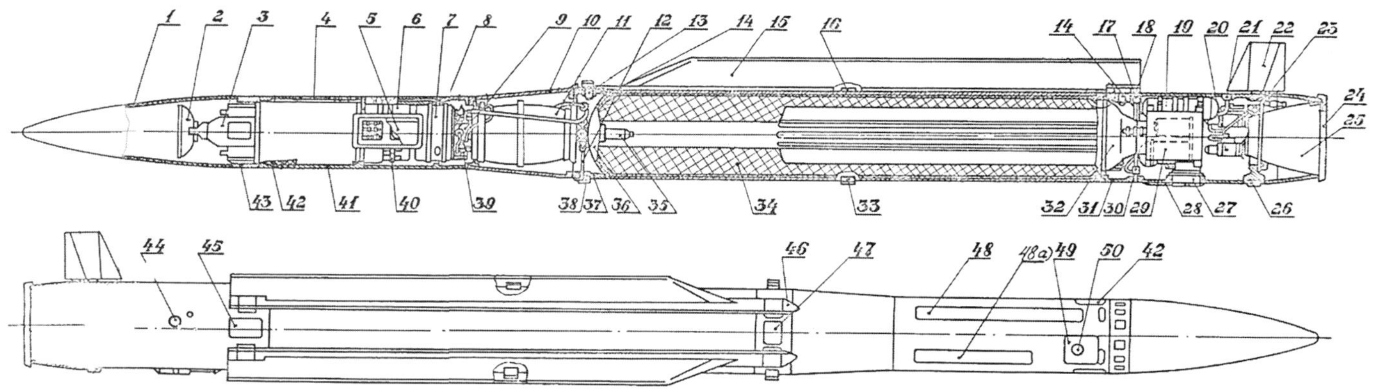

1 – radio waves transparent cone; 2 - target channel antenna - radar homing seeker; 3 - semi active radar homing seeker; 4 - proximity fuze antenna; 5 - hatch No. 1; 6 – autopilot control unit; 7 - radio fuse; 8 - compartment No. 1; 9 - safety-actuating mechanism; 10 - compartment No. 2; 11 - warhead; 12 - safety-starter; 13 - front rigging unit; 14 - electrical connector of the transit line; 15 - wing; 16 - rear rigging unit; 17 - absolute pressure signaling device; 18 – rear wing mount; 19 - gas generator of the gas supply system; 20 - steering gear; 21 - valve for checking steering gears with compressed air; 22 - steering wheel; 23 - steering wheel stopper; 24 - plug; 25 - nozzle block; 26 - rear yoke; 27 – detachable connector; 28 - protective device of the tear-off connector; 29 - turbogenerator; 30 - valve with a plug of the static pressure measurement system; 31 - compartment No. 4; 32 - rear bottom; 33 - middle yoke; 34 - rocket motor fuel charge; 35 - igniter; 36 - the front bottom of the rocket motor; 37 - transitional frame; 38 - front yoke; 39 - converter; 40 - electrical connectors; 41 - cylindrical part of compartment No. 1; 42 - radar homing seker antenna reference channel; 43 – frame radiotransparent fairing; 44 - valve for checking the turbogenerator; 45 - hatch No. 3; 46 - front wing mount; 47 - hatch No. 4; 48 - cover of the transmitting antenna of the radio fuze; 48a - cover of the receiving antenna of the radio fuse; 49 - hatch No. 2; 50 - transparent control window.

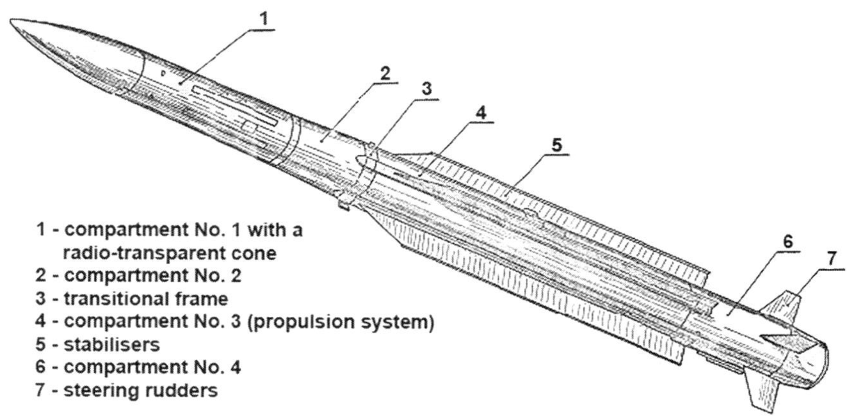

Figure 6-17: 9M38M1 missile. (*S.N. Elcin*, Raketa 9M38M1, Ustroistvo i funkcionirovanie)

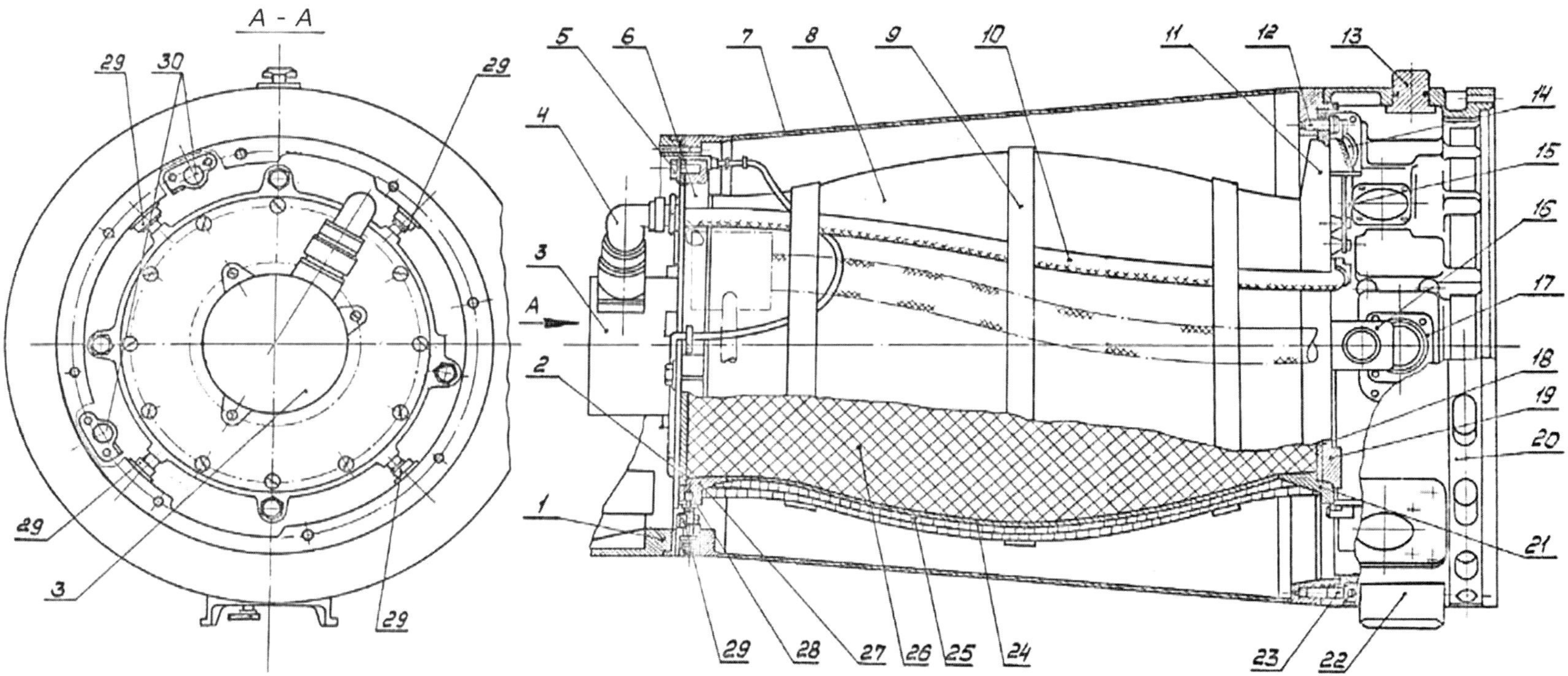

1 – compartment body; *2* – bottom; *3* – PIM; *4* – PIM (safety actuator) connector; *5* – bolt; *6* – warhead shell; *7* – compartment body; *8* – warhead body; *9* – bandage cover; *10* – electric harness; *11* – warhead lug; *12* – hairpin; *13* – lifting yoke; *14* – electrical harness connector; *15* – bracket; *16* – mounting lug; *17* – PIM (safety actuator) safety connector; *18* – pad; *19* – warhead cover; *20* – transitional frame; *21* – warhead plate; *22* – yoke; *23* – hairpin; *24* – warhead shell; *25* – striking elements; *26* – bursting charge; *27* – flange; *28* – thrust bearing; *29* – stop screw; *30* – SKD sensor.

Figure 6-18: 9M38M1 warhead. (*S.N Elcin,* Raketa 9M38M1 Ustroistvo I funkcionirovanie)

(Fig. 6-15) and the 9S470 combat command post. The 9S18M radar is designed to solve the following tasks:

- detection of air objects;
- measurements of three coordinates of air objects;
- IFF identification;
- determination of bearings for active jammers; and
- radar data transfer to the command post and individual launchers as well as to Polyana-D1 automated battle-management systems and PU-12 MP-25, PU-12 and PORI-P1 (P2) battle-management station.

During combat operations the 9S470M combat command post (Fig. 6-14) provides the solution to the following main tasks:

- collection, processing and displaying of information about the air situation coming from the surveillance and tracking radars and individual launchers;
- receiving and displaying data on the location and status of air defence systems, setting sectors of responsibility for the individual launchers;
- development of an optimal solution to the task of target distribution among the subordinate units;
- issuance of target designation of the individual launchers and control over the fulfilment of the assigned tasks; and
- overall control of operations.

9K317M – Buk M3 Viking

The latest version of the Buk family is 9K317M (Fig. 6-19), or the Buk-M3, also nicknamed 'Viking'. A medium-range surface-to-air missile system, it is a modernised version of the Buk-M2, featuring advanced electronic components and a deadly new missile, and could be regarded as a completely new system. It was designed, developed and manufactured by Almaz-Antey. The system boasts a new digital computer, high-speed data exchange system and a tele-thermal imaging target designator instead of the tele-optical trackers used in previous models. A battery of Buk-M3 missiles can track and engage up to thirty-six targets simultaneously, while its advanced 9R31M missile is capable of knocking down all existing flying objects, including highly manoeuvrable ones, even during active electronic jamming. The Buk-M3 can launch vertically and can also engage sea and land targets.

A Buk-M3 Viking missile battery consists of two 9A317M TELARs and one 9A316M TEL. The TELAR is based on the GM-569 armoured tracked chassis and carries six ready-to-fire missiles mounted on a turntable that can traverse a full 360°. The turret of the Buk-M3 TELAR includes the fire-control radar at the front and the launcher on top. In August 2018, at the Army-2018 International Military Technical Forum in Moscow, the latest variant of the Buk-M3 was shown for the first time to the

Figure 6-19: 9K317M Buk-M3 'Viking' with 9A317M TELAR and six 9R31M missiles stored in containers. (*Source: Vitaly Kuzmin*)

Figure 6-20: 9K317M Buk-M3 and S-300V integration. (*Source: Author*)

1 - 9S510ME command post; 2 - 9S18M surveilLance and target tracking radar; 3 - 9A317ME Transporter, Erector, Launcher and Radar (TELAR); 4 - 9S36ME low-level target tracking and acquisition radar; 5 - 9A316ME Transporter, Erector and Launcher (TEL).

Figure 6-21: 9K317M combat assets.

public with a new launcher turret equipped with two rows of three missile containers. The reloader vehicle of the Buk-M3 Viking is equipped with two blocks of six missiles, using the same tracked chassis as the previous version of the Buk family.

The Buk-M3 Viking uses the new 9R31M radar-guided surface-to-air missile. The system's target-destruction probability has been tested to 0.9999. It is able to destroy any type of air target at a range of 2.5km to 70km, with a speed of 3,000m/s at altitudes of 15m up to 35km. It has been optimised for the interception of low-flying cruise missiles. The system includes a high-speed data exchange system and a thermal-imaging target designator replacing the optical trackers on previous Buk models. The 9M317M missile, stored in the container, is fitted with a high-explosive fragmentation warhead.

The missile guidance system is very similar to that of the S-300V missile system, which led to a very interesting modification with the integration of one launcher with 9A383 radar with four 9M83M missiles from the S-300V system (Fig. 6-20).

In this configuration, the 9K17M Buk-M3 battalion can engage aerodynamic targets at ranges up to 100km, and ballistic targets at up to 40km, with 9M83M missiles, so that the system can be also considered as an ABM system (Fig. 6-21). These targets can be engaged with a maximum of two missiles at a time.

The operating principle is as follows: target surveillance and acquisition are performed by the independent 9S36M self-propelled target-tracking radar or by the individual 9A317M TELAR radar which scans the airspace and illuminates the target. Once the target is locked on and a 9M83M missile is launched by the S-300V battery, a 9A317M radar on the launcher or a 9S36M self-propelled radar illuminates the target, and guides the S-300V launcher 9A383M radar antenna, forming control commands that are sent to the missiles midway in its trajectory by the 9A383M radar.

In the final part of the missile guidance, the 9A383M radar on the S-300V system is activated, illuminating the target which enables the 9M83M missile's final semi-active radar self-guidance to the target.

Guidance system: inertial and radio command and semi-active radar self-guidance. Guidance method: proportional navigation.

Buk's extensive combat service in the Russian military will be discussed in detail in the book *Missiles and Rockets Over Ukraine* by the same author.

Chapter 7

Short-Range Air Defence

Operational experience with the first SAM defence systems gained by the late 1950s showed that they were ineffective against low-flying targets. This became particularly clear during the initial testing with air defence penetration by aircraft flying at low and very low altitudes. Following the initial results, some countries initiated the development of compact air defence missile systems intended to protect both fixed and mobile installations from low-flying aircraft only. Requirements for these SAM systems were similar in many respects and included above all maximum automation and compactness. The system's assets were to be mounted on no more than two cross-country vehicles, as otherwise it was expected that its deployment time would be unacceptably long for the intended purpose.

The 9K33 Osa (Wasp) (SA-8 'Gecko') system, the development of which commenced on 27 October 1960, was among the first such systems. The decision approved by the Soviet leadership envisaged the development of battlefield and shipborne small-sized self-contained SAM systems sharing the common 9M33 missile (Fig. 7-1). This self-propelled SAM system was intended to provide an air defence umbrella for mechanised forces such as armoured regiments, brigades, divisions and motorised infantry divisions (in Soviet terminology, motor rifle divisions) in various forms of deployment as well as on the march, and stationary installations. Among the basic requirements for the Osa system were its complete autonomy, which was to be ensured through the arrangement of all its combat assets – from the target-acquisition radar to the launcher with six missiles, as well as communications, navigation and survey control, computer, environment-monitoring and power-supply equipment – on a single self-propelled amphibious wheeled chassis, and the capability to detect low-flying targets which might suddenly appear from any direction (at a range of 0.8–1.0km to 10.8km and altitudes from 50m to 5,000m) while on the move and to engage them after only a brief halt.

The NII-20 (NIEMI)[1] Research Institute (chief designer M.M. Lisichkin) and the KB-82 Design Bureau (Tushino Engineering Plant, chief designer A.V. Potopalov) were assigned as prime developers. However, they faced serious problems because it turned out to be difficult for them to meet such high requirements, due to the available capabilities and many innovative solutions chosen at the initial development stage. As a result, on 8 January 1964, a commission was set up to provide necessary assistance to the 9K33 Osa developers. Based on its recommendations, a government decree was issued on 8 September 1964, under which KB-82 was suspended from work on the 9M33 missile, and its development was transferred to OKB-2[2] (Fakel Design Bureau) headed by P.D. Grushin.

Figure 7-1: 9K33 OSA (SA-8 'Gecko') mobile short-range missile system. (*Source:* Russian Air-Defence Systems)

The technical configuration and characteristics of the new missiles and modified components of the system were presented as early as the autumn of 1964. The development of the new missile relied on vast experience gained in the development of SAMs for the S-75 and S-125 systems, and several innovative technical solutions were implemented.

The first launch of a new version of the missile took place on 25 March 1965. However, when in the second half of 1967 the Osa SAM system was submitted for joint tests, some serious flaws were revealed and in July 1968 the tests were suspended. In this case, the unsuccessful layout of the combat vehicle with the SAM system components spaced across the vehicle hull was noted as one of the main drawbacks. As a result, it was decided to use the Bryansk Automotive Plant's model 937 self-propelled chassis to mount the Osa system. In the meantime, NIEMI Director V.P. Efremov was appointed chief designer and I.M. Drize became his deputy.

A virtually new short-range SAM system was developed within several months. In this case, a single antenna-launcher unit with four ready-to-launch missiles was placed on the roof of the vehicle. As a result, vehicle construction became simpler and more robust, less prone to oscillations and vibrations, and targets could be engaged with minimal

Such features of PGMs help them effectively withstand such systems as Osa, Roland and Crotale-NG. The first two circumstances impose new requirements on radars employed by the SAMs designed to fight the PGM, while the other two impose requirements on the flight ballistics and control loop of the systems as well as on the 'muscle' of their combat equipment.

The low values of effective RCS require a huge expenditure of energy by both target-acquisition radar (TAR) and target-tracking and missile-guidance radar (TTMGR or TTR, as often noted in Western literature), especially in case of electronic countermeasures undertaken by the enemy, as well as the implementation of new procedures to seek out and track targets. The TAR must be either three-coordinate or capable of measuring the target angle to an accuracy that minimises the fine search time by the TTR.

In addition, the TAR should realise the principle of criterional processing of the signals, thereby minimising the number of false alarms, such as clutter, and also examine the target flightpaths, categorise the targets, select the most dangerous ones from a group of detected targets and prioritise them.

Figure 7-2: 9A331 Tor-M1 combat vehicle. (Source: *Russian Air-Defence Systems*)

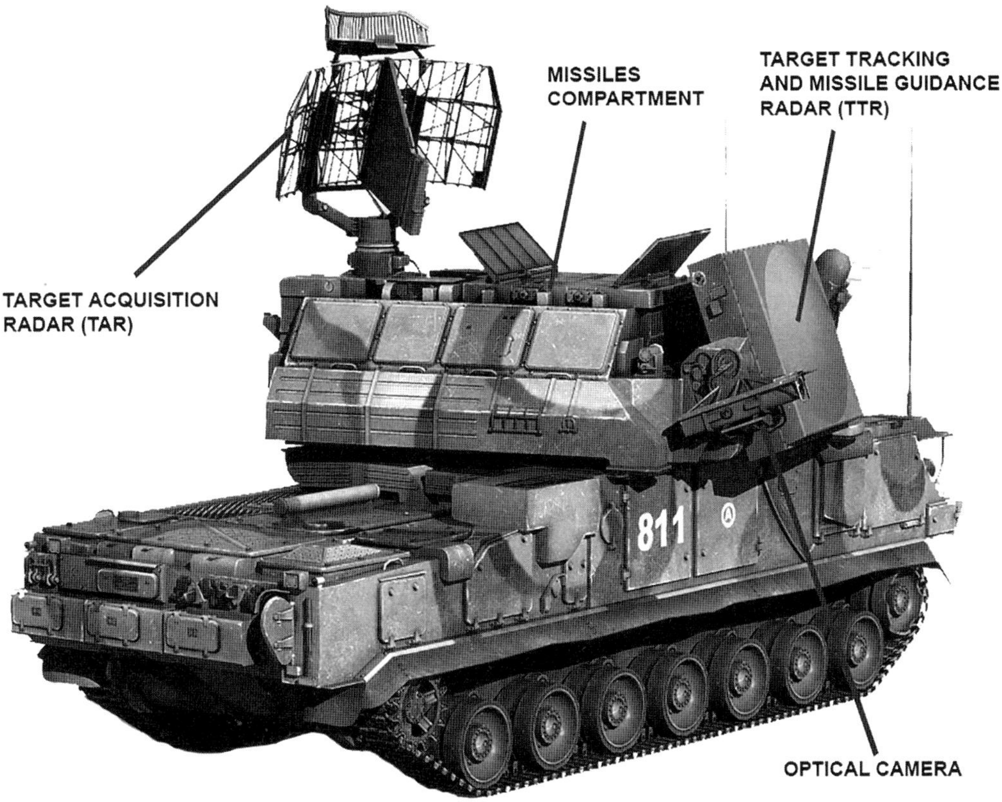

Figure 7-3: 9K331 components. (*Source:* Russian Air-Defence Systems *and 3D models*)

The 9K331 Tor-M1 (Fig. 7-2 and 7-3) system is a highly mobile rapid-reaction SAM built to replace the Cold War-era Osa-AKM system. Like the Osa-AKM, the Tor M1 is a fully self-contained package, with a search radar, a monopulse tracking and engagement radar, and a magazine of automatic command to line of sight (ACLOS) guided missiles. The design aims of the Tor were, however, broader than those for the Osa, and not only are low-flying aircraft and helicopters intended targets, but also cruise missiles, standoff missiles, and smart bombs during their terminal flight phase. Russian thinking is that long-range S-300V battery elements such as radars and command posts are to be covered by Tor point-defence systems, intended to engage and destroy guided munitions targeting the S-300V battery elements.

In turn, the aerodynamic configuration of the 9M330 missile remained similar to that of the 9M33 used in the Osa system, thus ensuring the necessary continuity of development. Also, during the development of the 9M330, as with other new-generation SAMs, the concept of guaranteed reliability of its maintenance-free operation in the army and navy throughout the entire warranty period was implemented (Fig. 7-4, 7-5).

The joint tests of the system were conducted in 1983–4, after which on 19 March 1986 it entered service. For the Tor system, the autonomous operation of batteries (four launch vehicles in each battery) was the main type of operation, although centralised and

9M330 SECTIONS

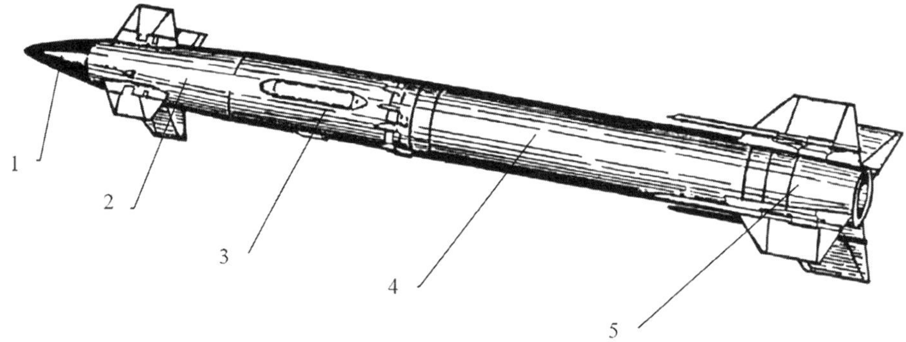

1 - missile radom (first section); 2 - controls section; 3 - instrumentation section;
4 - dual mode motor section ; 5 - tail fin block.

Figure 7-4: 9M330 components. (*Source:* Russian Air-Defence Systems)

Figure 7-5: 9M331 cutaway. (*Source:* Russian Air-Defence Systems)

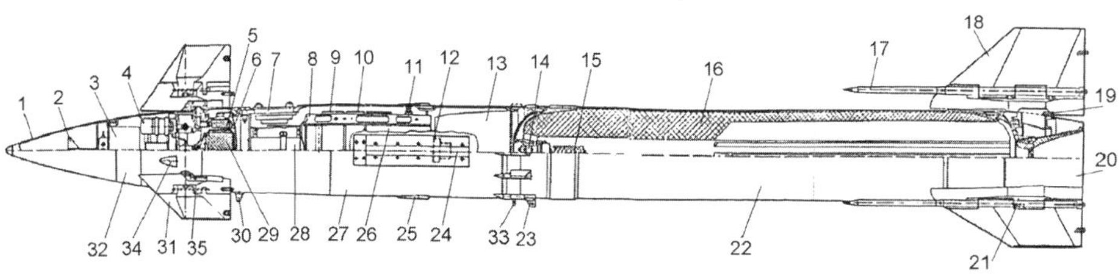

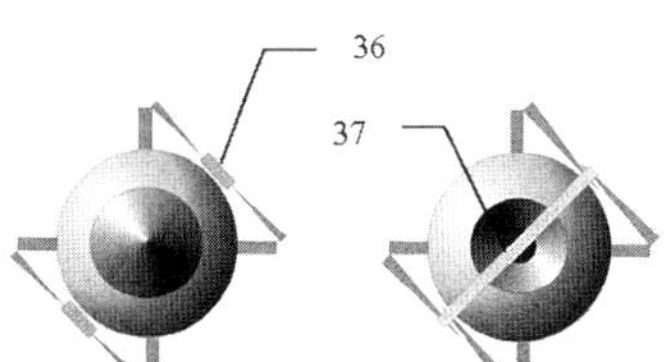

1 – radio wave transparent cone; 2 – proximity fuse antenna; 3 – proximity fuse receiver; 4 – canard mechanism and control; 5 - gas generator charge; 6 - hot gas source block; 7 - onboard electrical connector; 8 - on-board equipment stringer; 9 - autopilot; 10 - radio fuse receiver; 11 - booster disconnector; 12 - safety-actuating mechanism; 13 – fragmentation warhead; 14 - pressure sensor; 15 - igniter; 16 - solid fuel charge; 17 - torsion bar; 18 – Tail fin; 19, 21, 23 – missile yoke; 20 - tail compartment; 22 - solid fuel rocket motor; 24 - receiving antenna fuse; 25 - antenna on-board radio equipment; 26 - on-board radio equipment; 27 - hardware compartment; 28 - on-board power supply; 29 - gas generator power steering mechanism charge; 30, 33 - lever; 31 - rudder-aileron; 32 - control compartment; 34 - fitting; 35 - locking mechanism; 36 - rudders locking mechanisms spring; 37 - jumper

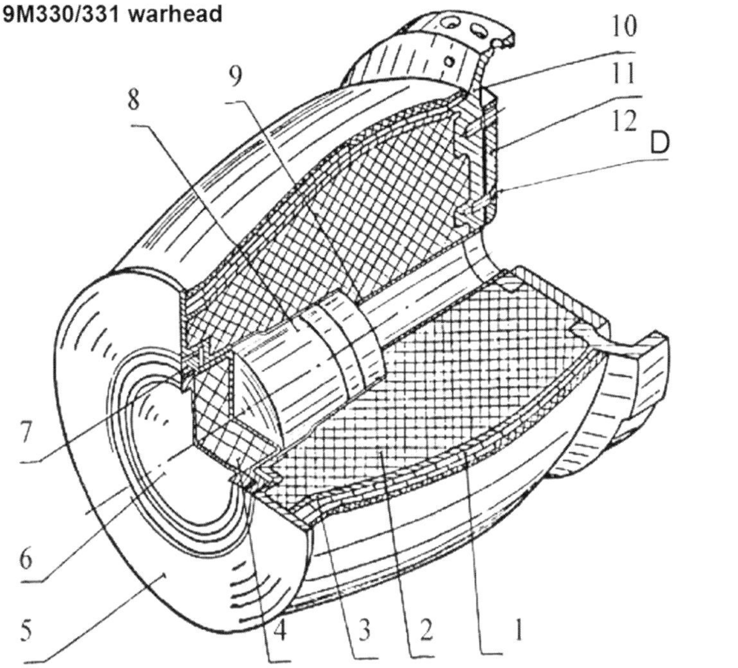

Figure 7-6: 9M330/331 warhead. (*Source:* Russian Air-Defence Systems)

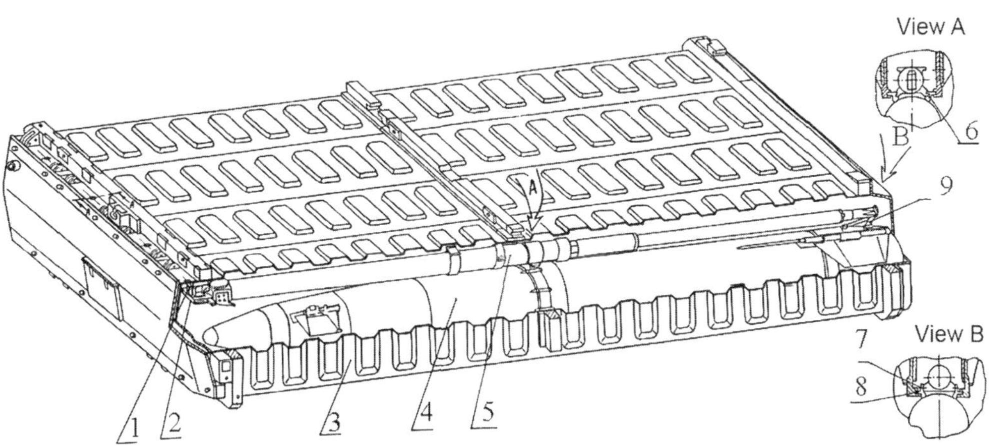

Figure 7-7: 9M334 missile transport and launch container.

mixed control of these batteries by an air defence division chief and air defence missile regiment commander was not ruled out.

Simultaneously with the adoption of the Tor system, work on its upgrade commenced. The Tor-M1 was the first improved version. It featured an additional second target channel, its missile carried a more effective warhead (Fig. 7-6), the engagement envelope and hit probabilities against low-flying targets were increased, etc. Also, for the first time in SAM system practice, a four-round transport-launch container was used instead of a launcher (Fig. 7-7).

Another distinctive feature of the Tor-M1 was the introduction of the 'Ranzhir' common battery commander post intended for automated control of its operations when it was used as part of an air defence missile regiment.

For the first time in a self-propelled system, the Tor and Tor-M1, capable of engaging aerial elements of PGMs, have repeatedly demonstrated their high combat capabilities during missile practice, field training exercises, and at weapons and military equipment exhibitions held in several countries worldwide (Fig. 7-2, 7-3).

The development and fielding of the Tor system and its upgraded versions have laid a solid foundation for effective engagement of the most sophisticated air threats on the battlefield. Today, this SAM system continues to improve.

The typical battery includes:

- 9A331 combat vehicle (CV) with 9M334 missile container module (9M331 missiles in the 9Y281launch container);
- 9T244 transport and loading machine;
- 9T245 transport vehicle;
- 9V887M and 9V888-1M maintenance vehicles;
- 9F116 mobile crane;
- 9F399-1M1 mobile maintenance shop;
- 9F678 autonomous combat simulator.

The 9A331 combat vehicle has the following main distinctive components (Fig. 7-3):

- two vertically-mounted 9M334 missile containers (four 9M331 missiles in each) (Fig. 7-7),
- 3D target-acquisition radar (TAR) – target-detection and tracking radar with a ground-based radar interrogator, and
- target tracking and missile guidance radar (TTR).

For the protection of stationary military objectives, as well as civilian and industrial facilities, modified versions of the basic system have been developed – towed container and wheeled versions. These modifications have the same tactical and technical characteristics but some limitations regarding mobility. These are cheaper than the basic self-propelled version.

Figure 7-8: Vertical launch with the missile deflection toward the target.

The Tor-M1 9A331 combat vehicle detects and selects air targets on the move and fires missiles at them from a short halt (Fig. 7-8). The newer version can do that while on the move.

The target acquisition radar (TAR) is a coherent-pulse circular radar. It works in the centimetre wave range with frequency control of the beam in elevation. The average transmitter power is 1.5 kW, the resolution is no less than 1.5–2.0° in azimuth, 4° in

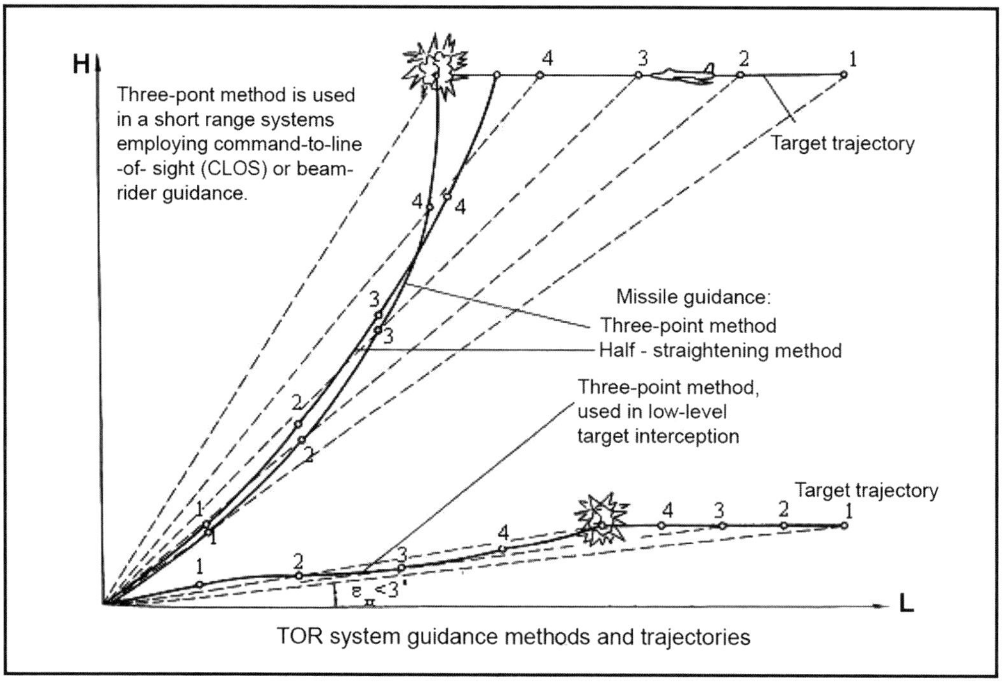

Missile trajectories for different guidance methods.

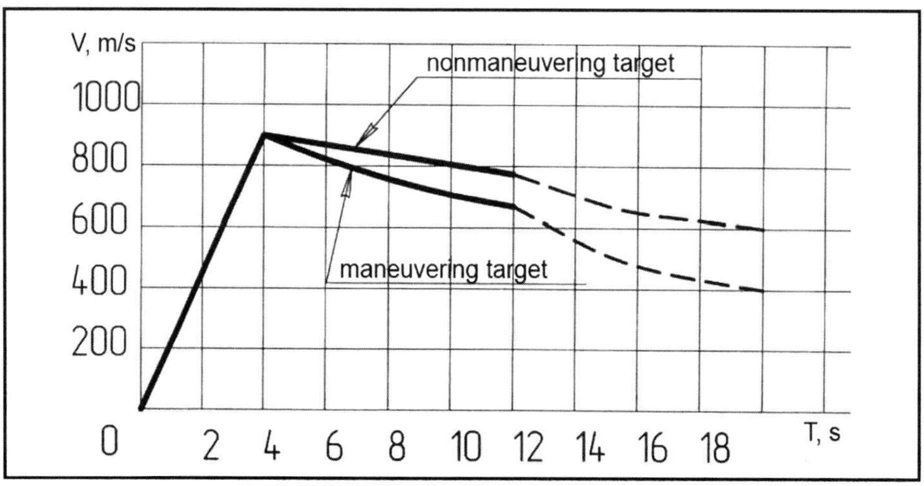

Missile velocity profile.

Figure 7-9: Guidance method (top) and velocity profile (bottom).

elevation and 200m in range. The maximum errors in determining the coordinates of the target are no more than half of the indicated resolution values.

There are two guidance methods applied to the system: 'half-way straightening' and 'three point'. Which method is selected depends of the target type and its parameters (speed, range, and angular position). When guided by the 'three-point' method, the missile, moving along a curved path, is constantly kept on the line of sight of the target. This guidance method is when the three points represents the target, the missile and the guidance station. When guided by the 'half-way straightening' method the movement of the missile at each moment of time is directed to the anticipated point of the interception of the target by the missile. As a result, the trajectory during guidance by this method is more 'straightened' and the required transverse overloads on the entire trajectory and at the interception point with the target are much smaller than

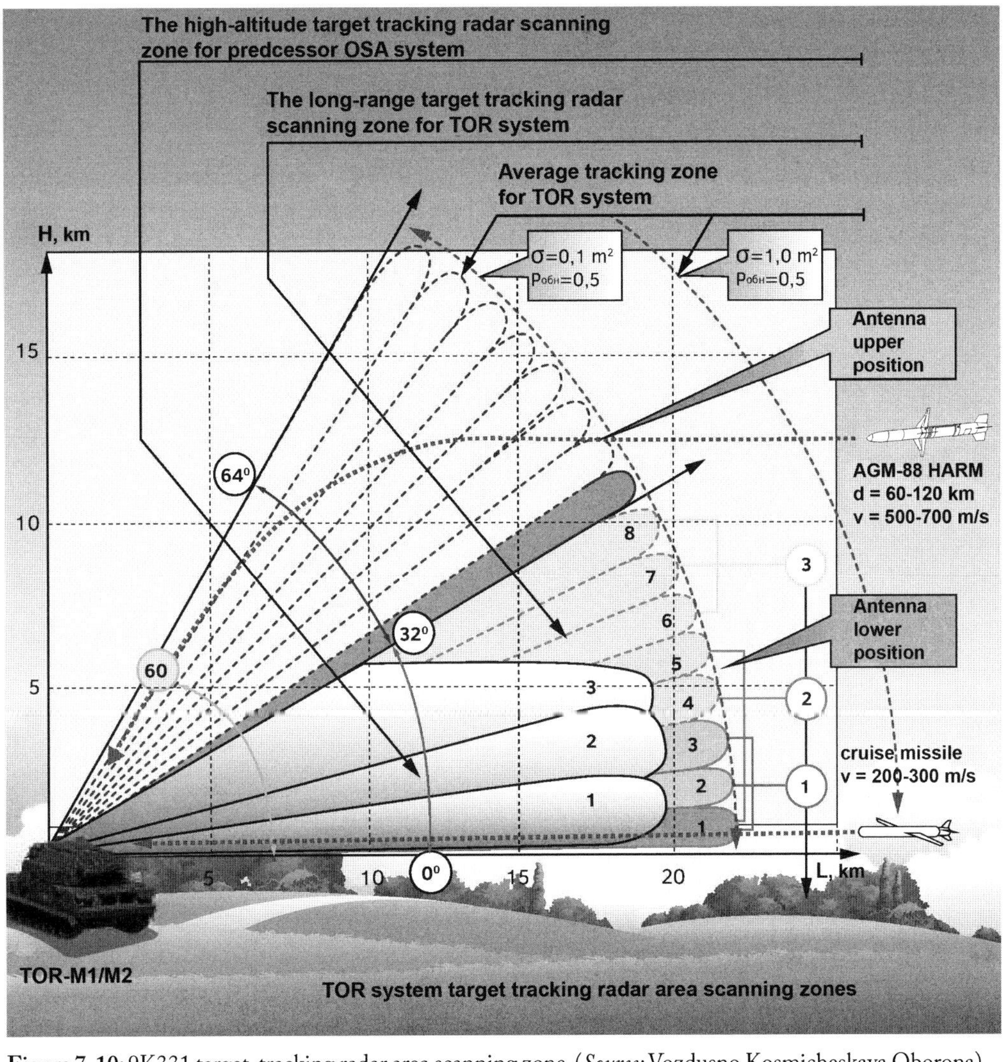

Figure 7-10: 9K331 target-tracking radar area scanning zone. (*Source:* Vozdusno Kosmicheskaya Oborona)

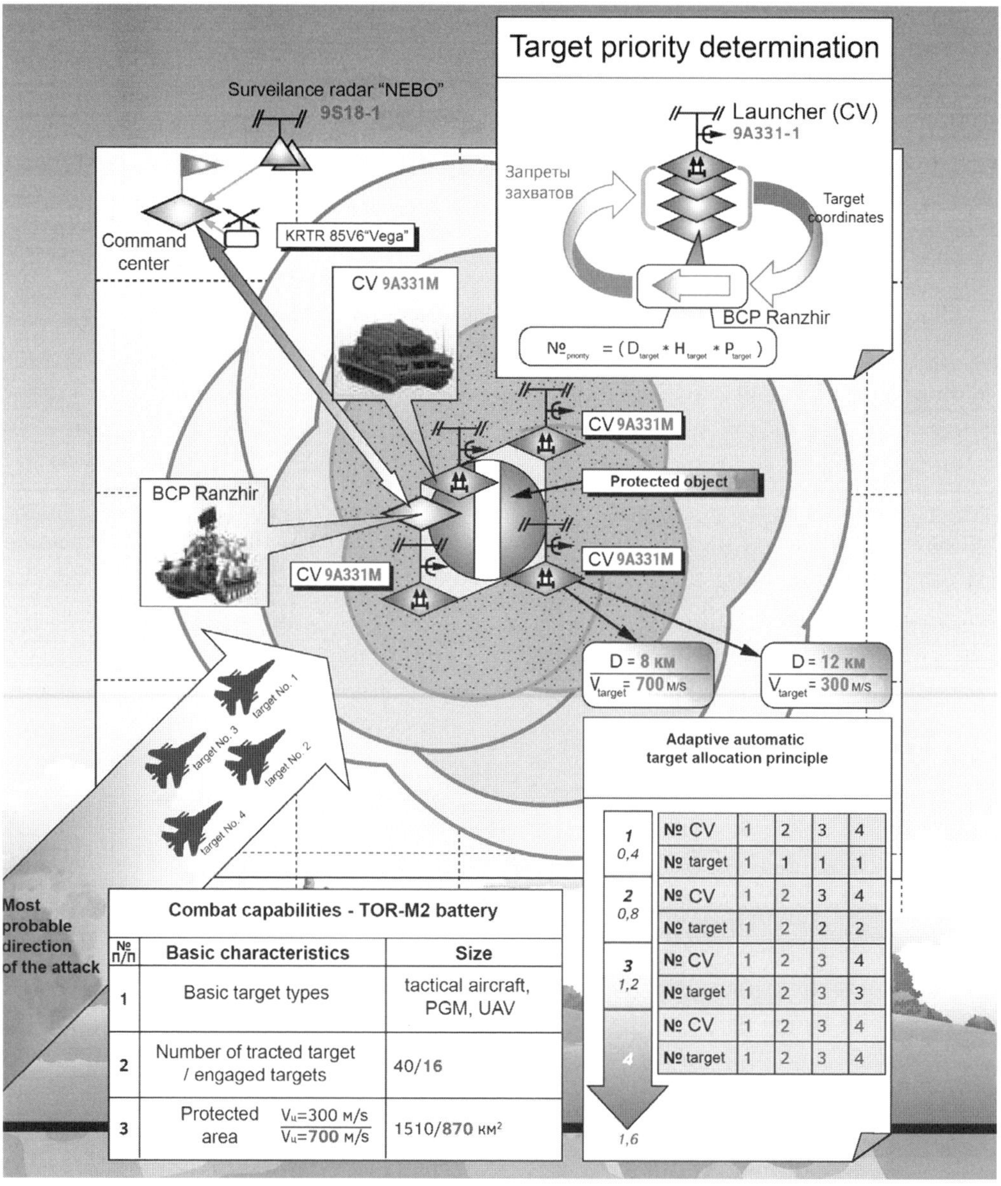

Figure 7-11: Target priority determination. The computer assets analyse detected targets, select the most dangerous targets for firing, and generate target data for the guidance station. (*Source:* Vozdusno Kosmicheskaya Oborona)

with the 'three-points' method (Fig. 7-9). The missile achieves maximum speed about 4 seconds after launch.

The antenna system of the TAR is stabilised. It produces an eight-portion battery command post radiation pattern (Fig. 7-10).

The scanning interval is 1 second, the beam flare (width) in the vertical plane is 4° and the portion switchover (scanning) mechanism is electronic. Any three portions of the radiation pattern can be scanned within one scanning interval. The entire elevation zone covers 32^0 and can be scanned within 3 seconds. The regular scanning programme is selected in such a way that, in order to increase the detection range for low-altitude targets, the first portion is scanned twice within three scanning intervals.

The station is capable of detecting an F-15 fighter flying at altitudes between 30m to 6,000m with a probability of at least P = 0.8 at a range of 25–27km; unmanned aerial vehicles with a probability of at least P = 0.7 at a range of 9–15km; hovering helicopters with a probability of P = 0.6–0.8 at a range of 13–20km; and helicopters on the ground with rotating rotors with a probability of P = 0.4–0.7 at a range of 13–20km.

The combat operation of the 9K331 air defence system takes place according to the scheme usual for anti-aircraft missile systems with a radio command guidance system. A detection station in motion or on the spot provides a circular overview of space, detects and identifies targets. The computer assets analyse detected targets, select the most dangerous targets for engagement, and generate target data for the guidance station (Fig. 7-11).

Four Tor combat vehicles (CV) are organic to one battery, which is the smallest tactical unit capable of executing combat missions independently. To control the combat actions and launch of the individual launchers, each SAM battery has a Ranzhir automated battery command post (BCP). Using coded communications and the navigation, survey control and orientation equipment of the CVs, the BCP produces target distribution

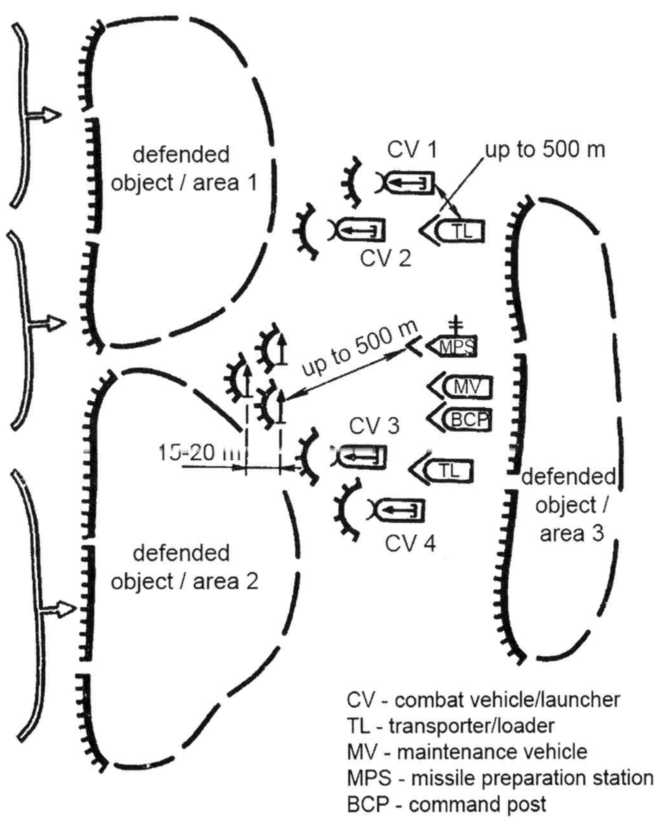

Figure 7-12: Tor missile battery in defence. Typical layout of the combat formation. This is applicable to other short-range mobile missile systems as well.

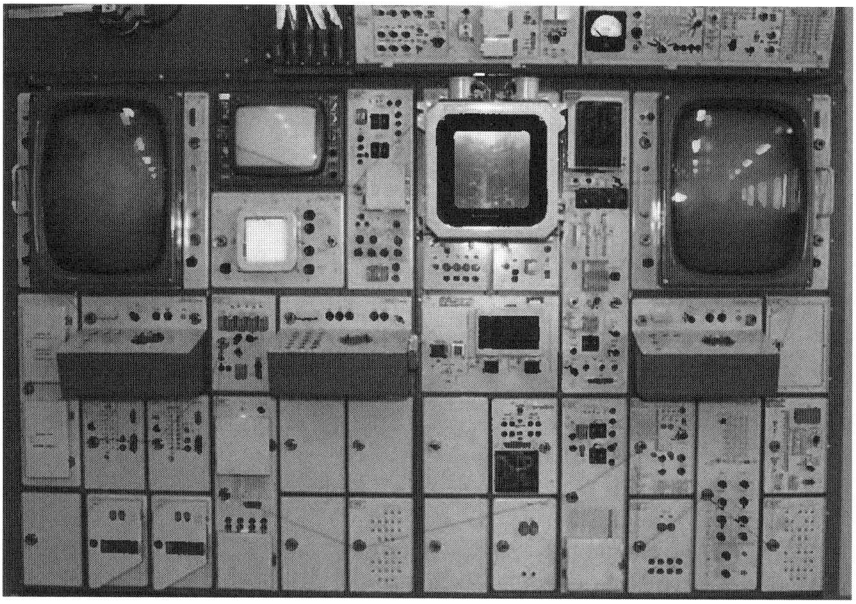

9F678 Operators training consoles. They are identical with the actual combat vehicle. Far left is the commander panoramic indicator, above right is the optical TV screen; bellow TV screen is the target distance tracking indicator above the operator station; screen in the middle is target tracking by angle indicator; right is the automatic tracking screen. Multiple scenarios can be simulated.

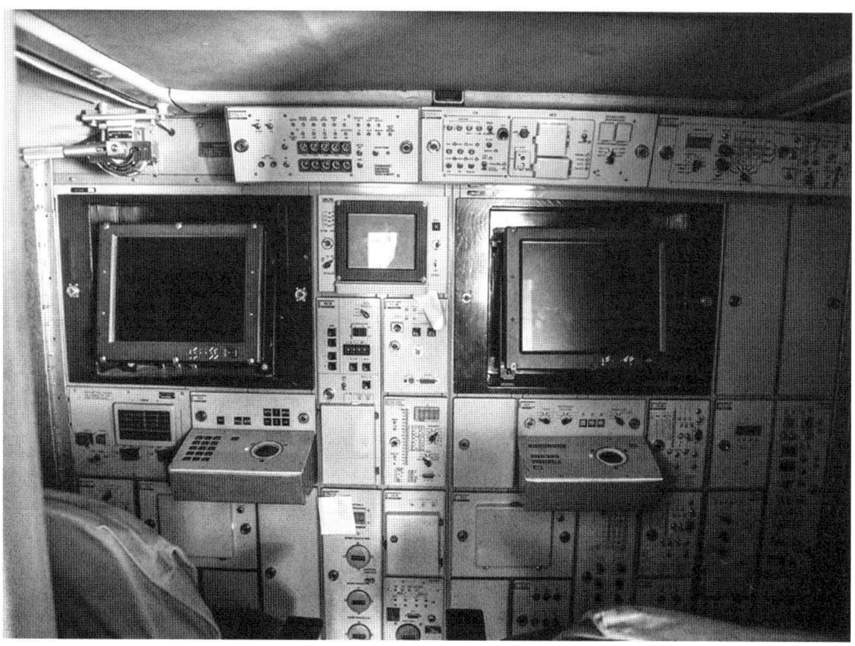

Fully digitalized workstations:
left - commander panoramic display;
middle - TV/optical tracking screen;
right - operator display for distance and angular target tracking and automatic by channel tracking (4 channels).

Figure 7-13: Tor-M1 (top) and Tor-M2 (bottom) interior (guidance station).

and precludes the accidental concentration of fire of several CVs on one target. The essence of target distribution resides in the automatic exchange of information on auto-tracked targets between the CVs via the BCP and automatic reassignment of priorities by the CVs with corrections made for received information. The target distribution system realises the step-by-step principle of adaptation of the CVs to the current air situation in real time. When necessary, the battery commander may intervene in the target-distribution process or execute other combat control tasks (Fig. 7-12).

The interior of the launcher (guidance portion) has evolved and has been modernised to include digital components (Fig. 7-13).

Tor System Variants

Some of the known Tor system variants which Russian ground forces had and still have include:

Tor, 9K330 – basic variant (phased out).

Tor M – improved basic version (in Ukrainian service, partially modernised).

Tor-M1, 9K331 – Tor M1 is a further improved version. It is based on a slightly different GM 5955 chassis and uses improved missiles. The Tor M1 is much more effective compared to the original Tor. It has a kill probability against aircraft of 45–80 per cent with a single missile. Its development was completed in 1989 and it entered service in 1991. It is equipped with a new two-processor computing subsystem. The TAR features an updated three-channel signal-processing subsystem. A few sub-variants have been developed: a containerised version, a towed version, and a wheeled version. They feature the same operational characteristics of the basic M1 system, except for mobility, and are also considerably cheaper than self-propelled versions.

Tor-M1T – this has been developed retaining all main performance characteristics to afford defence for static military and civilian facilities as well as troop-concentration areas against surprise mass air attacks. TOR-M1T is manufactured in three versions: wheeled, trailer and container mounted. These versions differ from each other only in the packaging of the combat vehicle systems. In the wheeled (self-propelled) version, Tor-M1TA is installed on the vehicle (equipment shelter) with a trailer (antenna-launch post). In the trailer mounted (towed) version, the Tor M1TB (Fig. 7-14) equipment shelter, and antenna-launch post are installed on two vehicle-towed trailers. In the container-mounted (stationary) version, all the Tor-M1TC elements are located in specially-design modular containers installed on the ground. The location of the Tor-M1T ADMS in two typical modules interconnected by cables expands the range of use of this system and scope of tasks it solves subject to the situation, and also improves the safety of the crew.

Tor-M2 – an upgraded M1 system which includes eight 9M331 or sixteen 9M338 missiles with increased altitude and range. Tor-M2 missiles have a range of 16km, maximum altitude of 10km and a maximum speed of 1000m/s. The system is capable

Figure 7-14: Tor M1TB. (*Source:* Air Defence Weapons and Electronic Systems of Russia)

Figure 7-15: Tor M2. Very different TAR antenna than earlier M1 version. (*Source: Vitaly Kuzmin*)

of firing from brief halts, which takes 2–3 seconds for the system to go from mobile to stationary and firing the missile (Fig. 7-15).

Tor-M2E – 9K332 – M2E (9M332ME). This is more effective against mass air attacks, and its firepower potential compared to the Tor-M1 is doubled. The combat vehicle is based on an off-road capable truck-type chassis. The Tor-M2E employs a new antenna wave waveguide system in the TAR, improved phased-array antenna in the TTR, and a Baget digital data computer with appropriate software and around-the-clock electro-optical target tracking system. It also uses a second channel for locking-in missiles, an improved data-processing system and new equipment and arrangement at the workstations (Fig. 7-16).

M2K – 9332MK is an export version, based on the Belarussian MZKT-6922 6x6 high-mobility wheeled chassis.

M2EK – the latest development with enhanced target engagement zone in the modular version, both independent and on a mobile chassis.

M2KM – 9M331MKM – also referred as Tor M2KM, is a modular system that can be accommodated on various chassis. It was revealed in 2013. The TELAR vehicle was based on an Indian Tata LPTA 3138 8 x 8 wheeled chassis but a Kamaz chassis can also be used.

Figure 7-16: M2E mounted on a truck chassis. (*Source:* Air Defence Weapons and Electronic Systems of Russia)

M1-2U – an improved version based on a tracked chassis. It can launch missiles while the TEL is on the move. The system is able to engage four targets simultaneously at an altitude of up to 10km. It was adopted by the Russian Army in 2012.

3K95 – Kinzhal – Naval Tor SA-N-9 – shipborne air defence system developed alongside Tor with which it has a number of interchangeable components. It entered service with the Soviet Navy in 1989, installed on some Soviet warships, notably the *Kuznetsov* class aircraft carrier, *Kirov* class cruisers, *Udaloy* class destroyers and *Neustrashymij* class frigates. The system was also retrofitted to some older ships.

M2TDT – specially designed to be used in Arctic regions at temperatures up to –50^{0} C. It is based on the chassis of the DT-30PM tracked all-terrain vehicle and is capable of detecting over forty air targets, especially PGMs, and to track and engage up to four of them simultaneously at a range of up to 12km and altitudes up to 10km with its sixteen missiles even on the move. Its development was completed in 2018 and the first delivery of twelve systems was made in November of the same year. This version is also nicknamed 'The Arctic Tor' (Fig. 7-17).

Tor-2E – an independent, mobile, all-terrain fighting unit that provides detection and identification of air targets on the march and at the halt, target lock-on and engagement at the halt, from a short stop, and on the move. A battery of the four-channel Tor-E2 system, consisting of four combat vehicles, can simultaneously engage up to sixteen targets flying from any direction at a range of at least 15km and an altitude of up to 12km. Each vehicle carries sixteen missiles, twice as many as previous versions. In addition, the two Tor-E2 combat vehicles can operate in the 'link' mode, which enables them to exchange information about the air situation at different altitudes and ranges and coordinate joint engagement operations. In this mode, one of the combat vehicles, acting from an ambush, receives information from the other one and does not reveal itself until the launch of the

Figure 7-17: Tor-M2TDT or 'Arctic Tor', based on the DT-30PM chassis. (*Source: Kupol*)

missile. A command post can be attached to a battery of four Tor-2E combat vehicles to control and coordinate them and interact with the air defence control system

Tor in Combat

Tor systems have seen use in combat. The first engagement is in the ongoing war in Syria. One battery provides short-range air defence for the Russian Khmeimim base in Latakia province. According to the Russian sources, so far it has engaged and destroyed at least forty-five drones launched by the militants. This is a very good example how this system can provide close protection for the S-400 and Pantsir-S systems (Fig. 7-18).

In the war in Ukraine, Tor provides AD for the motorised units. As the war is ongoing (at the time of writing) limited information is available about it efficiency. There are some reports of numerous engagements against drones (for example, one launcher claimed twelve drones and three helicopters in the first three months of combat). Tor's service in the Russian military will be discussed in detail in the book *Missiles and Rockets Over Ukraine* by the same author.

Figure 7-18: Tor-M2 at the Russian base in Khmeimim (Syria).

Chapter 8

Gun and Missile Systems, and Point Defence

2K22 Tunguska (SA-19 'Grison')

In 1973, the Central Committee and the USSR Council of Ministers passed a resolution to develop a detailed design and a prototype of the Tunguska self-propelled anti-aircraft gun (SPAAG). However, assessments made at the Instrument Design Bureau (KBP) at this time showed that the maximum efficiency of a new battlefield short-range air defence system could only be achieved with combined gun and missile armament. In this case, missiles had to be used to fire at air targets throughout the entire engagement envelope, while guns had to be employed to engage targets like aircraft flying at extremely low altitudes and helicopters suddenly emerging from behind cover at close range. In addition, it was appropriate to use guns to destroy cheap and numerous targets like UAVs and ground targets, due to the low cost of ammunition.

In 1975 this concept was approved and the performance specifications for the Tunguska (Fig. 8-1), equipped with both gun and missile armament, together with an optical sighting and radio remote control system for the SAMs, were finalised.

As a result, the key feature of the Tunguska, compared to existing AA systems, was that one combat vehicle mounted gun and missile armament, radar and optical detection, tracking and fire-control instruments using common equipment to support gun fire and missile guidance, target-acquisition radar, target-tracking radar, ground receiver/interrogator, optical sighting equipment, a digital computing system and laying drives. The Tunguska was to be armed with two liquid-cooled 30mm automatic cannon with ammunition load and the missile component was eight 9M311 missiles in transport and launch containers. The range of the guns was to be 3.5–4km; the missiles up to 8km. The Tunguska gun-missile system was to be the world's first twin-echelon self-propelled short-range air defence system.

KBP's development efforts on the 9M311 missile produced a single-stage SAM of an unrivalled bi-calibre configuration, with a separable booster and an unpowered sustainer stage. Such a layout ensured the extremely high performance of the missile. Thus, the absence of a motor in the sustainer stage eliminated smoke blocking the line of sight to the target, ensuring reliable and accurate guidance of the missile, reducing its weight and dimensions, and simplifying the layout of onboard equipment and the incorporation of the warhead into the design. This was also aided by the use of passive aerodynamic damping of the missile airframe during flight, provided by a control loop correction through sending commands to the missile from the SAM system's computer.

Figure 8-1: Tunguska-M 30mm automatic cannon firing. (*Source:* Air Defence Weapons and Electronic Systems of Russia)

In general, the use of the two-stage layout helped nearly halve the weight of the missile compared to a single-stage SAM and achieve higher ballistic characteristics. Along with KBP, the Tunguska programme also involved the Ulyanovsk Mechanical Plant, the Leningrad Optical and Mechanical Association (LOMO), the National Research University of Electronic Technology Design Bureau, the Kovrov-based Signal Research Institute, the Kirov-based Mayak Engineering Plant, the Izyum Instrument Plant, the Minsk Tractor Plant, etc.

The official tests of the SAM system began in September 1980. On 8 September 1982, the 2K22 Tunguska entered service. In the second half of 1990, an upgraded version, the Tunguska-M (2K22M), underwent tests. The basic improvements included the introduction of new radio sets and a receiver for communications with the Pantsir battery command post (PU-12M) and the PPRU-1M command post, as well as the replacement of a gas-turbine engine (part of the SAM system's power unit) with a new one with twice the service life.

In the process of further upgrades on the Tunguska, the vehicle received equipment for automated acquisition and processing of external targeting data from the 9S80 mobile control and reconnaissance post. This allowed automatic allocation of targets among the combat vehicles and significantly improved the effectiveness of the gun-missile battery when repelling a large-scale air raid. Upgrading Tunguska's digital computing system through the use of a new computer has expanded its capabilities to handle combat and monitoring tasks and also increased accuracy. In addition, a relief circuit was introduced that greatly facilitated the gunner's work in optical tracking of a moving aerial target.

The following components were added to the combat vehicle's equipment set: equipment for automated acquisition and processing of external targeting data coming from the battery command post, infrared missile locator-missile coordinate generation equipment, a new computer having higher speed and larger memory, and an improved rolling angle measurement system. Missile improvement was another focus of upgrade efforts. The upgraded missile received the designation 9M311-1M. Its sustainer stage was equipped with a continuous/pulsed light source. The missile equipment was also modified – its immunity while engaging targets that used optical jamming was increased, and the laser proximity sensor was replaced by a radar sensor with a circular antenna. All the above has increased the engagement range of the SAM system up to 10km, improved the immunity of the optical link in the missile control system and provided assured engagement of small targets like cruise missiles.

The high combat and operational capabilities of the Tunguska have been repeatedly confirmed during exercises and combat firing practice. The SAM system was repeatedly displayed at international military equipment exhibitions. Tunguska-M1 is designed to provide air defence both for land forces subunits in all types of combat engagements and for defence of fixed positions.

Tunguska-M1 is a modern short-range mobile air defence missile/gun complex that can engage aircraft, helicopters (including hovering ones), and other low-flying targets while on the move, at short halts, and while stationary, as well as ground targets.

Each launcher incorporates:

- combat assets,
- maintenance equipment, and
- training equipment.

A Tunguska-M1 battery includes:

- up to six 2S6M1 self-propelled platforms,
- 9M311-1M SAMs in container-launchers, eight per vehicle, and
- 30mm ZUOF8 rounds with a high-explosive incendiary projectile and 30mm ZUOR6 explosive tracer rounds.

Maintenance equipment includes:

- ADMGC maintenance and repair equipment and integrated automated missile test facilities, and
- facilities for temporary storage and transportation of missiles and gun rounds and loading of the self-propelled gun mounts.

The upgrade of Tunguska-M1 2S6M1 (Fig. 8-2) combat vehicle includes:

- full-time TV thermal imaging system with an automatic target tracker based on the targeting and optical equipment, and
- upgrade of the target-acquisition radar.

The Tunguska-M vehicle can be upgraded to M1 standard with:

- the automated external target designation equipment.
- updates for the turret, radar units, tracked chassis and the operational documentation,

Figure 8-2: Tunguska M1 gun/missile system. (*Source:* Air Defence Weapons and Electronic Systems of Russia)

- updates and replacements in the central computer system, targeting and optical equipment, radio command coder unit, automatic AA guns, motion-angle measuring system and cables, and
- modifications of the maintenance and repair facilities.

Tunguska-M1 can operate from a stationary position, at short halts and on the move. According to expert analyses, it has no equivalent in similar systems measured by the effectiveness of defence it provides for the army units on march and for stationary facilities against air attack weapons flying at low altitudes.

Point Defence and MANPADS

9K31 Strela-1 (SA-8 'Gaskin')

Development work on a light self-propelled surface-to-air missile system designated Strela-1 (Arrow) began following the USSR Council of Ministers' Resolution of 25 August 1960. The Moscow-based OKB-16 Design Bureau (Precision Engineering Design Bureau known also as KB TochMash) headed by A.E. Nudelman was its prime developer.

Unlike other similar systems, the 9M31 missile, which was developed for the Strela-1, used a photo-contrast seeker, which ensured target selection in the forward hemisphere, allowing head-on engagements. In this case, the Strela-1 with its engagement envelope of up to 5km in range and up to 3.5km in altitude fitted well into a regimental-level battlefield air defence system, which was under development, supplementing the Shilka SPAAG. Each combat vehicle, based on a BRDM-2 wheeled chassis, was equipped with a launcher carrying four missiles in transport-launch containers, missile-launching equipment and optical detection and aiming devices, as well as communications equipment.

With the 9M31M missile, the maximum engagement range was about 4.2km up to 3,500m altitude. The weight of the missile was 32kg. The warhead weight was only 2.6kg but it had a proximity fuze, unlike the contemporary 9K32 Strela-2 MANPAD. The official tests of the Strela-1 SAM system were carried out in 1967–8 and on 25 April 1968, it was adopted.

In 1968–70, the system underwent its first upgrade and received the designation Strela-1M. At the same time, a passive radio direction-finder was introduced into the system, providing target detection with on-board radio equipment, and target tracking and input into the field of view of the optical sight. This reduced the minimum engagement range of the system and increased homing accuracy and the target kill probability at low altitudes.

Later, the Strela-1 and Strela-1M systems were widely exported and supplied to dozens of states, where they repeatedly proved their high effectiveness and ease of use both in trials and in combat.

9K35 Strela-10 (SA-13 'Gopher')

The further evolution of the Strela-1 resulted in different versions of the Strela-10 SAM system. Building such simple non-all-weather systems was reasonable, both for economic and tactical reasons, as a supplement to more expensive battlefield SAM systems.

Tests of the first variant of this system, the Strela-10SV (9K35), were conducted in 1973–4. It became operational on 16 March 1976. It was mounted on a MT-LB multi-purpose tracked vehicle. In addition to the photo-contrast channel, the 9M37 missile used an infrared channel, which helped increase the effectiveness of the system in head-on and tail-chase engagements and also in a jamming environment. Moreover, its engagement area reached a range of 5km, with the launch weight of the missile being 40kg.

In 1977, the system saw another upgrade designated Strela-10M (9K35M). It received improved missile launching equipment on the combat vehicles and an advanced missile seeker, which became capable of discriminating targets in optical jamming. This version of the SAM system was fielded in 1979. Another few upgrades of the SAM system were carried out in the 1980s. The first of these, the Strela-10M2, entered service in 1981, the second, the Strela-10M3, in 1989 (Fig. 8-3).

The Strela-10M3 (9K35M3) SAM system featured a larger engagement envelope and higher efficiency and immunity in a severe optical jamming environment (at optical target visibility), and could engage all types of low-flying air targets (aircraft, helicopters, cruise missiles and UAVs). Combat vehicles of this SAM system were equipped with a new optical sight having two channels with a variable field of view, as well as improved missile-launching equipment, which allowed a more reliable target lock-on.

Figure 8-3: Strela-10M3.

For its 9M333 missile, the propulsion system and transport-launch container was modified and a new three-channel seeker was introduced which comprised photo-contrast, infrared and 'jamming' channels, with the latter providing target discrimination in an optical jamming environment. The 9M333, 9M37M and 9M37MD missiles could be used with all versions of Strela-10.

Like the Strela-1, various versions of the Strela-10 were delivered to several foreign countries and were widely used in armed conflicts in the Middle East and Africa and recently in Ukraine. The system is intended for the protection of army units in both static positions and on the march, against air threats and reconnaissance assets flying at low and extremely low altitudes.

The objective of the upgrade was to provide operational capability in the daytime and at night and under conditions of low visibility and also to realise the performance of autonomous automatic sector target search. It is achieved by the inclusion of the thermal-imaging system, automatic target acquisition and tracking unit and scanner. The spectral range of thermal imaging channel comes to 3–5 μm and corresponds with the spectral range of 9M333 (9M37M, 9M37MD) SAM seekers.

The photo contrast channel (also used by the Strela-1M) did not require cooling and could be used against both incoming and departing targets but was not protected against natural optical interference (heavy clouds with strong contrast, for example). The IR channel required prior cooling and could be used only against departing targets, but it was effective against natural optical interference (because the 9M37 missile used a PbS detector with IR guidance it was not possible to perform a lock-on against an incoming target).

The parabolic antenna between the missile containers is the target distance meter/rangefinder radar. While the Strela-1 relied solely on the human eye to determine whether the target was in the engagement zone, for the Strela-10M this additional equipment was provided. The millimetre-wave rangefinder radar provided firing-zone and lead-angle calculation.

The 9M37 missile is a bit heavier than the 9M31M (40kg vs 32kg) and has a slightly larger warhead (3kg vs. 2.6kg). It is equipped with a proximity fuze. The vehicle carries four missiles ready to launch and four more reloads inside the hull. The maximum engagement range is 5km for up to 3,500m altitude. The system can engage incoming targets with a maximum speed of 415m/s, and departing ones at 310m/s.

Strela-10 has received many upgrades since its introduction, as well as other SAM systems. While the 9M37M had only IR/photo contrast guidance with a 9E47 type guidance section, it was replaced with the 9M333 variant which was also fitted to R-27T/ET (AA-10B/D Alamo) air-to-air missiles. The missile received a laser proximity fuze making it more effective against targets with a small radar cross-section. The latest Strela-10M (M4) variant is equipped with a night-vision camera and the target coordinates can be provided via digital datalink so the target can be tracked.

Sosna

Developed by the same design bureau as the Strela system, Sosna is a successor to 9K35 Strela-10, and is a cheaper alternative to the Tor missile system for army air defence as well as Pantsir-S1 for the aerospace defence forces.

Designed to work in passive mode utilising different imaging systems such as a thermal camera, an optical TV camera and a laser rangefinder in order to find and engage targets, Sosna-R is able to operate effectively under the control of various types of old, modern and planned battery command posts, the most preferable of which is the FPU 'Assembly-M1-2' (9S80M1-2), and is resistant to jamming. It uses a tracked SAM launcher with twelve missiles with a maximum engagement range of 10km and altitude of 10km. During the development phase initial launcher was based on the MT-LB vehicle (similar to Strela-10). It is equipped with twelve missiles that can be reloaded in 12 minutes. The serial production version is based on the BMP-3 IFV. The Sosna can also deliver fire while on the move. The system has a crew of two: the driver and operator (Fig. 8-4).

The system is armed with 9M340 missiles in their transport-launch containers and arranged in two banks of six. The missile is two-stage type, weight 38kg, utilising beam-rider guidance and is capable of engaging and destroying aircraft, helicopters, cruise missiles, guided bombs, small-sized air attack weapons including elements of high-precision weapons, and light armoured vehicles. It also has a combined impact/proximity laser fuze. Its payload is made up of two warheads weighing a total of 7kg.

Figure 8-4: Sosna. (*Source:* Air Defence Weapons and Electronic Systems of Russia)

The fragmented-rod warhead is designed for proximity detonation when flying close to the target, while the armour-piercing/fragmentation (AP-Frag) warhead goes off on impact. The system has high resistance to jamming and besides its passive mode of operation it can be equipped with an additional small-size acquisition radar.

The new Palma AAA system developed from Sosna features integrated armament that comprises eight Sosna-R precision surface-to-air missiles with laser beam guidance and two AO-18KDE rapid-fire guns. As a defence component, the Palma is designated to defend both ships and naval bases, coastal infrastructure, airbases and other vital facilities.

Self-Propelled Anti-Aircraft Guns (SPAAGs)

ZSU 23/4 Shilka

Development of the ZSU-23/4 Shilka (Fig. 8-5) SPAAG began on 17 April 1957. This rapid-fire SPAAG was to provide effective air defence of infantry units against low-flying aircraft and helicopters in different combat situations, including on the march, at any time and in all weather conditions. The Shilka programme involved a team of enterprises led by the chief designer of the chassis and mount N.A. Astrov (Mytishchi Engineering Plant's OKB-40 Design Bureau).

Figure 8-5: ZSU 23/4 Shilka. (*Source:* Air Defence Weapons and Electronic Systems of Russia)

Among the most significant innovations implemented in the programme was the use of an acquisition and guidance radar from LOMO and the Tula Radio Components Plant's Design Bureau (currently NII Strela Research Institute).

The Tula-based TsKB-14 (KBP Instrument Design Bureau) developed the 2A7 autocannon for use in the Shilka, which was a modification of the 2A14 autocannon used in the ZU-23 AA gun mount. A water-cooling jacket, an air charger and an electric trigger were introduced into the 2A14 design. The service life of the autocannon was 3,000 shots, and the rate of fire of the four autocannons reached 3,800 rounds per minute. The first Shilka prototype intended for field testing was completed in December 1960. The official tests were conducted between 26 August and 24 October 1961. The statement of their completion noted: '. . . In terms of firing effectiveness, one Shilka is superior to a battery of four 14.5mm ZPU-4 AA guns and a battery of six 37mm Model 1939 automatic AA guns'. A year later, on 5 September 1962, the new SPAAG entered service under the designation ZSU-23-4 Shilka and its series production was launched at the Ulyanovsk Mechanical Plant. Its development was a big success for Soviet designers. At that time none of the foreign armies had anything like it. Soon the Shilka became increasingly known not only as an independent fire unit but also as part of air defence missile/gun groups.

It was used in this role for the first time in the late 1960s in the Middle East, when small-calibre AA artillery and primarily Shilka SPAAGs began to be used for providing close-in air defence cover for SAM battalions to ensure the required survivability of air defence missile groups. The disposition of SPAAGs was selected with due regard to the terrain and tactics already demonstrated by the Israeli air force. The Shilkas were placed 400–800m from the centre of a SAM site for immediate protection of the SAM battalion from low-altitude attacks.

When six SPAAGs were allocated for this mission, three of them were at 1.5–3.5km from the SAM battalion along the most probable directions of Israeli air attacks. Such an arrangement provided simultaneous engagement of the target by several guns at once. This tactic proved very effective. The emergence of Shilka guns forced the Israeli aircraft to fly at medium altitudes. At the same time, for aircraft the mission over target time became minimal and almost did not exceed 1.5–2 minutes and the accuracy of target approach and bombing decreased. The Shilka also proved to be a highly mobile vehicle offering a good cross-country capacity in the desert and mountainous terrain. The Shilka was capable of firing on the move. The chassis of the ZSU-23/4 is the same as the PT-76 amphibious recon tank but the ZSU-23 does not have amphibious capability.

The fire-control radar operate on a 2cm wavelength and it can detect a MiG-21 size target from about 13km, the maximal possible target tracking range being 20km. The fire-control system can perform target acquisition but only in sector-search mode and with very limited capability because the pencil beam is only 2° wide. During target acquisition, the pencil beam of the antenna mechanically scans a degree sector vertically (elevation). The system is most efficient when it gets coordinates from the 9S482

BTR-60 PU-12 mobile air defence command post via radio. The CP receives the coordinates from higher-level radars via a digital datalink.

During the most intense Israeli air raids, from 29 June to 3 August 1970, the Shilka guns were actively used to cover missile battalions deployed east of Cairo, having proved themselves as a simple and effective weapon, especially for countering pop-up low-flying air targets. During this period, Shilkas conducted seven engagements, resulting in two damaged aircraft. One of them was damaged on 3 August 1970 in the Suez Canal area, where two SPAAGs located at 1.5–3.5km from a missile battalion fired on three surprised targets and forced them to abandon bombing. Shilkas were used also in all the subsequent armed conflicts in the Middle East. On 7 October 1973, one shot down two Israeli Phantoms. In October 1973, they downed a total of eleven planes. In the spring of 1974, they were responsible for another five aircraft. Nowadays, Shilka is considered outdated but still can found in use in many countries. Even in the recent Russian-Ukrainian war, Shilkas have been observed on both sides. Beside the original role, these guns have been proven in urban combat.

2S38 Derivatsiya

The 2S38 Derivatsiya (Fig. 8-6) is a new-generation SPAAG system relying on a tracked, lightly armoured vehicle with a fast-firing 57mm automatic gun. It has been developed by Uralvagonzavod of Nizhny Tagil, to meet a military demand for a lightweight, low-level self-propelled airspace denial system.

The novelty of the 2S38 is that it relies on the gun of a much larger calibre than the 30mm of other systems. Smaller-calibre weapons do not have sufficient range and

Figure 8-6: 2S38 Derivatsiya.

are not that effective against present-day armoured targets, but the principal advantage enjoyed by the 57mm is the gun's guided-projectile ammunition. The development of the round was far more difficult than developing a similar round for the 152mm Koalitsiya-SV SP howitzer.

Tochmash developed its guided projectile for the Burevestnik improved artillery system based on the S-60 gun. The guided projectile's airframe has a canard aerodynamic configuration. The round is loaded and fired in the same manner that 'dumb' rounds are. The projectile has four wings folded in the casing and controlled by the actuator in the projectile's nose section, using the energy of the airflow. The laser sensor for guided the projectile to its target is in its rear and covered by a sabot that separates in flight.

The warhead weighs 2kg, with 400g being the weight of the high explosive, which corresponds to that of the HE of the organic 76mm artillery projectile. A proximity fuze-equipped multifunction projectile is being developed for the ZAK-57[1] Derivatsiya that will be able to fire ordinary 57mm fragmentation/tracer and armour-piercing rounds as well. The guided projectile is fired via the rifled barrel toward the target or to a calculated set-forward point and is laser guided. Its range is between 200m and 6–8km against manned aircraft and 3–5km against UAVs (Fig. 8-7).

The ZAK-57 has a TV/thermal-imaging system to acquire and track targets and to cue projectiles to them. The system has automatic target lock-on and tracking capabilities, a laser rangefinder and a laser guidance system. The electro-optical control system affords the SPAAG round-the-clock all-weather operating capability. The Derivatsiya can fire both on the move and at the halt. The gun has a high rate of fire – 120 rounds per minute. The process of repelling air attacks is completely automatic from target acquisition to round selection to firing. The gun's elevation varies from -5° to +75°. The Derivatsiya-PVO reaches targets at an altitude of 4.5km and eliminates lightly armoured ground

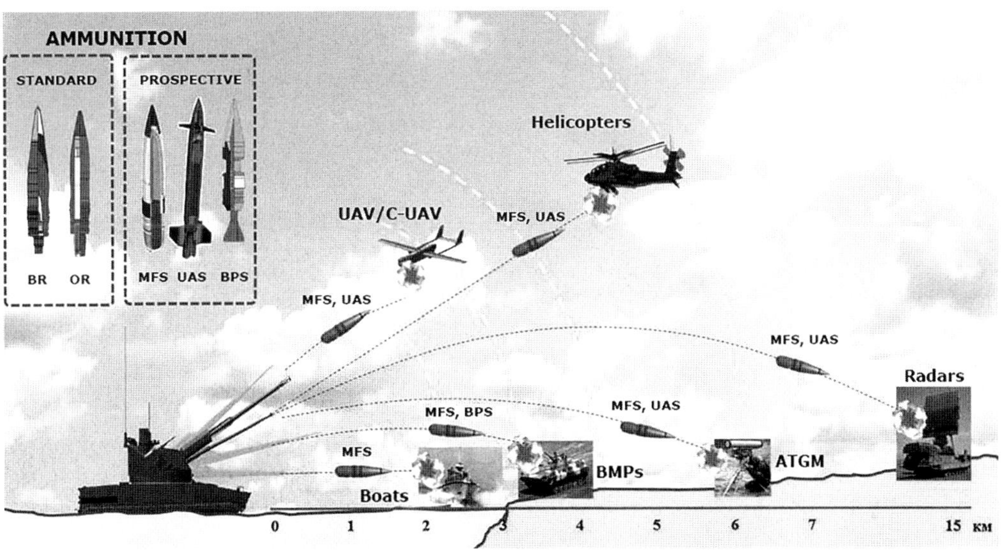

Figure 8-7: 2S38 engagements.

vehicles at a range of 3km. The SPAAG's strengths include its low weight – just over 20 tons – which contributes to its high mobility, off-road capability, speed and buoyancy.

For decades, the Russian Armed Forces have used either SAM systems or SPAAG/M systems with the gun being supplemented with SAMs in the short-range air defence role. They are the Tunguska and Pantsir-S1. The Derivatsiya is more effective than the smaller-calibre rapid-fire guns of both systems. The hull is based on the late-model BMP-3 series infantry fighting vehicle (IFV) which is proven for cross-country mobility and general road travel. The general shape of the hull is consistent with the low-profile BMP series as a whole: a near-horizontal glacis plate at the bow, flat roof line on the hull, and flat sides and rear panels. Armour protection is up to small-arms fire and artillery fragments with attention given to mine absorption underneath. An unmanned remote-controlled turret sits atop the vehicle hull with full 360° traverse as well as an undisclosed elevation span.

The driver sits front left in the hull with the vehicle commander to his right. The powerpack is at the rear of the hull. Six double-tyred road wheels are on each hull side with the drive sprocket at the front and the track idler at the rear. Three track-return rollers are fitted and protected by side 'skirt' armour.

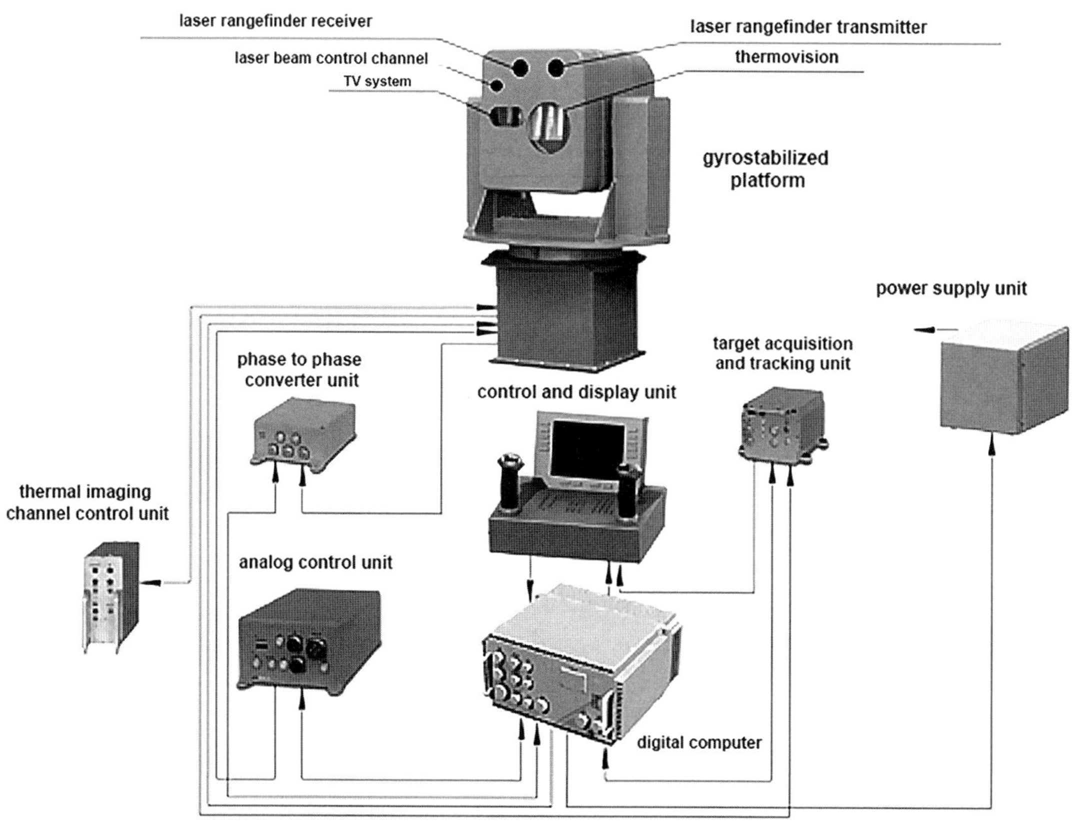

Figure 8-8: 2S38 fire-control system.

The vehicle is armed with a single, rapid-fire, high-angle 57mm S-60 autocannon. An independently-operated 7.62mm machine gun is installed along the right side of the turret with its own separate elevation capability. Twelve smoke-grenade dischargers provide the vehicle with a self-screening measure – all of these launchers are contained on the turret. The primary weapon is based in the towed form of the AZP S-60 single-barrelled AAA gun system and is proven against low-flying targets, light armoured vehicles, and other 'soft' targets to be found on the battlefield. The crew has access to High-Explosive, FRAGmentation (HE-FRAG) rounds for soft targets and Armour-Piercing (AP) rounds for armoured targets. Both types are said to have a guided mode for accuracy-at-range and remote fuze-setting for precise, controlled detonation of individual rounds (Fig. 8-7, 8-8).

MANPADS

9K32 Strela-2 (SA-7 'Grail')

In the early 1960s existing missile systems were slow to deploy to combat formations. This was the gap the attack aircraft could exploit. There was no 'point' defence missile protection for the 'big players' especially at extremely low altitudes. This also applied to smaller tactical units and military installations. Because of this, the idea of a man-portable air defence missile system (MANPAD) arose. The USSR Council of Ministers' Resolution 946-398 of 25 August 1960 tasked the Kolomna KBM Engineering Design Bureau to develop the first Soviet MANPAD named Strela-2, officially designated as 9M32 (Fig. 8-9, 8-10). The basic idea was for a shoulder-launched short-range infra-red guided missile. This work began with a series of brainstorming sessions that involved leading engineers of the design bureau led by S.P. Nepobedimy. As a consequence, the first of its kind in the Soviet MANPAD category was developed in the 1960s and entered in service in 1969. It was quickly followed by the improved Strela-2M.

A canard aerodynamic layout was chosen for the missile, with the control surfaces placed in only one plane, while control of missile attitude was done by deflecting the control surfaces in concert with the angular position of the missile. To place the missile inside the launch tube, the control surfaces retracted into the missile airframe, while the fins were folded behind the missile. Once the missile left the launch tube, its control surfaces and fins unfolded and were locked by spring devices.

After activating the power supply to the missile, aiming can be performed. The lock-on of the IR seeker to the target is indicated by a buzz indicating that the missile is ready for launch. The missile's uncooled lead sulphide (PbS) passive infra-red frequency modulated seeker head detects infrared radiation at and slightly below 2.8μm in wavelength. It has a 1.9° field of view and can track at 9° per second. The seeker restricted the Strela-2 only to tail-on engagements and also had very limited effectiveness against helicopters.

The 9K32 has a maximum engagement range of 3.7km up to 1,500m altitude, the upgraded 9K32M 4.2km and 2,300m respectively; the maximum target speed is 220–260 m/s against departing targets. Maximum speed is 420m/s and 500m/s for the upgraded

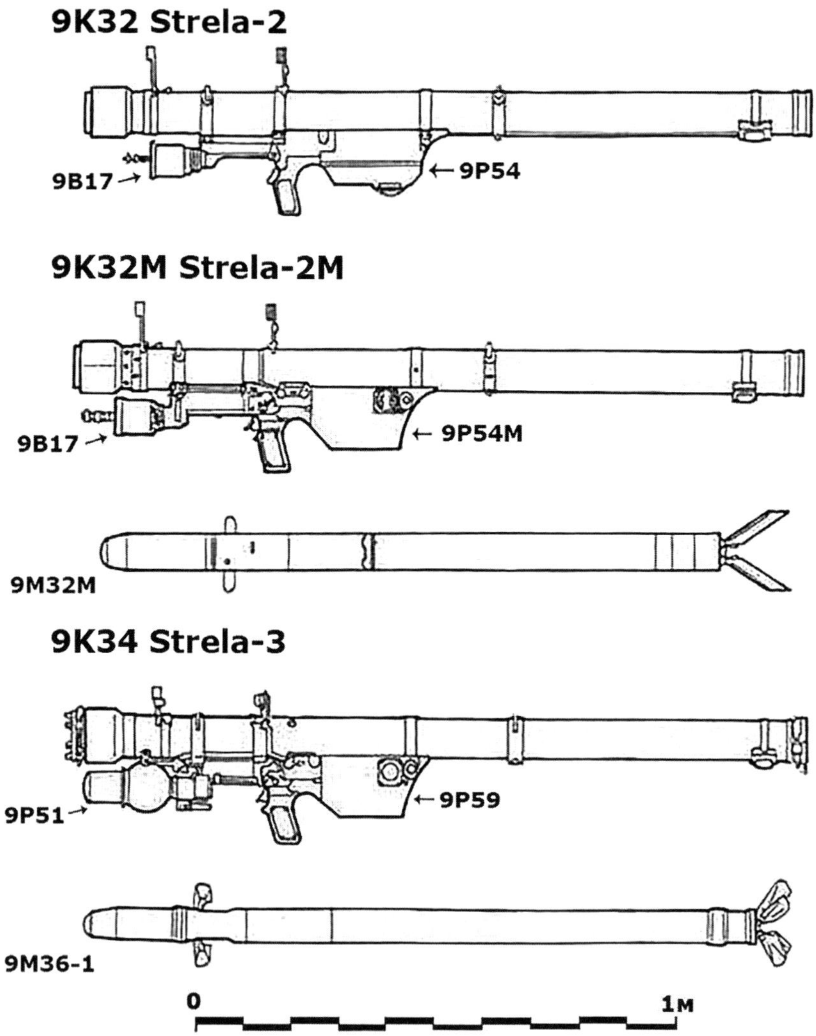

Figure 8-9: 9K32, 9K32M and 9K34 Strela models.

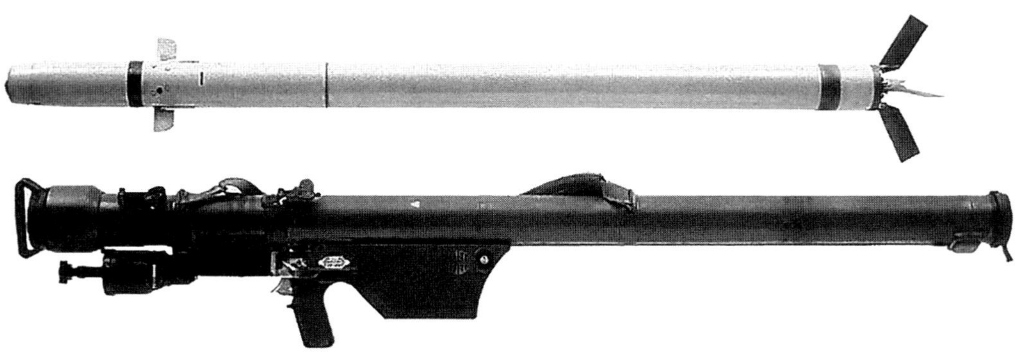

Figure 8-10: 9K32M.

type. The reaction time of the Strela-2M is about 15 seconds but it greatly depends on the situation and the skill of the crew. If the launcher is already mounted on the shoulder, the covers removed and sights extended, the reaction time is roughly halved.

The Strela-2 family soon saw combat and it was used in every major conflict of the Cold War (Vietnam, the Arab-Israeli Wars etc). In Afghanistan the Mujahideen used the captured weapons against the Soviet forces as well as those supplied by the CIA network. The results were mixed depending on the environment and types of targets. Strela-2 variants were susceptible to flares and jammers such as AN/ALQ-144. The Warsaw Pact and Soviet client countries even used them on small warships such as corvettes or patrol boats. The naval variant received the SA-N-5 designation from Western agencies.

The second generation of the Soviet MANPAD development was introduced in 1974. The seeker still used the PbS detector technology, but it was cooled, and the amplitude-modulated (AM) guidance principle was replaced with the frequency-modulated (FM) method. It was a bit less vulnerable to flares and thermal jammers had only limited use against the FM guidance comparing to AM.

The 9K34 had a maximum engagement range of 4.1km up to 2,700m altitude with the maximum target speed of 225m/s for departing targets and 150m/s against incoming ones. The maximum missile speed is 41 m/s. The missile did not have a proximity fuse. It has very limited capabilities against helicopters and slow propeller aircraft. The Strela-3 is not a really an all-aspect missile. The deployment of Strela-3 was not as widespread within the Warsaw Pact as earlier MANPADs. Strela-2 was replaced by the 9K310 Igla-1 (SA-16).

9K310 Igla-1 (SA-16 'Gimlet')

This represents the third generation of Soviet MANPADs and was introduced in 1981. The seeker technology of the Igla-1 was totally different from all of its predecessors. The detector is InSb (indium antimonide) which made possible lock and launch against both incoming and departing targets. Besides the new detector material, it got a new type of FM modulated guidance (linear reticule). The new seeker design were made highly resistant against flares and the thermal jammer is totally ineffective against the Igla-1 (Fig. 8-11).

The 9K310 has a maximum 5.2km engagement range of 5.2km up to 3,500m altitude. The maximum incoming target speed is 320m/s and for departing targets 360m/s. Maximum missile speed is 570m/s. The missile still has only an impact fuze. The Igla-1 was an interim step because of the development issues of the 9K38 Igla (later called SA-18). East Germany bought 270 launchers and 550 missiles from 1988, Hungary acquired 36 launchers and 432 missiles. Poland and Czechoslovakia did not buy any during the Cold War.

9K38 Igla (SA-18 'Grouse')

The 9K38 Igla (Fig. 8-11), which fulfilled the original design requirement, was fielded in 1983. It uses the same FM guidance principle as the 9K310, but it was designed with

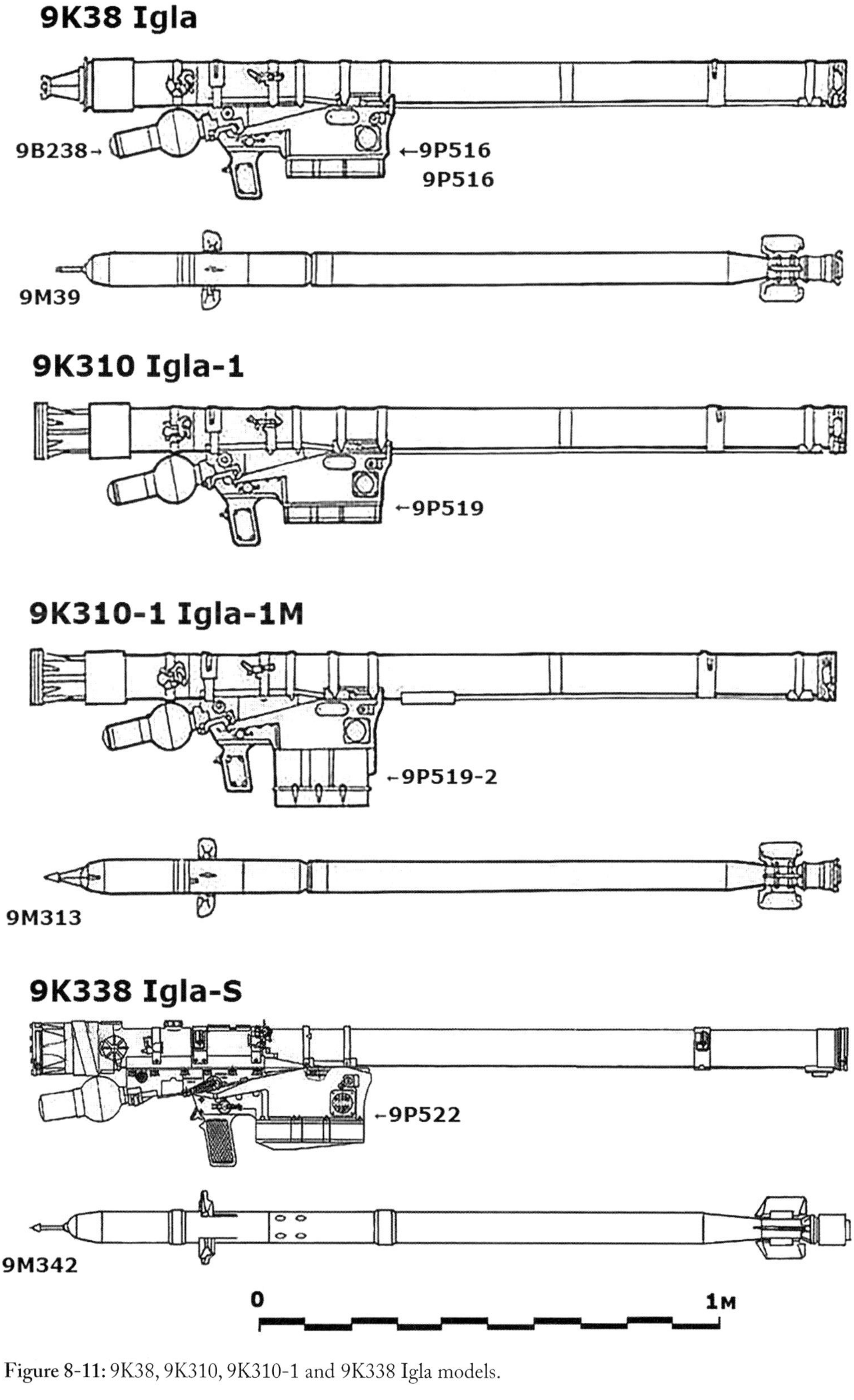

Figure 8-11: 9K38, 9K310, 9K310-1 and 9K338 Igla models.

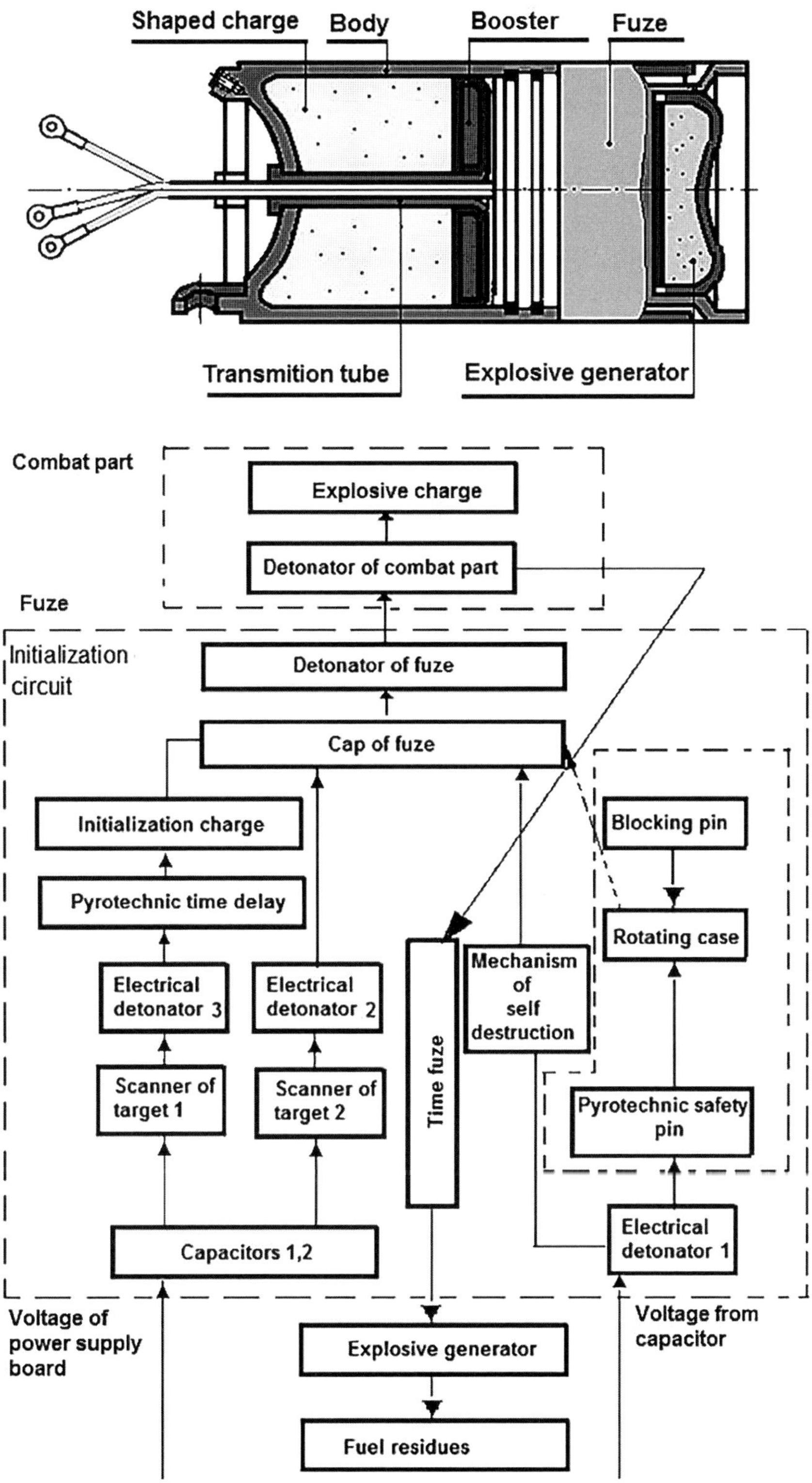

Figure 8-12: 9M313 warhead (top) and fuze structural schematics (bottom).

a dual seeker which put the missile in a totally different category in comparison to any other missiles at that time, not only in the Soviet Union. The system was named after the small spike at the nose of the missile. 'Igla' in Russian means 'needle'. The engagement zone of the Igla is identical with that of Igla-1.

The seeker incorporated sensitivity, vibration- and shock-resistant characteristics that were unique for that time. As with the Igla-1, compressed nitrogen was used to cool the seeker to a working temperature of –200°C. The new seeker was carried in a needle-like spike installed in the nose of the missile to reduce drag.

The KBM-developed family of the Strela-2, Strela-2M, Strela-3, Igla-1 and Igla MANPADS made it possible to effectively solve the problem of combating low-flying air targets. In this case, each of the subsequent versions far exceeded the capabilities of its predecessor, becoming the answer to aircraft design improvements, changes in air-attack tactics, and the advent of effective air defence system countermeasures.

These MANPADS are almost undetectable by reconnaissance equipment, can be employed suddenly and quickly, and are highly accurate. As a result of their widespread use, military aircraft cannot dominate airspace altitudes up to 3,500m, where the majority of close-support attacks against ground targets are performed. The warhead and fuze are shown in Fig. 8-12.

This led to a significant change in air attack tactics and the massive use of relatively low-cost cruise missiles. Engaging the latter required weapons whose number exceeded the number of cruise missiles several times, with high accuracy and relatively low cost, that could be quickly moved and deployed.

9K338 Igla-S (SA-24 'Grinch')

In the early 2000s, the Igla-S (9K338) MANPADS adopted in 2001 proved to be among such weapons. It has embodied all the best from its predecessors and, through a series of new design solutions, has provided qualitatively new combat capabilities (Fig. 8-13). Like the previous MANPADS, the Igla-S can be launched from any unprepared open area, an emplacement, trucks and platforms, and even from pools of water.

For this variant, LOMO developed a compact seeker, the 9E435. The Igla-S also differs by having a far heavier warhead both in the explosive weight (2.5kg for the IGLA-S against 1.1kg for the Igla) and the number of fragments, as well as by the use of a contact/proximity fuze, whose operation algorithm selects the optimum time of detonation, both in contact and proximity modes. To this end, a laser proximity target sensor was added to the warhead to provide its detonation when the missile reaches a distance of 1.5m from the target. This has considerably increased killing efficiency against small targets like cruise missiles and UAVs. In turn, the replacement of the existing explosion-control actuator with an electric proportional one reduced the drag coefficient of the missile and increased its average speed and target engagement range.

A detachable night sight was additionally introduced for the Igla-S. It allows the use of the MANPADS at night, providing target detection and identification by the gunner, and aiming and target tracking before missile launch. In addition, there is maintenance

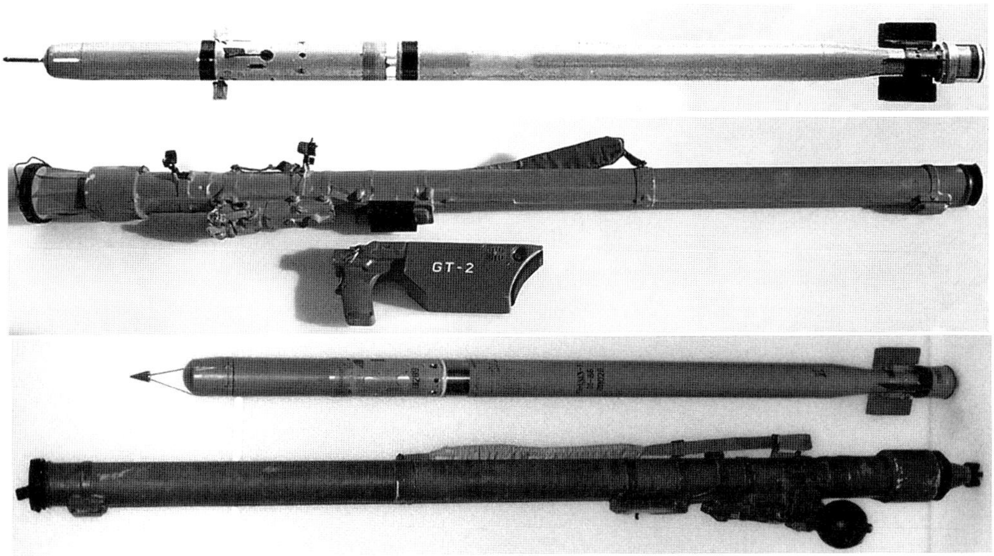

Figure 8-13: 9K310-1 with 9M39 (top) and 9K38 with 9M313 (bottom).

equipment used to periodically check the system's combat assets. The Igla-S retained a high level of operational continuity with the Igla and Igla-1: the overall dimensions of the MANPADS, mounting seats and shipping container dimensions remained the same. These MANPADS have interchangeable fire-control units. The pre-launch, launch and maintenance procedures are also identical.

The Igla-S remains operable under extreme temperature and high humidity conditions, at sudden changes in ambient temperature, in case of condensed precipitation, after immersion in water and the ascent in an unpressurised aircraft cabin to an altitude of 12km, and after prolonged carriage by any kind of transport, including in automotive and tracked vehicles, on all types of roads and terrain. If the missile in the launch container is accidentally dropped on concrete from a height of 2m, it will remain operable.

The Igla-S development process has incorporated many trends in the evolution of these weapons, in particular, the use of a MANPADS missile as part of the various ground-, sea, and air-based platforms ('Dzhigit' pedestal launcher, 'Gibka' shipborne launcher and 'Strelets' launch module, respectively). This allows light, mobile guided missile systems to be built around them. In these installations, missile establishment and firepower of the platform can be significantly increased owing to the small size and weight of the missile; furthermore, in terms of their performance MANPADS have approached short-range air defence systems.

9K333 Verba (Willow) (SA-25)

The primary new feature of the Verba (Fig. 8-14) is its multispectral optical seeker, using three sensors – ultraviolet, near infrared, and mid-infrared – as opposed to the Igla-S's two. Cross-checking sensors against one another better discriminates between relevant targets and decoys, and decreases the chance of disruption from countermeasures, including lasers that attempt to blind missiles.[2]

Figure 8-14: 9M333.

According to a KBM, the Verba can engage fixed- and rotary-wing aircraft and 'new types of threats' such as UAVs and cruise missiles. The 9K333 can effectively engage aerial targets with low infrared signatures. The system can be coupled to an external IFF unit. The Verba's containerised 9M336 SAM can be integrated into ground- and sea-based short-range air-defence systems. It can also be used by air platforms.

The system is in serial production for the Russian armed forces, with several ground force and airborne formations receiving Verbas since 2014. It first appeared with the Ivanovo VDV division after passing Army testing in the summer of 2011. Officially, it was adopted into service in 2015. KBM signed a long-term contract with the Russian Ministry of Defence to supply Verba and carries out its production.[3] In the recent Russian-Ukrainian war, Verbas successfully engaged and downed a couple of Ukrainian Su-25s as well as numerous UAVs and loitering munitions.

Appendix

NATO Codenames for Missile Systems

S-25 Berkut	SA-1 'Guild'
S-75 Dvina/Volkhov/Desna	SA-2 'Guideline'
S-125 Neva	SA-3 'Goa'
2K11 Krug	SA-4 'Ganef'
S-200 Volga	SA-5 'Gammon'
2K12 Kub/Kvadrat	SA-6 'Gainful'
9K32 Strela-2	SA-7 'Galosh' and 'Grail'
9K33 Osa	SA-8 'Gecko'
9K31 Strela-1	SA-9 'Gaskin'
S-300P/PS/PT	SA-10 'Grumble'
9K37 Buk	SA-11 'Gadfly'
S-300V	SA-12 'Gladiator' and 'Giant'
9K35 Strela-10	SA-13 'Gopher'
9K36 Strela-3	SA-14 'Gremlin'
9K330/9K331/9K332 Tor	SA-15 'Gauntlet'
9K310 Igla-1	SA-16 'Gimlet'
9K37 Buk-M1-2	SA-17 'Grizzly'
9K38 Igla	SA-18 'Grouse'
2K22 Tunguska	SA-19 'Grison'
S-300PM/PMU Favorit	SA-20 'Gargoyle'
S-400 Triumf	SA-21 'Growler'
Pantsir-S1	SA-22 'Greyhound'
S-300VM 'Antey-2500'	SA-23 'Gladiator'/'Giant'
9K338 Igla-S	SA-24 'Grinch'
9K333 Verba	SA-25
9K317 BUK M3 Viking	None Assigned ('Viking' used)
S-350 Vityaz	None Assigned
S-500 Prometheus	None Assigned

The US DoD has different designations for naval surface-to-air missiles (SA-N series) with Soviet designations. However, these are not standard NATO names. NATO uses the regular SA series for naval SAM. The US DoD refers to them by these names:

4K90 Volna	SA-N-1 'Goa' (SA-3)
M-2 Volkhov-M	SA-N-2 'Guideline' (SA-2)
4K60/4K65 Shtorm	SA-N-3 Goblet
9M33 Osa-M	SA-N-4 'Gecko' (SA-8)
9K32 Strela-2	SA-N-5 'Grail' (SA-7)
S-300F Fort	SA-N-6 'Grumble' (SA-10)
9M38/9M38M Uragan	SA-N-7 'Gadfly' (SA-11)
9K34 Strela-3	SA-N-8 'Gremlin' (SA-14)
3K95 Kinzhal	SA-N-9 'Gauntlet' (SA-15)
3M38 Igla	SA-N-10 'Grouse' (SA-18)
3M87 Kashtan	SA-N-11 'Grison' (SA-19)
3K37 Smerch/Shtil	SA-N-12 'Grizzly' (SA-17)
9K38 Igla	SA-N-14 'Grouse' (SA-18)
S-300FM	SA-N-20 'Gargoyle' (SA-20)

NATO Codenames for S-300 and S-400 Missiles

5V55K/KD	'Grumble' mod 0
5V55R/RD	'Grumble' mod 1
48N6/E	'Gargoyle' mod 0
48N6D/E2	'Gargoyle' mod 1
48N6DM/E3	'Growler'
9M96/E/D/E2	None assigned
40N6	None assigned

NATO Codenames for S-300, S-400, S-500 Systems Radars

5N64	'Big Bird A'
5N64S	'Big Bird B'
5D6E	'Big Bird C'
64N6/E/E2	'Big Bird D'
91N6	'Big Bird E'
5N66/5N66M	'Clam Shell'
76N6	'Clam Shell'
5N63	'Flap Lid A'

5N63S/30N6E	'Flap Lid B'
30N6/E1/E2	'Tomb Stone'
92N6	'Grave Stone'
36D6	'Tin Shield'
19Zh6	'Tin Shield'
ST-68U	'Tin Shield'
96L6/96L6E	'Cheese Board'
Yenisei (77T6)	None assigned

NATO Codenames for S-300V Radars

9S15/9S15M (1RL140)	'Bill Board'
9S32	'Grill Pan'
9S19	'High Screen'

NATO Codenames for Radars that are in Use (Including Older Types used by Other Countries)

Nebo-SV/P-18M	'Box Spring'
Nebo-M 55Zh6M	'Tall Rack'
P-15 (1RL13)	'Flat Face'
39N6E Kasta	'Flat Face X'
P-40 (1S12/1RL128	'Long Track'
SNR-125	'Low Blow'
P-18 Terek (1RL131)	'Spoon Rest D'
P-19 (1RL134)	'Flat Face B'
PRV-16 (1RL19)	'Thin Skin'
PRV-13 (1RL130)	'Odd Pair'
1S91	'Strait Flush'

Most Common Russian Abbreviations

ASU	Avtomatizirovanya Sistema Ulravleniya	Automated Control System
F	Flot	Fleet, Navy
GKAT	Gosudarstveni Komitet Aciacionoy Tehniki	State Aviation Technics Committee
GRAU	Glavnoe Raketno Artilerisko Upravlenie	Main Rocket and Artillery Directorate

KBP	Konstruktorskoe Biro Proborostroeniya	Instrument Design Bureau
KBU	Kabina Boevoga Upravleniya	Combat Control Cabin
KP	Komandniy Punkt	Command Post
KPS	Komandni Punkt Sistema	System Command Post
MOBD	Modul Obespecheniya Boevogo Dezhurstva	Combat Shift Living Module
NII	Nauchno-Isleditelyskii Institut	Scientific Research Institute
NIEMI	Nauchno-Issledovatel'skiy Elektromekhanicheskiy Institut	Scientific Research Electromechanical Institute
NPO	Naucho-Proizvodstveno Obyedinenie	Scientific and Manufacturing Enterprise
NVO	Niskovisotni Obnaruzhitely	Low-level Surveillance Radar
OKB	Opitnoe Konstruktorskoe Biro	Research Design Bureau
PBU	Punkt Boevogo Upravleniya	Combat Command Post
PKB	Proektno-Konstruktorkoe Biro	Project-Design Bureau
PO	Proizvodstvenoe Obyedineniye	Manufacturing Enterprise
PU	Puskovaya Ustanovka	Launcher
PVO	Protivovazdushnaya oborona	Air Defence
PZRK	Perenosni Zenitni Raketni Kompleks	MANPAD
REB	Radio-Elektronaya borba	Electronic Warfare
RLS	Radiolokatsionaya Stanitsa	Radar Station
RPN	Radilokator Podsveta i Navedeniya	Surveillance, tracking and guidance radar
RLO	Radiolokator Obnaruzheniya	Surveillance/tracking radar
SNR	Stanitsa Navedeniya Raket	Missile Guidance Station
SPU	Samohodnaya Puskovaya Ustanovka	Self-propelled Launcher
TPK	Transportno-Puskovoi Kontainer	Transport-Launch Container
TsKB (CKB)	Tsentralnii Konstrukorskoe Biro	Central Design Bureau
TsNII (CNII)	Tsentralnii Naucho-Isledovatelskii Institut	Central Scientific Research Insttute
VKS	Vozdusho-Kosmicheskoi Sili	Aerospace forces
VMF	Voeno Morskoi Flot	Navy
V-PVO	Voiskova Protivovazdusha Oborona	Army Air Defence
VVKO	Vozdushno Kosmicheskaya Oborona	Aerospace Defence
VVS	Voeno Vazdushiy Sil	Air Force
ZAK	Zenitniy Artilleriskiy Kompleks	Air Defence Artillery Complex
ZRK	Zenitno-Raketni Kompleks	Air Defence Missile Complex
ZRS	Zeninto-Raketnaya Sistema	Air Defence Missile System

Notes

Chapter 1

1. Protivovazdushnaya i Protivoraketnaya Oborona – Enciklopedia XXI Veka.
2. The Russian Aerospace Forces (Cyrillic – Воздушно-космические силы – *Vozdushno-kosmicheskiye sily*) or VKS (ВКС) comprises the aerospace branch of the Armed Forces. Russia established it as a new branch of its military on 1 August 2015 with the merging of the Air Force (VVS) and the Aerospace Defence Forces (VVKO).
3. ПВО Сухопутных Войск.
4. J. Bronk, *Modern Russian and Chinese Integrated Air Defence Systems: the Nature of the Threat, Growth Trajectory and Western Options*, RUSI, 2020.
5. A target-acquisition system typically includes target-acquisition radars and engagement and fire-control radars. The radar detects and follows the intended targets so as to determine their trajectory, a function that is put to use in a wide range of civilian and military applications. Radar is used to monitor enemy targets to determine if they represent an immediate threat. In case of an imminent threat, radar may track the target and then use the track information to employ suitable defensive or offensive countermeasures such as using guided missiles or aircraft to intercept the enemy targets. Engagement and fire-control radar is a 'target tracking radar' specifically designed for integrationwith air-defence weapon systems. The radar component of the platform measures the coordinates of the intended target or targets in terms of their azimuth, elevation, height, range and velocity, which may be used to determine the target trajectory and to predict its future position. These radars provide continuous position data on a single or multiple targets enabling the associated guns or guided weapons to be directed and locked on to targets.
6. RCS of a target, denoted by 'σ' (sigma), is measured as a ratio of the transmitted radar signal power back scattered from the target per unit solid angle in the direction of radar to the radar signal power intercepted by the target. Conceptually, RCS is measured by comparing the strength of a reflected signal from the target to the reflected signal from a perfectly smooth conducting metal sphere with a frontal or projected area of $1m^2$. RCS is measured in m^2 and is therefore the projected area of an isotropically radiating perfectly conducting sphere that would reflect back the same power in the direction of radar as the one that is actually reflected by the target for a given incident power. RCS is also measured in dBsm (or dBm^2), which is decibels relative to $1m^2$ RCS in dBsm.

Chapter 2

1. Центральный научно-исследовательский институт – Central Research Institute
2. The kill chain refers to the sequence of detection, tracking, locking onto target, launching, guiding and hitting. If any of these parts can be eliminated or obscured, the aircraft has a chance of avoiding being hit.
3. M. Mihajlović and Dj. Aniĉić, *Shooting Down the Stealth Fighter*, Pen and Sword Air World, 2021.
4. Dielectrics that exhibit electromagnetic loss at microwave frequencies.
5. Mihajlović and Aniĉić, *Shooting Down the Stealth Fighter.*
6. Ibid.
7. Jonas Kjellen, *Russian Electronic Warfare – The Role of Electronic Warfare in the Russian Armed Forces*, Försvarsdepartementet/Ministry of Defence, 2018.
8. Kjellen, *Russian Electronic Warfare.*

Chapter 3

1. Войска противовозду́шной и противораке́тной оборо́ны – Войска ПВО-ПРО.
2. https://sites.google.com/site/samsimulator1972/home.
3. ГРАУ – Гла́вное раке́тно-артиллери́йское управле́ние – Main Missile and Artillery Directorate
4. Сухопутный Войск – Ground Forces – SV.
5. Флот – Navy (Flot) – F .
6. ПВО-PVO – Противовоздушная оборона – air defence.
7. www.armyrecognition.com/russia_russian_missile_system_vehicle_uk/s-350e_s-350_vityaz_50r6_air_defense_missile_data_pictures.html
8. Ibid.

Chapter 4

1. Progressive development of tactical air defence weapons and systems (source: S.V Druzin, V.V. Mayorov and B.N. Gorevich, 'An advanced new-look tactical air defence armament system', *Journal of 'Almaz – Antey' Air and Space Defence Corporation* No. 4, 2019).

Chapter 5

1. http://www.ausairpower.net/APA-Russian-SAM-Radars-DKB.html#mozTocId363282
2. http://www.ausairpower.net/APA-'Giant'-'Gladiator'.html#mozTocId402288
3. Ibid.

Chapter 6

1. KB is an abbreviation of the Russian initials of 'Конструкторское Бюро'– Konstruktorskoye Biro, meaning Design Bureau. During the Soviet era, KBs were closed institutions working on design and prototyping of advanced technology, usually for military applications. A bureau was officially identified by a number, and often semi-officially by the name of its lead designer.
2. OKB is a transliteration of the Russian initials of 'Опытное конструкторское бюро' – Opytnoye Konstruktorskoye Biro, meaning Experimental Design Bureau.
3. GKAT is the abbreviation for the Государственный Комитет по Авиационной Технике (ГКАТ) 'State Committee for Aviation Technologies'.
4. NII is an abbreviation for Научно-Исследовательский Институт – Scientific and Research Institute.
5. GKRE – State Committee for Radio Electronics.
6. A design bureau of plant No. 134 GKAT, which originally specialised in the field of aviation small arms and bombs and had already accumulated some experience in the development of the K-7 air-to-air missile, was instructed to create a guided missile for the complex. Subsequently, this organisation was transformed into GosMKB 'Vympel'. The development of the Kub missile complex began under the leadership of the chief designer I.I.Toropov.
7. 'Kvadrat' is the Russian word for 'Square'. Export versions differ from the system designated for use in the Soviet Army.
8. http://www.ausairpower.net/APA-Engagement-Fire-Control.html#mozTocId110872
9. Ibid.
10. Ibid.

Chapter 7

1. NII-20 – R&D Institute No. 20; NIEMI – Electrical Mechanical R&D Institute.
2. OKB is a transliteration of the Russian initials of 'Опытное конструкторское бюро' – Opytnoye Konstruktorskoye Buro, meaning Experimental Design Bureau. During the Soviet era, OKBs were closed institutions working on design and prototyping of advanced technology, usually for military applications. A bureau was officially identified by a number, and often semi-officially by the name of its lead designer.

3. Tor ('Top' in Russian Cyrillic) is a geometric figure torus. Soviet practice includes naming missile systems after geometric forms such as Kub or Kvadrat.

Chapter 8

1. ZAK – Zenitniy Artileriskiy Kompleks – Air-Defence Artillery Complex.
2. https://www.armyrecognition.com/july_2017_global_defense_security_news_industry/all_russian_airborne_troops_equipped_verba_manpads_82707173.html
3. https://en.wikipedia.org/wiki/9K333_Verba

Bibliography

Airpower Australia, http://www.ausairpower.net, miscellaneous articles.

Andersen, Yu. A., Drozhkin A.I. and Lozik P.M. (1979), *Protivvozdushnaya Oborona Suhoputnih Voisk*, Voeno Izdatestvo Ministerstvo Oboroni SSSR, Moskva.

Apalkov, Yu. (2010), *Udarni Korabli*, Morkniga.

Arhangelski I.I. (2001), *Proektirovanie Zenitnih Upravlyaemih Raket*, Moskovskii Aviacioni Institut (MAI).

Armeiski Sornik journal.

Board, Warren J. and Hoffman, John B. (2016), *Air and Missile Defence System Engineering*, CRC Press.

Bronk, Justin (2020), *Modern Russian and Chinese Integrated Air Defence*, RUSI.

Dobrinkin, V.D, Kupriyanov A.I., Pomomarev V.G. and Shustov, L.N. (2007), *Radiolektronaya Borba*, Vuzovskaya Kniga, Moskva.

Elcin, S. (2008), *Zenitna Raketnaya Sistema S-300V, Raketa 9M83, Ustroistvo i Funkcionirovaniye*, Sankt Peterburg.

Ganin, S.M. and Karpenko, A.V. (2001), *Zenitnaya Rketnaya Sistema S-300*, Bastion Press, St. Petersburg.

http://simhq.com/forum/ubbthreads.php/topics/3900842/1

http://www.mycitymilitary.com

Jenn, D.C. (2005), *Radar and Laser Cross Section Engineering*, AIAA.

Kjellen, Jonas (2018), *Russian Electronic Warfare – The Role of Electronic Warfare in the Russian Armed Forces*, Försvarsdepartementet/Ministry of Defence.

Knott, Eugene F. (2006), *Radar Cross Section*, SciTech Publishing.

Knyazkov, V.S. and Rozhkov, V.V. (1977), *Boevie Raketi*, DOSAAV, Moskva.

Korovin, V.N, Afanasyev P.P and Svetov V.G. (2011), *Petr Grushin, Znameniti, Konstruktori Rossii*, Politehnika, St. Petersburg.

Kulikov, A.I. (2006), *Voenoe Iskustvo v Lokalnih Voinah*, Ministerstvo Oboroni RF.

Martino, Andrea de (2012), *Introduction to Modern EW Systems*, Artech House.

Mihajlović, M. (2020), *Jetliner Down: Tor-M1 Missile System*, report.

—— (1994), *Proporcionalno vodjenje* ('Proportional Guidance'), Faculty of Technical Sciences, Novi Sad, Serbia.

——, and Aniĉić, Djordje (2022), *Shooting Down the Stealth Fighter*, Pen and Sword Air World.

——, Vukosavljevic, Z. and Borojevic, D. (2022), *Three Fingers of Death: Soviet 2K12 Kub (SA-6 'Gainful') missile system*, Toronto.

Pervov, Mikhail (2012), *Raskazi o Ruskih Raketah*, Stolichnaya Enciklopedia, Moskva.

'Progressive development of tactical air defence weapons and systems', Druzin S.V., Mayorov V.V. and Gorevich B.N. (2019), 'An advanced new-look tactical air defence armament system', *Journal of 'Almaz-Antey' Air and Space Defence Corporation*, No. 4, 2019.

Raketi fakela (2003) ('Fakel Missiles'), Fakel Engineering Design Bureau, Moskva.
Richards, M.A. (2005), *Fundamentals of Radar Signal Processing*, McGraw Education.
RosOboronEksport catalogues.
Russia's Electronic Warfare Capabilities to 2025, Estonian MoD.
Skolnik, M.I. (2002), *Introduction to Radar Systems*, McGraw-Hill Education.
Sukharevsky, O. (2009), *Raseyanie Elektromagnetnih Voln Vozdushim i Nazemnim Radiolokacionim Obyektam,* Kharkov Air Forces University.
Taktika Zenitnih Raketnih Voisk, Uchebnik (1969) ('Air Defence Forces Tactics') Ministerstvo Oboroni SSSR.
Tehnika i Voruzhenie (1999–2018) ('Equipment and Weaponry' magazine).
Teperin, L.L. and Vozhdaev V.V. (2018), *Kharakteristiki Radiolokatsionnoy Zametnosti Letatelnih Aparatov*, FizMatLit, Moskva.
Toomay, J.C. (2004), *Radar Principles for Non-specialists*, SciTech Publishing.
Ufimtsev, Pyotr (2007), *Fundamentals of the Physical Theory of Diffraction*, Wiley-Interscience.
Vakin, Sergei A., Shustov, Lev N. and Dunwell, Robert H. (2001), *Fundamentals of Electronic Warfare*, Artech House.
Various technical manuals, MoD SSSR.
Video material: Samiy-Samiy Video material: Udarnaya Sila.
Video material: Sdelano v SSSR.
Video material: TV Zvezda, Voennaya Priyomka.
Voiskovaya Protivvozdushanay Oborona 1915–2015, Zbornik (Army Air Defence Journal).
Voruzhenie PVO i RES Rossii (2011) (Air Defence Weapons and Electronic Systems of Russia) *Rosoboronexport* (2011), Almaz-Antey, Moskva 2011.
Vozdushno Kosmicheskaya Oborona (2007–2015). (Air & Space Defence Journal).
Vozdusho-Kosmicheski Rubezh journal.
Zenitni Raketni Kompleksi PVO Suhoputniy Voisk (1997) ('Air Defence Missile System of the Ground Forces'). *Tehnika i Voruzhenie*, Special Edition.

Index

1S91 34, 172
19Zh6 34, 62
2K11 Krug 52, 128, 142, 169, 171
2K12 Kub/Kvadrat 128, 142, 169, 171–4
2K22 Tunguska 212, 213
30N6/E1/E2 23, 34, 62, 72–4, 82
36D6 34, 62, 65
39N6E Kasta 32, 34
3K37 Smerch/Shtil 234
3K95 Kinzhal 210, 234
3M38 Igla 15, 234
3M87 Kashtan 234
40N6 13, 14, 88, 91, 93
48N6/E 234
48N6D/E2 234
48N6DM/E3 234
4K60/4K65 Shtorm 234
4K90 Volna 234
5D6E 234
5N63 54, 55, 57, 234
5N63S 54, 55, 57, 235
5N64/5N64S 71
5N66/5N66M 59, 60
5V55K/KD 54, 62, 68, 82
5V55R/RD 56 ,62, 82, 97, 234
55Zh6M 37, 234
64N6/E/E2 23, 34, 69, 71, 79, 81
76N6 83, 234
91N6 87, 88, 98, 234
92N6 87, 88, 90, 235
96L6/96L6E 79, 80, 83, 87, 90, 92, 98, 103, 104
9A82 146, 148, 150, 152, 161, 162, 166
9A83 146, 148, 150, 152
9K31 Strela-1 129, 142
9K310 Igla-1 227
9K317 BUK M3 Viking 177, 180, 188–90
9K32 Strela-2 216, 225
9K33 Osa 142, 192, 193
9K330/9K331/9K332 194, 197, 202, 207, 209
9K333 Verba 231, 234
9K338 Igla-S 228, 230, 238
9K34 Strela-3 226, 234
9K35 Strela-10 216
9K37 Buk 174, 175, 177, 180
9K37 Buk-M1-2 175
9M33 Osa-M 234
9K38 Igla 227, 233
9K81 142
9M38/9M38M Uragan 175, 176, 180, 185–7, 234
9M82 142, 146, 152, 153, 155, 156, 158, 160
9M82MD 13, 14
9M83 146, 152, 153, 155, 156, 158, 160, 161, 190
9M96/E/D/E2 13, 72, 88, 91, 93, 103
9S15/9S15M 145, 147, 150–2, 164, 235
9S19 145, 146, 150–2, 164, 235
9S32 34, 146, 148–52, 166, 167, 235

Active Homing Head (AHH) 120,
Active Phase Antenna Array (APAA) 120
Aerospace Attack Weapon (ASAW) 1, 121,
Air Defence Missile System (ADMS) 77, 85, 142, 173, 191, 225
Airborne Warning And Control System (AWACS) 10
Anti-Aircraft Artillery (AAA) 120, 140,
Anti-Aircraft Missile System (AAMS) 69, 93, 94, 121, 142, 162, 170, 205

'Big Bird' 34, 98, 234
'Bill Board' 150, 235
'Box Spring' 235
Buk 7, 12, 15, 125, 133, 137, 174, 175–83, 185, 188–91

'Cheese Board' 98, 235
'Clam Shell' 234
Combat Control Post (CCP) 69, 105, 124
Combat Vehicle (CV) 106, 108, 114, 150, 160–2, 164, 193, 194, 200, 202, 205, 207, 209–12, 214–17
Command Post (CP) 6, 10, 11, 54, 58, 60, 63, 70, 76, 79, 85, 90, 98, 102, 114, 121, 124, 139, 140, 142, 145, 150, 152, 180, 183–5, 188, 197, 204, 205, 211, 213, 214, 219, 222
Continuous Wave (CW) 50, 56, 152
Counter Very Low Observable (CVLO) 37

Destruction of Air Defence (DEAD) 15, 16

Electronic Countermeasures (ECM) 1, 6–8, 10, 11, 137, 139, 194, 196
Electronic Intelligence (ELINT) 4, 41, 43, 45
Electronic Warfare (EW) 97, 118, 125, 126, 140, 150, 194

'Flap Lid' 34, 234
'Flat Face' 34, 235

GRAU (Main Rocket and Artillery Directorate) 52, 143, 177, 235
'Grave Stone' 235
'Grill Pan' 34, 150, 151, 235

'High Screen' 150, 235

Igla 15, 133, 135, 139, 140, 227, 228, 230, 231, 233
Integrated Air Defence System (IADS) 1, 4, 10, 39
Intermediate Range Missile (IRM) 120

KBP (Instrument Design Bureau) 54
KBU (Combat Control Cabin) 54
KPS (System Command Post) 60, 76, 77
Kupol 133

Legacy systems 34, 91, 127, 169
'Long Track' 34, 235
Long-range missile 120, 142
'Low Blow' 34, 235

M-2 Volkhov-M 234
Man-Portable Air Defence System (MANPAD) 14, 15 135, 139, 140, 216, 225–31
Ministry of Defence (MoD) 13, 125, 232

Nebo-M 6, 14, 34, 37, 90, 235
Nebo-SV/P-18M 133, 162, 235
NIEMI (Scientific Research Electromechanical Institute) 51, 192–4, 236
NII (Scientific Research Institute) 51, 192–4
NPO (Scientific and Manufacturing Enterprise) 69, 76
NVO (Low-level Surveillance radar) 59, 60, 77, 236

OKB (Research Design Bureau) 142, 171, 192, 216, 220, 236
Optoelectronic Device (OED) 119

P-15 (1RL13) 34, 134, 235
P-18 Terek (1RL131) 31, 34, 131, 235
P-19 (1RL134) 131, 235
P-40 (1S12/1RL128) 34, 131, 132, 235
Pantsir-S1 7, 15, 90, 105, 106, 108, 110, 125, 219, 224, 233
PBU (Combat Command Post) 69, 188
Precision Guided Munition (PGM) 7, 40, 139, 195, 196, 200, 210
PRV-13 (1RL130) 235
PRV-16 (1RL19) 131, 235

Radar Cross Section (RCS) 14, 17–20, 23–6, 28, 29, 30, 90, 98, 110, 125, 141, 143, 151, 158, 162, 195, 196, 218

S-25 Berkut 47, 48, 50, 51
S-75 Dvina/Volkhov/Desna 47, 48, 50, 51, 56, 193
S-125 Neva 48, 50, 51, 56, 101, 171, 193
S-200 Volga 12, 49–51, 90
S-300F Fort 52, 94, 97
S-300FM 234
S-300P/PS/PT 51, 54, 56, 60, 62, 66, 69, 72, 75, 101

S-300PM/PMU 69, 72, 76,
S-300PMU/PMU2 Favorit 69, 72, 78, 79, 81, 83, 90, 233, 234
S-300V 12, 13, 15, 52, 133, 134, 137, 139, 142–68
S-300VM 'Antey-2500' 12, 133, 168, 233
S-350 Vityaz 7, 101–04, 113, 233
S-400 Triumf 7, 12–15, 29, 51, 83, 85, 86, 90–4, 98, 101, 103, 113, 117, 211, 233, 234
S-500 Prometheus 7, 14, 51, 98, 99, 101, 117, 233, 234
SA-1 'Guild' 47, 233
SA-2 'Guideline' 34, 47, 233
SA-3 'Goa' 48, 171
SA-4 'Ganef' 34, 142, 169–73, 233
SA-5 'Gammon' 49, 50, 90, 233
SA-6 'Gainful' 142, 169, 177, 233
SA-7 'Galosh' and 'Grail' 225, 233
SA-8 'Gecko' 142, 192, 193, 233
SA-9 'Gaskin' 142, 233
SA-10 'Grumble' 34, 98, 233
SA-11 'Gadfly' 174, 233
SA-12 'Gladiator' and 'Giant' 34, 142, 233
SA-13 'Gopher' 216, 233
SA-14 'Gremlin' 233, 234
SA-15 'Gauntlet' 15, 194, 233
SA-16 'Gimlet' 227, 233
SA-17 'Grizzly' 15, 174, 175–8, 233, 234
SA-18 'Grouse' 227, 233
SA-19 'Grison' 15, 212, 233
SA-20 'Gargoyle' 233
SA-21 'Growler' 12, 233
SA-22 'Greyhound' 105, 233
SA-23 'Gladiator/Giant' 12, 233
SA-24 'Grinch' 240, 233
SA-25 15, 231
SA-N-1 'Goa' (SA-3) 234
SA-N-2 'Guideline' (SA-2) 234
SA-N-3 'Goblet' 234
SA-N-4 'Gecko' (SA-8) 234
SA-N-5 'Grail' (SA-7) 234
SA-N-6 'Grumble' (SA-10) 234
SA-N-7 'Gadfly' (SA-11) 234
SA-N-8 'Gremlin' (SA-14) 234
SA-N-9 'Gauntlet' (SA-15) 234
SA-N-10 'Grouse (SA-18) 234
SA-N-11 'Grison' (SA-19) 234
SA-N-12 'Grizzly' (SA-17) 234
SA-N-14 'Grouse' (SA-18) 234
SA-N-20 'Gargoyle' (SA-20) 234
Self-propelled Anti-Aircraft Gun (SPAAG) 142, 171, 212, 220
Short Range Missile (SRM) 13, 193
SNR-125 34, 235
'Spoon Rest' 34, 235
ST-68U 235
'Strait Flush' 235
Suppression of Air Defence (SEAD) 15, 16
Surface-to-Air Missile (SAM) 6, 47, 88, 93, 98, 106, 118, 131, 188, 190, 216, 220, 234

'Tall Rack' 34, 37, 235
'Thin Skin' 235
'Tin Shield' 34, 235
'Tomb Stone' 235
Tor 137, 139, 195, 205, 207
Tor/Tor-M1/Tor-M2 90, 125, 133, 136, 140, 196, 197, 200, 202, 206–09
Transport and Launch Container (TLC) 53, 56, 153, 156, 161, 194, 199, 212
TsKB (CKB) (Central Design Bureau) 97, 101, 221, 236
TsNII (CNII) (Central Scientific Research Institute) 17, 20, 236

UCAV (Unmanned Combat Aerial Vehicle) 141
UHF (Ultra High Frequency) 30, 34, 39, 90, 91, 110, 119, 236
Universal Automation Equipment System (UAES) 124
Universal Battery Command Post (UBCP) 124
Unmanned Aerial Vehicle (UAV) 40, 41, 46, 94, 98, 101, 103, 119, 120, 121, 125–7, 174, 194, 205, 212, 217, 223, 230, 232

VHF (Very High Frequency) 17, 30, 34–7, 39, 100, 101